Case Studies in Library Security

Case Studies
in
Library Security

BRUCE A. SHUMAN

2002
Libraries Unlimited
A Division of Greenwood Publishing Group, Inc.
Westport, Connecticut

*To Ann Cameron Shuman—wife, best friend,
critic, and consigliere.*

∽

LIBRARIES UNLIMITED
A Division of Greenwood Publishing Group, Inc.
88 Post Road West
Westport, CT 06881
1-800-225-5800
www.lu.com

ISBN 1-56308-936-X

Contents

The Cases

Introduction

Why This Book?

Several professional books have been published in recent years dealing with various aspects of library security; this one is different. This work teaches its lessons painlessly, presenting useful information through conversational monologues and dialogues about various library security problems. It then offers follow-up, thought-provoking questions, permitting the reader to ask, "What would *I* do in such circumstances?" The 40 case studies presented are designed to assist library staff members and students in contemplating various security challenges that could occur in library buildings.

Unlike other library-oriented texts on security, which present information in a straightforward, narrative manner, this work employs the conversational approach, allowing the principal characters to speak in their own words, describing security problems in which they played a part, their reactions to those problems, and their views on how those problems were—or might be—resolved. This format is designed to make for easy reading, while at the same time provide a focus for assessing and evaluating problems and contemplating various reactions to them. The conversational technique promotes involvement through empathy, removing much of the detachment found in merely reading about problems that other libraries have encountered and how they decided to deal with them.

The case study method is a proven technique for considering various courses of action and for choosing from among them, according to one's specific situation. Practitioners and students in library and information science programs are afforded the chance to consider potential problems in a "safe" reading environment or classroom situation, preparing themselves for situations that may later have actual, real-world consequences.

To accomplish these tasks, I have created a fictional community and a public library system within it. The Pecan Grove Public Library system, in which these events happen, is representational; it is no particular library, but rather an amalgam of several libraries. Although the employees of this library system may seem to have to cope with more security problems in a single season than real-world libraries might have to face in decades, their situation is intended to be realistic enough that anyone working in a public or academic library might feel some sense of connection or empathy to the protagonists and thus be able to critique their actions and decisions. Contemplating such plausible scenarios is a form of "rehearsal," intended to prepare the reader to deal with similar problems, should they arise on the job.

In this work, learning about various security aspects of library operation is accomplished through a familiar method of exposition—the case study—but then these cases diverge from the traditional by employing conversational monologues and dialogues as an expository teaching device. In each case, a fictional (but plausible) character explains in his or her own words what happened, what part he or she played in the unfolding drama, the sequence of events, what was done about the problem, and how the situation resolved itself and with what ramifications. Readers get opportunities to visualize problems that may threaten the security of modern libraries and to consider and propose their own workable solutions.

Because budgetary constraints are constant, libraries frequently must content themselves with merely the best among several unappetizing alternatives to security problems. Occasionally, a security problem may not involve an outside "bad guy," but rather an employee. This realization is well stated in the words of Walt Kelly's *Pogo*, "We have met the enemy and he is *us!*"

Heightened Awareness

There has always been a need for security in libraries, but since the events of September 11, 2001, that need is being felt even more. People tend to be more watchful (and sometimes more nervous) about their security nowadays, and one can hardly blame them. The events of that day serve to illustrate the point that libraries as public buildings (and the people within them) may be more at risk now than they were before. If there is any silver lining behind the resulting cloud of fear and suspicion, it may be that librarians have entered (along with the rest of American society) into a new era of awareness of others and general security consciousness. In short, we're more vigilant now.

Such acts have also, unfortunately, discouraged people from visiting public places because they fear being caught up in the next atrocity. As public places, libraries are potential targets. We have seen what can happen when we let our guard down, and we are anxious about it happening again. Library security, therefore, is an area that needs to be bolstered in the face of terrorism. As just one example, traditionally, a major focus of library security has been watching what people walk out the door with; not what they may be bringing inside. Nowadays, some spilled powdered sugar or baby powder can bring panic and even an all-out police response.

Clearly, the world has changed, and libraries must change with it. People who work in such buildings need to think about their security more than they did before, because although security problems have always been with us, new ones have been brought to our attention now. It is to the changed and potentially frightening library milieu of the future and the new problems that librarians must face that this work is dedicated.

By way of introduction, as author of these cases, I have worked in or taught about libraries for more than 30 years and have dealt personally with or spoken with people who participated in dramas like many of the ones to follow. That in no way means that I have all of (or even any of) the "answers." It does, however, suggest that I'm in a rather advantageous position to ask some of the pertinent questions. The "answers" are your department, dear reader!

In an Ideal World

In an ideal world, there would be no need whatsoever for library security (or for any form of law enforcement, for that matter), because people who work in and operate libraries would never encounter crimes, misdemeanors, or other threats to the safe, secure operation of their facilities. In an ideal world, larceny, robbery, rape, murder, and even theft would never occur. What is more, the thought of *committing* such acts would never even occur to the citizens of a community. Everyone would be completely trustworthy, no one would be impelled toward crime, and there would be no hunger, poverty, greed, or addictive drugs on the streets. And since we're fantasizing about an ideal world, every time you went to the library and wanted to put your hands on a specific library material that you wanted or needed, there it would be, sitting in its appointed place, waiting for you.

But we do not live in an ideal world. Not even close.

Put away any utopian fantasies about the perfectibility of humankind. While most people may indeed be honest, benevolent, sweet-natured, and gentle, there are still crooks, criminals, and sociopaths out there (who sometimes come through the library's doors). It's a mean old world we live in, and those who work in libraries must not only be aware that a wide spectrum of security problems exists, but that such problems can and do arise or occur without warning.

Therefore, library personnel should be informed (and drilled) on effective coping strategies to combat such problems. They should also understand that no single solution to a given problem is likely to be universal. At minimum, it is important for library staff to understand the causes of security and safety problems, to recognize or anticipate them where possible, to consider plausible responses, and, where possible, to cope with them effectively when they occur.

Pretty Good Security

Some years ago, I served as a library and information science faculty member in a large urban university surrounded by a vast and dangerous city with an alarming crime rate. The safety risks of working there were manageable as long as one took certain sensible precautions, such as rarely venturing into certain parts of town and never doing so at night. Nevertheless, there was an ethnic carry-out restaurant in a particularly dangerous part of town that beckoned our department's faculty and staff frequently, especially on Fridays. This storefront eatery offered exotic and delicious food at such affordable prices that we, having survived an all-morning Friday faculty meeting and being hungry, would frequently phone in an order for these fascinating tastes that couldn't be found anywhere else. The problem was that the place didn't deliver, and someone brave (or foolhardy) enough had to be designated to venture downtown to collect our lunches.

Frequently, I would volunteer (or be "volunteered") either to drive or "ride shotgun" on the food run, when missions to retrieve our lunches were organized. Aside from the remarkable food, what I remember best from a professional standpoint is having been deeply impressed with the level of physical security for employees that the restaurant had in place:

- Food orders were phoned in or could be placed in person through a small window cut into a huge, transparent, and presumably bulletproof wall, completely separating the kitchen from the lobby, where customers were required to remain.

- Workers inside the transparent wall had a clear view of everyone waiting outside. Loitering in the shabby, sparsely appointed lobby was discouraged, a sentiment underscored by a large posted sign saying "NO LOITERING."

- Personnel involved in food preparation worked in their kitchen safely behind their shield, seemingly safe against robbery or assault.

- Customers were required to pre-pay for their orders, passing money (cash only) through a small window in the impenetrable wall.

- Individual orders, when ready, were passed out of the kitchen to customers through another, somewhat larger window.

- Group orders (like ours) requiring cartons were hand-delivered to customers through a doorway in the wall; but the man bringing food outside of the protected area was huge and rippling with tattoos and muscle, his entire demeanor saying, "Don't even *think* of messing with me!"

- True, the occupants of the kitchen had to emerge from their cocooned enclosure at the close of the business day, but when employees left the safety of their bulletproof enclosure, the aforementioned large man was presumably there to protect them as they walked to their cars, their homes, or the bank.

Now, is that good security, or what?

If you discount any possibly adverse public relations aspects of having staff working in a fortress, such strict preventive measures, under the circumstances, seem to constitute an effective coping strategy for running a successful business both safely and profitably in one of the most dangerous parts of a dangerous city.

Libraries Are Not Restaurants

Our interest, however, is not with the security concerns of restaurant workers. It is with the security of the people, property, and information of libraries, which operate on entirely different assumptions from those of commercial services, one of the more salient being that working in a library normally entails physical proximity to, and often actually rubbing elbows with, the general public. No library can attempt to follow that restaurant's example, effectively walling off its staff from the people they serve. The library's aim, in fact, is not that of creating a fortress-like stronghold from which staff can run their operations in almost complete physical safety. That would be diametrically opposed to the objectives that libraries are striving to achieve. Here are some of the ways in which security for a public library differs from that of commercial enterprises:

- In a public library, people are free to enter for no stated or particular reason, roam around more or less at will, and spend considerable time inside the building without spending money.

- In a public library, "loitering," in the sense of spending time without transacting any business is generally tolerated and even encouraged.

- In a public library, patrons (customers) are normally not stopped, frisked, interrogated, detained, or turned away as ineligible for entry into the building.

- In a public library, it is possible—and even common—to spend hours without explaining your reason for being there, justifying your presence, or even speaking to anyone else.

- In a public library, you don't need money to partake of most services offered. There are exceptions, but most library services are free of direct cost to the public.

- In a public library, security guards may be present, but such personnel are neither armed nor authorized to use physical force to control visitors.

- A public library is a public service operated not for profit (little cash is present), making libraries much less likely as potential targets for burglars or thieves.

Such differences in both goals and ambiance lead to corresponding differences in attitude toward a strong and vigilant security posture. With both lives and money to protect, commercial establishments in dangerous neighborhoods may seek (and invest considerable money) to protect employees against crime by walling them away from physical threats.

They don't do that at McDonald's or Burger King restaurants, but some restaurants do take such extreme measures. People working in library buildings, however, are more vulnerable to predators and thieves because libraries exist to serve "everybody," admission requirements are minimal, and security presence may be inadequate or even completely absent due to a multiplicity of factors, many of which involve financial constraints.

Because of its purpose and atmosphere, the library's visitors are free to enter and roam about unchallenged so long as they observe certain basic rules (such as appropriate dress and behavior), but the rules of eligibility and conduct are intentionally few. No public library would ever want to defend itself against the charge that it erects unnecessary barriers between its workers and those whom they serve. In the modern library, openness and free access are common operating principles, but those virtues, though they sound appealing, entail risk. The more open one's workspace is, the more building occupants are at risk due to the actions of others.

Perhaps most important from a security point of view is that, unlike that fondly remembered inner-city carry-out restaurant, libraries do not separate staff physically from the people they serve. To the contrary, the duties of many librarians routinely require that they interact and mingle with their clientele. The public has the expectation that library staff are there to be helpful, and few citizens would accept it without complaint if a public library enacted stringent new rules keeping staff and the public separated by physical barriers. Many libraries opt for a generally "open" style of architecture and ambiance.

Library staff sometimes need to protect themselves from their visitors—and visitors from one another—because it is a regrettable facet of human nature that not everyone who enters a library building is there to use the services and collections offered, nor are all visitors full of good will toward others. When people freely mingle and interact, some few may occasionally commit acts that can lead to harm or disturbance. That is a good reason why library employees need to be ever mindful of security concerns. That's the way it is. Wishing that it weren't so is a futile exercise, and clearly, the simple expedient of walling ourselves safely off from those we serve is not an option.

Risk

Entering any public building entails risk, and library buildings are no exceptions. What we must accept realistically is that risk is a part of life and that a proactive security posture and level of preparedness in a library is both necessary and desirable. Protecting people and property well in a library building is an effective countermeasure to risk. For various reasons, library security is a tricky issue; or rather, multiple interconnected issues. No one is suggesting that library work is a high-risk vocation, or that staff members and visitors are in constant or even frequent peril. In most circumstances, people working within a library building (or visiting one) have little need to fear for their physical safety. Library work is arguably among the safest of professional vocations, but at the same time, one must understand that the job of protecting people and property in so public a place is often tricky and difficult.

A common thought of many librarians working with the public in urban settings runs, "This would be a pretty good place to work if we only didn't have to unlock the doors every morning and let the thundering herd enter the building." If you've ever run a public service desk, you know what I'm talking about and will probably concede the point. People enter libraries out of different motives, and once inside, they act out varying behaviors. Yet it is never possible to sort out precisely which visitors are likely to become troublemakers just by looking at them (although a couple of the following case studies, in fact, deal with the issue of developing ways to do just that). Wishful thinking? Perhaps, but technology marches on, and solutions with potential application to the problems of library security are in the works. You ain't seen nothin' yet.

Most of the time, thankfully, people working, studying, and otherwise engaged within library buildings may freely go about their business in comparative safety. The incidence of crime in libraries is, thankfully, rare when compared to statistics for such places as bus stations, sports venues, bars, or nightclubs. Unfortunately, *because* they are rare, when such incidents do occur, they frequently receive major play in the local media, and frightening news accounts or negative publicity can discourage users from visiting library buildings. Consider these frightening, if isolated, recent examples, taken from various library newsletters and periodicals over the past decade:

- A librarian is murdered while working alone in a small town library. A 16-year-old youth from a nearby town is arrested and charged with armed robbery, murder, and felony murder. His motive, he explains, was the desire to possess the staff member's expensive jewelry.

- A patron suddenly draws a firearm and shoots and kills two reference librarians in a branch public library. The gunman, a transient, homeless person is later described as a regular patron of the library.

- A gunman, carrying a pistol and what he says is a bomb, takes 18 people hostage in a downtown urban library. An alert off-duty deputy, who manages to sneak in among the hostages, subsequently shoots and kills the gunman. Luckily, no hostages are hurt despite a tense five-and-a-half-hour standoff, but the bomb found on the dead man's person proves to have been "live" and big enough to have, if detonated, blown up most of the building.

- A branch library clerk working the evening shift is beaten to death by a young man who has been harassing several of the women on the library staff, making obscene telephone calls, and exposing himself to female staff members. The victim had complained to police a week earlier that the man had been harassing her, but the police pointed out that, unless an actual crime has been committed, they could do nothing.

- In New York City, powdered sugar from a dropped doughnut sets off anthrax fears, leading to the temporary closing of a library building. As a result, some libraries that used to search patrons on the way out (to prevent book theft) begin searching them on the way in—to prevent the unthinkable.

Most of the time, working in a library is a walk in the park compared to the risks run by those who deal in commercial goods and services, but incidents can and do happen. Librarians like to boast about their institution's place in the community as a source of information, recreation, and enlightenment, but sometimes, one can't help envying the employees of privately owned establishments who protect themselves against crime by erecting impenetrable barriers between themselves and their clientele. Still, libraries are generally safe places to work and visit. The reasons for this vary, but in general, visitors to libraries (and staff) tend to be better-educated people, a trait that usually correlates positively with the avoidance of criminal behavior.

Additionally, because libraries do not handle or store large amounts of cash, thieves and burglars overlook them in favor of restaurants and banks in making their robbery plans. In this regard, libraries are fortunate in that they do not generally attract felons. In another regard, protecting people from coming to harm because of the actions of others, libraries are at risk because of the very openness that is their main selling point in a democratic society. All sorts of people each day may freely walk, stroll, lurch, stumble, or slither through the library's front door, and once inside, they are free to exhibit their behaviors or impulses as they see fit.

The Case Study Method

To get the reader thinking about security problems for libraries, 40 case studies are offered here, each scenario involving a different security problem and suggesting one or more approaches to a workable solution. Each case is supplemented with pertinent questions to think about and, where appropriate, to discuss with others. Regarding those questions, it is fruitless to search for perfect solutions or to try to find singular "correct" answers to the challenges presented by these cases. In actuality, the word "correct" is irrelevant here. In each case, it's not about "right"; it's about "fit." In any incident involving library security, there are various courses of action possible for staff members ranging from trying to ignore the problem to taking immediate and forceful action (such as calling the police). Approaches to effective solutions will vary with the individuals involved, their perceptions and assessments of the threat, and various environmental situations.

Each of the following cases provides a brief scenario involving (fictional) people who are coping (or have coped) with a particular library security problem, and what they have to say about it. The reader is then invited to think about and critique the decisions and actions made by the protagonists. The anticipated effect of role-playing such situations is (in the event that a similar problem ever arises on your "watch") not that you will necessarily find and implement the correct solution quickly and without effort, but that you will at least have previously thought about the problem, including the issues involved in the decisions to be made, alternative coping strategies, and foreseeable consequences. Thinking about problems *before* they occur puts you one up on anyone to whom that same situation may come as a surprise or shock. Forewarned is forearmed, and all that.

The unique format used in this work—the conversational case study—presents a mini-drama and then affords the reader an opportunity to contemplate the problems raised therein in the comparative safety of the mind or of class discussion. The cases are intended to encourage the reader to think problems through to their logical conclusions and to develop strategies for solving them. That much is nothing new. Many case study books have been written before; in fact, I personally have written four such works. What is unique (and hopefully refreshing) about this book is that each case is presented not as straightforward recitation of a problem, a reaction, and a solution, but rather as a conversational monologue or dialogue—each one in a different voice—in which the person relating the incident uses his or her own words to explain what happened, how it was dealt with, and what repercussions ensued.

Typical (and Not So Typical) Security Problems

Security problems arising in library buildings run the gamut of types from mere nuisances and annoyances (people who steal library books, people who won't stop talking or humming aloud, people who don't smell sweet) to those who are actually dangerous (stalkers, or people who turn belligerent or abusive). Here are some hypothetical cases in point to suggest the range and scope of the overall problem of library security. In each case, assume that no trained security personnel or law enforcement officers are available to handle the problem for you. It's happening on y*our* watch, and you have responsibility for dealing with this problem. You need to do *something,* and quickly, but *what?*

- A patron is caught removing library books from the library without authorization.

- A man is reportedly exposing himself to others in the library stacks.

- A library patron becomes angry, threatening, and verbally abusive to a staff member.

- A patron ignores (or forgets) repeated warnings to hold her voice down and persists in speaking aloud, disturbing those around her.

- Illegal drugs are being sold or used in the public restrooms.

- A homeless patron's personal odor is offensive to everyone else.

- A patron is observed tearing pages out of a reference book.

- A fistfight breaks out between two patrons.

- A sudden fire (or tornado) disrupts the usual quiet of the library.

- A staff member becomes highly emotional as a result of an incident in the library.

- A stalker is bothering female staff members.

- An anonymous hacker has found a way to access personal and private electronic library records and seems to be "visiting" the various files at will.

These illustrative examples are only a dozen of the myriad potential and hypothetical security problems that arise in the case studies that follow. The purpose of showcasing these dilemmas is to give the reader some idea of how varied and complex security problems can be for libraries, and how difficult finding solutions can be. The case study method allows you, the reader, a chance to tackle such problems and to work out for yourself how you would deal with them if they occurred in your library. A word of warning: Don't be lulled into feeling that finding solutions to any of these cases is a "piece of cake" simply because the person describing the problem seems convinced that he or she has found a solution.

Welcome to Pecan Grove, the city where everything happens. First, we'll get you acquainted with the city and its officials, then we'll move on to the library system—our venue for various security problems.

City of Pecan Grove, Government Officials

> The Honorable Joy Nees, Mayor
> Judy Newhouse, Head of Human Resources
> Carole Miller, Vice Mayor
> David Rubin, Head of Internet Services
> Pat Sanchez, City Manager
> David Wacker, Legal Counselor
> Kristina Simon, Comptroller/Budget Officer

The city of Pecan Grove (named for the abundance of pecan trees that, interspersed with evergreen live oaks, line the Pecan River's banks for miles, upstream and downstream), a mid-sized southwestern city, was founded in 1849 by settlers moving westward from the Atlantic Coast, attracted by the fertile soil and undaunted by the dry summers where stretches of more than 50 days without rainfall are not unknown.

The Pecan Grove metropolitan area has a population of more than a quarter million people. Pecan Grove, proper, with a population (according to the 2000 census) of approximately 210,000 residents, is not a satellite or suburb of a major metropolitan city such as Dallas or Houston, but lies no more than a three-hour drive from either of those major metropolitan areas. The terrain is mixed—rolling hills and flatlands—and the area is heavily agricultural, boasting (in years when there is adequate rainfall, at least) crops of cotton, corn, soybeans, and vegetables. A significant area outside the city is given over to dairy and cattle herds.

The Pecan River flows through the heart of Pecan Grove, normally at a sluggish pace, but in occasional times of flood, as a raging torrent. The climate is temperate, with relatively mild winters, less rainfall than coastal cities have, the odd ice storm, but little or no snow. While Pecan Grove lies too far inland to worry about the hurricanes that threaten coastal cities, tornados and hail storms sometimes cause major damage. Transportation in and out of Pecan Grove is adequate as two main interstate highways intersect within the city limits, a nearby airport serves the needs of commuters, and Amtrak passenger service, once curtailed, has recently returned to the area. Intercity bus service also provides transportation to such major cities as Dallas, Fort Worth, Little Rock, Shreveport, Oklahoma City, Houston, San Antonio, and beyond.

There has been a gradual shift in the city's demographics since settler times. While the populace was originally Anglo and Protestant, more Catholic residents, especially Hispanics from Mexico and Central America have moved to Pecan Grove in recent years. Politically, the surrounding area is predominantly conservative ("family values" are preached by the more successful office holders). The city, however, is more politically diverse, thanks to the growth of the technology industry that attracts "outsiders" from most everywhere.

This trend toward moderation is exemplified by the fact that Pecan Grove's current mayor, Joy Nees, soundly defeated a "good old boy" opponent in the 1996 election. Ms. Nees was born and raised in New Zealand but has been a resident of the United States for the past 30 years. In 2001, she won a second term of office, over a field of Hispanic and African-American candidates, due to a widely held perception that she wields a firm hand on the controls of economic growth, the environment, education, and various social problems.

A recessionary economy of recent years, however, has caused major disruptions in the city's economic health, and several technology and "dot.com" companies have gone bankrupt, moved away, or laid off hundreds of workers. Migration to Pecan Grove of Mexican-born people has accelerated over the past decade, and there is a degree of unrest between the various ethnicities as they jostle with one another for power and their economic "piece of the pie." When Ms. Nees steps down in 2006, after her second and statutorily final term, the next mayor could well be from the ranks of the minority groups in town.

Pecan Grove, while having its own personality and culture, generally shares many qualities with cities of similar size and boasts nothing particularly distinctive that might make its array of urban problems stand out. Consider it a typical community with typical problems of growth. In its six-square-mile urban setting, people worry about the economy, crime, and, more recently, terrorism; the community is otherwise vexed with the usual variety of economic, demographic, and social problems found in other American cities.

The Pecan Grove Public Library System

Board of Trustees

Bryan Pepper, Chair
Patricia Barrett
Mark Palumbo
Phyllis Owen
Shirley Petrey
Scott Lucas

Administration

Ann Cameron Bowman, Director
Karen Southern, Administrative Assistant
Michael Chitwood, Associate Director
Donna Starnes, Secretary
Jonn Dalton, Head of Extension Services
Jan Asuquo, Grants Officer
Kyle Bozeman, Human Resources
Seymour Zweigoron, Administrative Intern
Robin Lewis, Head, Lake Highlands Branch
Glenda Short, Head, Lakewood Branch
Steve Fierros, Guard, Lakewood Branch
Lee Brooks, Head, East River Branch
Linda Villareal, Head, Southlake Branch

Circulation Department

Apollo Joven, Head of Circulation
Mary Lou Thurmon, Circulation Librarian
Josh Amdur, Circulation Librarian
Karen Klaus, Circulation Clerk
Michelle Davis, Circulation Clerk
Hildagard Powell, Circulation Clerk
Patricia Ridley, Circulation Clerk
Bill Hunter, Circulation Clerk

Reference/Adult Services Department

Mary Rhoades, Head of Reference
Andy Michlin, Reference Librarian
Steve Glass, Reference Librarian/Head of Electronic Services
Harold Pennigan, Reference Librarian
Dee Segrest, Reference Clerk
Nancy Bratcher, Reference Librarian
Carl Davis, Reference Librarian
Hugh Benton, Curator of Pecaniana Collection

Children's/Young Adult Services Department
Ruth Sawyer, Head of Children's Services
Patricia Hiller, Children's Librarian
April Engel, Children's Librarian
Beulah Cooper, Children's Librarian
Yolanda Arista, Children's Librarian/Story Hour Specialist

Technical Services Department
Paul Holser, Head of Technical Services
James Barrett, Acquisitions Officer
Andrea Meeden, Webmaster
Shirley Petrey, Internet Services
Waheed Thompson, Cataloger
Mic Barron, Systems Analyst
Sam Dick-Onuoha, Computer Technician/Support Specialist

Physical Plant
Christopher Cree, Chief Engineer and Custodian
Carl Hickerson, Janitor

Security Force
Matthew DeWaelsche, Head of Security
Michael Early, Security Guard, Central Branch
T. A. Sanders, Security Guard, Central Branch
Steven Fierros, Security Guard, Lakewood Branch

The public library system consists of a large downtown central library and four branches, serving residents in four areas: north, south, east, and west. Some years ago, there were more branches and a large, well-equipped bookmobile, extending service to remote parts of Pecan County. But recent years have seen budgetary problems for both the city and the library system alike, resulting in economic contraction for both.

Just when the library system needs increased security the most, the overall budget has decreased as a result of years of recessionary economic times. In addition, other—more urgent—priorities for the city council to spend money, such as fighting crime and street repair, have arisen. In this climate, taxpayers are understandably disinclined to see their tax rates rise.

The downtown Central Branch puts library services and collections within a convenient driving or public transit time for most citizens. The limited number of parking spaces around the building can make finding a place to park a challenge, but there are several parking structures within three or four blocks of the central library, and their rates would be considered moderate by big-city standards.

The downtown, three-story building is large and roomy, with well-appointed reading rooms and adequate (if aging) collections of materials. It is in full compliance with recent laws concerning access for disabled persons. The library is open to the public from 9:00 A.M. to 9:00 P.M. Monday through Thursday, and from 9:00 A.M. to 5:00 P.M. on Friday and Saturday. The structure was built in 1971, and is, to put it charitably, showing its age. Still, it does what it can with what it can afford, due to the hard work and public relations efforts of Director Ann Cameron Bowman and her staff.

One definite problem is that the library's security presence is not well funded. Consequently, there are only two full-time guards to maintain order and handle situations in the Central Branch. The budget simply cannot stand hiring more, and there is ongoing debate between the library director and city hall over whether it is feasible to forego security guards entirely in favor of buying more books, recordings, and videos to meet the demands of the public. Director Bowman is unalterably opposed to removing security guards from the library budget, but she knows that she may lose this battle and shudders to think about the consequences.

There is an old saying, "You can't have guns and butter." The library system's leaders are aware that there may not be enough money to permit, on one hand, an adequate selection of services and collections, and on the other, to also have good security. Therefore, the library's leadership needs to think through its options carefully in offering protection to patrons, materials, and the building itself, especially emphasizing creative or inexpensive options. Moreover, the library needs to "sell" the importance of security to the thrift-minded city administration and council. The jury is still out on what will eventually transpire.

Levels of Security

There is no such thing as perfect security; there are only different degrees of insecurity. In libraries, insecurity is a given: Minimizing that insecurity is a worthwhile goal. The objective of this book is to expose the reader to a good selection of potential threats, problems, and challenges for library security. The reader is invited both to second-guess the decisions and actions taken by the characters in the dramas presented and to try to think of workable ways of combating or defeating such risks without much in the way of additional money.

The final four cases in this work explore some new security technologies developed or being developed in other fields—borrowed and applied herein to a library context and setting. Such solutions may seem fanciful, impractical, or even improbable, but as George Bernard Shaw wrote in *Back to Methuselah* (1921), "You see things; and you say, 'Why?' But I dream things that never were; and I say, 'Why not?' " Indeed, why not? Today's speculation sometimes becomes tomorrow's reality.

When Jules Verne first published his books *Un Voyage dans la Lune* and *Twenty Thousand Leagues Under the Sea,* both back in the 1860s, dealing respectively with vehicles capable of space travel and ships that could remain underwater for weeks, both ideas were widely dismissed as pure fantasy, things only dreamt but not worth practical consideration. Today, however, submarines and space travel are part of common experience. Ideas expressed now in the earliest years of the twenty-first century, therefore, may seem improbable and far-fetched, but it's possible that they'll be accepted notions in the not-too-distant future. Consider the Internet and the World Wide Web, which now, with the help of libraries, are within the reach of all citizens. If you're over 40, would such a possibility have even occurred to you, say, 20 years ago? I rest my case.

Finally, the names of the library employees and other people in these cases, rather than having been invented, were borrowed (with tacit permission) from members of the author's extended family of Texas Scrabble™ players, who meet at weekly clubs and about once a month at tournaments over designer boards with specialty tiles, racks, and time clocks. No attempt has been made to match the traits or habits of characters in these cases with the actual natures of the persons for whom they are named. Should anyone not particularly care for the way in which his or her namesake has been represented, I consider this the usual boilerplate disclaimer about pure coincidence and lack of malicious intent and am hoping for the best. I'm grateful to be able to use their names. Thanks, y'all.

The Cases

And now, let's get down to cases. Each is listed here with a brief excerpt from its conversational narrative, providing a hint of its unique flavor. The situations that follow are designed to present 40 different—but related—aspects of security for a modern library, involving persons seeing things from their unique perspectives. I have plunked these actors down in my fictional public library within a fictional community, so that their problems and coping strategies can be seen clearly. Let us pray that such a large number of headaches would never befall any one real library, at least within the same decade, anyway.

1. Braggadocio

"Today, I'm pleased to tell you that no one—except possibly the most sophisticated information bandits—could succeed in penetrating our firewall and getting into our private and valuable information, no matter how resourceful they are or how hard they try."

2. Any Minute Now

"And today—payday—when the staff payroll is missing my name—*gotcha!*"

3. An Offer You Can't Refuse

"What kind of favor am I asking? Not much. A very small matter, actually. All I'm asking is that you move one of your employees from one job to another, that's all. Nobody gets fired, nobody is demoted. Everybody's pay stays the same."

4. "Borrowing" Privileges

"No, see, I was just, you know, like, borrowing it, uh, temporarily? But I totally intended to bring it back at the end of the term."

5. An Ill Wind

"How were we supposed to know? The weather forecast yesterday called for rain, and a 50 percent chance of thunderstorms."

6. Guard, Off Guard

"And instead of saying that she was sorry or she'd try to do better in the future, she snarled, 'Come on, gimme a break! I can't be everywhere at once, can I?' "

7. A Harmless Eccentric

"I figure the only difference between this place and Bughouse Square is that you got warmer seats!"

8. Breaking Up Is Hard to Do

"And my insanely jealous jerk of an ex has been stalking me ever since the separation. "

9. No Time for This @#$%&!

"Yeah, right. Like I'm supposed to spend my whole lunch hour waiting in your stupid check-out line! As my daughter likes to say, 'As if!' "

10. It Rhymes with *Witch*

"And then he used foul language like I haven't heard since my late husband's navy days."

11. Security Is Everybody's Job

"So in response to his question about the lack of security presence in our branch, I got a little sarcastic, maybe. What I said was, 'We're all security officers, here, honey.' "

12. Just Like at the Airport

"What's up with the metal detector at the front door? This ain't Metro Airport, you know."

13. Noonchook Boy

"I mean, me first thought was, here's a bloke's been watching too many Kung Fu films."

14. In Loco Parentis

"Suddenly, this really big guy rushes in, grabs up the kid, shouts, 'It's all right. I'm her father!' and runs out again. What was I supposed to do about it?"

15. Gulag West

"Surveillance cameras? Great. Just what we need—another step toward Orwell's *1984*!"

16. Cyrus the Virus

"If word of this problem ever gets out, we'll probably be kissing the likelihood of any future rare book donations good-bye."

17. Colors

"I guess it's like that old song goes, 'When you're a Jet, you're a Jet all the way.' "

18. Pornucopia

"But when I turned to look at the monitor—there they were—what my father used to call unspeakable practices and unnatural acts, in living color!"

19. No Place Else to Go

"Hey, they turn us out of the shelter after breakfast and tell us we can't come back until dinnertime. I need a warm and safe place to hang out for the day, and I'm sorry but I don't got no private shower or designer soap!"

20. Best Rates in Town

"Why here at the library? Well, for openers, it's a lot cheaper than the Holiday Inn."

21. Stealing Is Stealing

"Whether it's from a public library or a bookstore, I say that stealing is stealing and the same rules apply."

22. Everybody Out!

"So, even when the fire alarm went off—and kept on blasting—almost nobody ran—or even walked—outside."

23. Here's Lookin' At You, Kid!

"Then he just grins and says, 'So, you're saying I stole your information? Fine. But how come you still have it, then?' "

24. Death Threat

"But this message was different: This one said, 'Mr. President, enjoy your Christmas, because it's for sure that you're not going to be around to welcome in the New Year.' "

25. Just Paperweights

"Listen, lady, I'm telling you—this is the kind of virus that chicken soup isn't going to fix."

26. She Said/He Said

"She's crazy, man! Crazy or a liar, one. I was just scratching myself, is all. Ain't that allowed?"

27. *Sieg Heil!* or Whatever

"Maybe now you see how, without our knowledge, this library became de facto state Nazi Party headquarters!"

28. Who Watches the Watchers?

"We're pretty good at catching our theft-minded visitors before they make off with our property, but what do we do about inside jobs?"

29. *Un Nouveau Espèce de Voyeur*

"Hey, all I'm doing is using my powers of observation. How is it my fault if other people are careless?"

30. The Customer Is Always Right

"Who has time to write all that stuff down? Besides, I didn't have a pen with me."

31. One Hail of a Night

"And then he says, 'It was late, we were drinking, we were waiting out the rain, and then it started to hail like mad!' "

32. Stark Staring Mad

"Well, no, he didn't touch me or actually say anything or make obscene gestures. But the way he kept staring at me made me crazy. I couldn't just let him get away with it, could I?"

33. Honesty as a Policy

"Before I gave the green light for you to hire her, I ran the usual standard background check, which may not be enough to spot the troubled ones ahead of time."

34. It Takes a Thief

"So, my question is, what'd it be worth to you if I showed you the holes in your electronic security, and how to plug 'em?"

35. See You in Court

"Well, yes, the idea was to get tough on delinquents, as a direct way of recovering our missing books. But threaten anybody? Never!"

36. The Schpritz

"Now, if anybody is stupid enough to try to remove a rare or expensive book from the building without permission: *WHAM!*"

37. The Latest Thing in Eyewear

"Here's all you do: Just put on a pair of these goggles, adjust the strap until they fit comfortably, look up, and you'll be amazed at what you can see!"

38. Thou Shalt Not Steal

"Ethical, schmethical! All I can tell you is that since we installed that new subliminal system, theft of materials has dropped over 30 percent!"

39. Out-U-Go®

"But if he ignores that warning, a big robotic arm drops down out of the ceiling, grabs him by the ear, and quick-marches him out the front door."

40. Somebody Else's Problem

"Our aim is to make it so difficult, risky and time-consuming to get into our system that would-be hackers will give it up and decide to try breaking into other libraries' files."

Case 1

Braggadocio

Ann Cameron Bowman, library director, to the Pecan Grove Rotary Club at their monthly breakfast meeting

Good morning, ladies and gentlemen of the Pecan Grove Rotary, a group, as most of you know, in which I have proudly claimed personal membership for many years. Now, it's a privilege and a wonderful opportunity for me to be able to come here and address y'all this morning and to talk about one of my favorite subjects: my library. Perhaps I should have said, "*your* library," or better yet, "*our* library." I like that last one better, because the Pecan Grove Public Library, for which I've served as director for almost a dozen years, is everyone's library. As a tax-supported municipal institution, it belongs to us all. I've just been the chief caretaker over the years, but you and your friends and families and all the other citizens really own the place.

While I could talk endlessly about the library system, I have been granted only half an hour to address this august gathering and then get off the podium, because this is, after all, the monthly rotary meeting, and there's business to transact. So I've decided to focus my attention on one issue, for it is a priority concern of mine and is something I am convinced that everyone—not just the staff and patrons of the library—should be concerned about. That issue is library security.

You don't need to be reminded that security of various sorts has been on everybody's mind lately, and library security is part of the overall problem. Now I see that a few of your faces wear what just might be puzzled expressions. "The *library?*" you may be thinking, "Who needs to worry about security in such a sedate, quiet place?" My contention is that library security is relevant to the crisis into which our nation has been plunged, and I'll give you my reasons. I've given the matter a lot of thought and decided that it might be well for me to define library security in my own way, so that even if we don't have time to discuss it in all of its ramifications, at least we can establish a frame of reference. Library security, at least from our perspective at

1

the public library, may be subdivided into three basic classes: materials and equipment, physical security, and electronic security.

The first and most traditional security problem concerns the combination of the methods and practices that we use to retain the materials and equipment that we buy with public funds—and that's not just books, but also magazines, computer programs, and entertainment and educational videos, just to name a few. It also means doing what we can to preserve and protect the computers you see everywhere in our buildings, equipment designed to provide the public word processing capabilities, e-mail access, and Internet access to a whole universe of information. Clearly, we don't want any of those items stolen, damaged, vandalized, or . . . well, let's just say . . . walking off.

But despite our best efforts to hold onto our materials and equipment, we are suffering from a considerable rate of loss. Now, I won't bore you with precise figures, but here are some round numbers to make a point. The library system now has a grand total of approximately 250,000 books, counting our big downtown building and all four branches. Call that figure "year one." Now, some of you may recall a news item in *The Pecan Grove Observer* a few months ago that reported the alarming fact that a full 13 percent of the library's book stock and other materials had gone missing during the past year or at least didn't show up during our annual inventory in August. Think about it: 13 percent! To frame that statistic in practical terms, subtracting 13 percent from a total of a quarter million volumes means that the libraries of this city will be able to count, by year two, a book stock of approximately 217,000 volumes. Discounting new and replacement purchases, at the present loss rate, only 189,000 volumes would still be available in year three. To cut to the chase, if the library were to continue to lose books at the present rate over the next eight years, without replacement, we'd have just over 94,000 of those original 250,000 left! That's fewer than 40 percent of the books we have now!

Appalling, isn't it? I mention this one aspect of security to demonstrate the importance of holding onto our materials and keeping valuable property—publicly owned property, let me remind you—from being stolen or vandalized. Although we are attempting to take vigorous countermeasures to prevent theft and loss, I don't have time to go into the details now. But if anybody here feels like calling me about it, I can provide information about what we're doing to stop or interdict the theft and loss of library materials. Let me add that even though our budget provides precious little money for such solutions, we're doing what we can. That's where I could use a little help. Many of y'all are business leaders, and a word with the city government might do wonders for us.

But time's a-wasting, so let's pass on to the next aspect of security, one much more serious than the one I've just touched on: the physical safety of library building occupants, both those who work in the libraries and the hundreds of our fellow citizens who visit our libraries each day. After all, a book or a computer can be replaced, something that can't be said for human beings. Physical security is something we probably all think about every day when we watch the evening news or pick up a newspaper. When I was a kid, the library was a safe haven, a tranquil place to go and find a book or a place to study. That's why my parents let me go there to do my homework after school. I felt safe, and in that quiet atmosphere, I could really concentrate on my books or essays. Nobody back then really worried that bad things could happen to anybody in the library. The bus station, maybe. The post office? Possibly. But the library? It just didn't seem possible.

Today, however, it's a different ball game, as you know. People are nervous about their personal safety, and unless they are reasonably assured a degree of freedom from threat or violence, they will avoid public places like the library, and that's bad for business. Realistically, however, although there is always a risk of becoming a victim of violence in the library as anywhere else, I am pleased to say that, statistically, you are much safer inside one of the libraries here in our community than you would be walking around on the streets or driving on the freeways. The risks people take visiting the library are not all that different from the risks they face when attending sporting events or traveling on airplanes.

But I'm talking now about physical security, and no one needs to remind y'all that life entails risk. Library security is an issue of public safety. We do what we can to keep people in our buildings from being hit over the head or having their purses ransacked or pockets picked while they're visiting us. But libraries, while comparatively safe, can be more dangerous than other places where people congregate, such as office buildings, theaters, and other private sector settings. Why? It all comes down to the line item budget for security.

Let me give an example: This city, like every other city, has its fair share of homeless people. You've all seen them sleeping in downtown doorways or shambling around, maybe panhandling. Most of them are harmless however unsightly or poorly groomed they may seem. Unfortunately, some of the homeless suffer from drug or alcohol addiction and are possibly also mentally ill, and unless they find accommodations in our city's few shelters, they may be forced to spend their nights sleeping on the streets or under one of the river bridges downtown. Admittedly, the plight of the homeless is a great national disgrace, but even while our hearts may go out to them, many of us probably find ourselves trying to ignore them.

Where am I going with this? Well, guess where many of those homeless people spend their daylight and early evening hours. If you've ever visited my downtown library building, you'd know. Why the library? Well, for one thing, the library has no admission requirements, and all are free to enter and use the collections and services, as long as they observe a few certain rules of conduct.

Here's a scenario for you to envision: In one of the reading rooms of the main library on a cold, rainy evening, a soaked and shabbily dressed homeless person (most are male, but a few are female) has shuffled in and sits down in a chair. This poor unfortunate doesn't do anything against the rules—like hustle you or anybody else for spare change—doesn't speak a word or even appear to take any notice of other people. He's just sitting there, wearing several layers of sodden, threadbare and dirty clothing, maybe rubbing his hands together to get the circulation going because it's cold outside, but now, in here, he's at least warm. But as he begins to warm up, his strong odor intensifies in the warmth. As he sits, his head hangs lower and lower, and soon he has fallen asleep and begins snoring quietly. Other people in the room are showing signs of being aware of the odor and are either leaving the room or leaving the library. Get the picture?

Of course, we can deplore the situation, point fingers and blame society for the fact that homeless people exist, or we could rail at the misplaced priorities of a city government that permits such people to roam the streets and public buildings, but we can't solve all the problems of society. At least not all at once. All we can really do is accept this as a basic problem of public places everywhere: rights in conflict; one individual's right to enter freely and roam unbothered in a public building versus everybody else's problem with the way he smells.

Now here's the challenge: You're this evening's librarian in charge, responsible not only for your own comfort and safety but for that of everyone else in the building. Given all the circumstances, what do you do? I can think of several options, and perhaps y'all can think of more. The possibilities are almost endless. For example, you might

- Ignore the sleeping man and hope he'll leave soon.
- Go to your locker in the back and find your atomizer full of perfume or cologne and spray it liberally all around.
- Call the local police and ask to have him removed from the building.
- Summon a library security guard to escort the man to the door.

- Engage him in conversation; try to make him ashamed of his appearance and odor and make him aware of the effect he is having on others.

- Offer him money as charity (or a bribe, or the price of a new shirt) to get him to leave.

- Direct him to the nearest mission or shelter where he might, at least, get a hot meal, laundry services, and possibly a set of new clothes.

- Think to yourself, "There but for the grace of God go I," and be grateful that it's not you in such a plight. Tell as much to anyone else who complains.

- Call the police and have him removed for sleeping, since sleeping in the library is on the list of prohibited behaviors while smelling bad is not.

See the difficulty? Many of these solutions are plausible enough, but none of them, I think you will agree, is really desirable. A library operates under different rules than a large office building, where under normal circumstances, uniformed security guards are seated behind a desk, carefully watching everyone who comes in or leaves, and, who are under explicit instructions from building management not to tolerate shabby, smelly people. Guards in such buildings might also have a bank of television screens showing different views of the lobby from surveillance cameras.

Fortunately, or unfortunately—take your pick—the library is not like that. The burden of proof for keeping someone out or making someone leave falls on the staff. True, we have established rules of conduct, and anyone breaking them may get the old heave-ho from our security guy on duty. In rare cases, we've even had to make a quick call to the police. But the library operates under a set of rules and regulations that you're not going to find in the vast majority of public office buildings. As we are funded by public money, we are expected to be inclusive rather than exclusive and open rather than closed, with respect to whom we permit to enter and move freely around the building.

Now as I said, we have security guards (although far from the number we'd like) to see to it that people obey the rules, but beyond that, there's not much they can do. As an example, our guards are instructed to be polite and welcoming to the public, and the term *public* extends from the mayor to those men and women who, out of dire necessity, have to sleep under those downtown bridges I was talking about. And as for the people who are emotionally troubled or even mentally ill, do we have a way to screen them out before they enter the library? No. That's not the way it works. First, someone must do something against the rules, and then—only then—our guards are allowed to act. But none of that precludes or hinders close surveillance, however, and I am proud to say that incidents of violence in any of our libraries are so rare as to be statistically negligible, and we intend to keep things that way.

I could hold forth on this topic for hours. Some of y'all, in fact, have heard me do it. But I feel it's worth talking about as much as possible. Clearly, public safety, in this era of terrorist threats and high crime statistics, is an important topic. But that's not what I plan to spend the rest of my time talking to y'all about.

It's time now to acquaint you, my fellow rotarians, with a different type of security, one I'm sure you've heard about and read about increasingly in recent years: electronic security. Electronic security broadly refers to all the measures and countermeasures that we take in order to keep our electronic information secure and safely locked away from unauthorized intrusion and prying eyes. Putting it another way, we want to keep our files untampered with and our borrowers' personal information personal—it's as simple as that.

There are information bandits out there—call them hackers or crackers or what you will—practicing various forms of information theft, identity theft, unlawful access to records (both public and private), and electronic manipulation of funds (constituting embezzlement). These bad guys sometimes try to introduce crippling viruses into our programs that can turn a hard drive full of important information into gibberish or just screen-after-blank-screen of nothing, in seconds. Keeping our information secure—and don't kid yourselves, it's your information, too—is as a priority, right up there with ensuring that our patrons and staff are not assaulted or robbed.

But don't think that we who work in your community library just sit around wringing our hands about the various security problems that confront us. In the area of bolstering our electronic security, for example, we have taken the positive step of installing a state-of-the-art firewall on our main computer server that requires all persons seeking access to our files to identify themselves. In the event that a person seeking access turns out not to be an authorized user (and we have levels of users ranging from general to high security insider), the firewall traps and isolates the username and password of the suspected intruder, walls it off from the information he or she seeks, and sets about attempting to ascertain the true identity of the intruder. It doesn't always work out the way we'd like, but it's reliable enough to make a hacker think twice, and that's the point of the exercise.

So what do we get in return for our large investment in electronic security? We used to be afraid (even if we didn't go on and on about it) about what a hacker or cracker with too much time on his hands and sophisticated knowledge of computers might do to penetrate our system. But no longer. Before, we felt vulnerable and afraid when we thought about the mischief that could be done to our system, without either our knowledge or consent.

Today, however, I'm pleased to tell you that no one—except possibly the most sophisticated information bandits—can succeed in penetrating our firewall and getting into our private and valuable records, no matter how resourceful they are or how hard they try. Does that sound like boasting? Braggadocio, perhaps? Possibly, but I hope it demonstrates the level of confidence I have in our new electronic security system. Mind you, I hope nobody actually puts our new firewall to the test, but I say that should anyone be so rash or so foolish as to try it, well, bring it on!

Oh! Just look at the clock! See how time passes when you're having fun? My time's just about up, and I've hardly scratched the surface of what I could tell you about our library had I the time and you the patience. There's so much more I could mention, but I fear that I might become like one of those infomercials they show on late night television. So let me exit by repeating my invitation that y'all come and visit or revisit the wonderful, hard-working, and ever-changing Pecan Grove Public Library, whose downtown site is just a few blocks from where we are meeting this morning. Call ahead, in fact, and one of my talented staff will be happy to take you on a guided tour. Thanks again for inviting me here today and for the chance to talk about our library. I'm outta here. Come on down!

Questions for Discussion

1. What methods might be most effective in retaining library materials and equipment without entailing much in the way of additional funding?

2. Are there some ways of dealing with malodorous library patrons that do not appear on Ann's list?

3. Do you believe it was wise for Ann to boast that the library's electronic security is so strong that she is confident that almost no one could penetrate it? Why or why not?

Case 2

Any Minute Now

Mic Barron, systems analyst, to his personal tape-recorder at home

Let's see, here. Hmm, it's 6:50 A.M., Pecan Grove time, and that means that we're just ten minutes away from the moment when the payroll gets printed out over in Sumnerville at 8:00 A.M. sharp. Ten minutes to go. The last few days have been an agony of waiting, but soon, very soon! Oh, it's going to be so . . . It's just a pity I won't be seeing it, myself. That's the only sad part. I wish I could be there to watch.

Here's something about me: I don't take insults or injuries lying down. Nobody is going to do me wrong and get away with it. *Nobody*. I always get payback when someone treats me unfairly. It's just the way I am. Anybody wrongs me, they'd better watch out. And this time, vengeance is going to be mine! I didn't take all those high-level programming courses back in college for nothing. Nuh-uh baby, no way! All those grueling hours of writing code, running programs, eliminating bugs, troubleshooting errors, and more recently, making a library system hackproof have given me some really useful skills. That's why I'm a star in my profession (whether others realize it or not). And now, all that work is finally about to pay off, big time, even if I'm the only one to know all the details.

Ten minutes now and it's payback time!

I'm recording this for posterity even if nobody else ever hears it. So here's how it all went down: Last year, when I was hired by the Sumnerville Public Library as a programmer/systems analyst, I went happily to work and quickly became the "go-to guy" for a small staff of technically unsophisticated librarians. Most of my colleagues were clueless when it came to technology. So I acquired a deserved reputation as an absolute genius at fixing technical problems, although what I did wasn't really all that hard. The staff in Sumnerville came to depend on me more and more. I was their utility infielder, programmer, systems analyst, repairman, whatever. I did it all. As

8

my boss became increasingly aware of my value to the library, my salary grew and became quite respectable (competitive with private-sector pay, anyway) and second only to the director's. This really bugged the associate director who had served the institution for years and had acquired a couple of advanced degrees along the way. Helms, that pompous, strutting fool, with his starched collars and his fancy, high-toned way of speaking. While I thought it only fair that I was well paid for what I did, I figure it may have been the principal reason why he picked me to fire: paycheck envy.

Helms resented the fact that I earned more than he did, and he never tried to conceal it from me. He should have understood that it's all about supply and demand, but I guess he didn't and probably never will. But it wasn't just my salary. The other reason I was targeted for extinction at the Sumnerville Library, I admit, is that I don't suffer fools gladly. I refuse to kiss up to bosses or socialize with dull people who haven't the faintest idea of how hard it is to pull off my accomplishments, even though I make what I do look effortless.

Helms was always treating me with condescension. Bloody snob. But it's true—I don't mix well with others. Still, I didn't quit—he fired me. Well, that's one way to look at it. In many ways, though, I fired *him!* Just about now, I'm sure they'd like to talk to me about recent events back in Sumnerville. Well, they can question me, but first they have to find me, the fools! I'm working here now in Pecan Grove, almost 2,000 miles away from the scene of the crime and sporting a brand new identity. I figure I'm going to be a bit hard to locate. After all, I left work, left town, left the time zone, and moved way down here, leaving no forwarding address. So let them look.

Now I know there are plenty of my former fellow employees who just loved it when I got cashiered and sent packing. Helms, in particular, had the knife out for me since day one. He's a nasty piece of work, Helms, a stuffed shirt, who never bothered to conceal his dislike for me, even before he looked closely at the payroll printout one day and found out that I made $5,000 a year more than he did, despite all those advanced degrees of his. That's gotta hurt, I suppose, but too bad for him. It's simply a matter of supply and demand. Anyway, Helms was a sneaky micromanager, always snooping around, trying to catch me at something I shouldn't be doing and talking me down to others in the staff room. Some of the people I worked with at that library were all right, I guess. Limited, but basically all right. But Helms? If I ran that place, I wouldn't pay him nickel one. That library would be better off without him; not without me. It just isn't fair. Anyway, that's all going to change any minute now, and today—payday—when the staff payroll comes out and is missing my name: gotcha! I'm going to record all the details while they're still fresh in my mind. But first, another look at my watch.

Five minutes to go. Sweet!

The director back in Sumnerville wasn't so bad. Pretty good, actually, for a boss. I'm sorry that she's going to suffer along with the rest of them when my little land mine goes off. I hope she doesn't lose her job over it, but hey, in a war, there's always a certain amount of collateral damage, right? Who said that? Some general, maybe. Anyway, that's the way of the world. Collective guilt: the innocent have to pay the price along with the guilty. That's just the way it is.

But Helms—that pompous twit in a three-piece suit and "old school" tie—will soon be running around like the proverbial headless chicken when he sees what's happened to the library's irreplaceable system of electronic recordkeeping. Who knows? Maybe he'll get fired for not protecting better against the actions of insiders, those trusted employees with password access to sensitive information and files.

People like me.

Oh, I'd just love to be a fly on the wall, watching and listening when he gets called in to explain the catastrophe. They'll say he was negligent in allowing this to happen. He'll be blamed because such a tragedy wasn't prevented. Oh, payback is a wonderful thing! It was only a matter of time until Helms found a way to get rid of me, after city hall announced the need for job cuts and layoffs to balance the municipal budget. I knew my name headed the list on his personal excremental roster. So I took . . . precautions, while waiting for the chop. Let's say anticipated, because I didn't really want to leave. Not just yet, anyway. I had to be ready before Helms had a chance to can me. I had to prepare my nasty little surprise to initialize now, not then—with the ax coming down on my neck. Now there's nothing any of them can do to prevent it. In just a matter of minutes, unless something goes seriously wrong, I'll have my payback in a really subtle way because after my Trojan Horse activates itself, it'll delete the sequence that caused it to attack and destroy the files in the first place. Is that cool, or what? Any minute now.

Hmm, three minutes to go.

Don't get me wrong, I'm not an evil person. Well, not always, anyway. At least, I'm not your conventional villain. After all, firing me didn't have to happen. Until it did, I was content—more or less—just to keep it all status quo, and nobody would have been hurt. I would've worked hard for them over in Sumnerville. My little subroutine would have drowsed quietly forever in the bowels of the mainframe, if they'd just kept me on—that's all they had to do! Just kept me on the payroll, and I'd have given 'em a good day's work for their money. But layoffs were necessary, according to the city. Fine, go ahead, fire somebody. But why me? I was the indispensable man! Anybody else and my terrible swift sword of justice would have stayed in the scabbard, so to speak.

I know, that image is melodramatic hyperbole, but what the hell.

See, nobody in the executive suite suspected it, but my biweekly paychecks were, in a sense, premiums on an insurance policy—an insurance policy that virtually guaranteed that the library's technical operations ran smoothly, just as long as my name stayed on the system's payroll. That's all I required: survival. And if it'd been *my* idea to go somewhere else, no problem. On my last day, I would have simply deleted the lines of code I'd secretly put in the system, and we could've parted with smiles and handshakes all around. Maybe even a staff going away party for me, with a cake and spiked punch! Why not?

But, no! Helms went ahead and fired me just out of jealous spite, and because he didn't like me, and now he and all the rest of them are going to pay dearly! Because any minute now, it'll be payday and payback time back in Sumnerville, and when my Trojan Horse automatically triggers itself, they're guaranteed not to like the results. Not even a little bit.

I was so cool that day! I'd prepared for it carefully, so when I got canned, I took it like a man. I smiled, even, to Helms's obvious astonishment. That's the beauty part. Sheer genius, if I do say so myself. I'd arranged my homemade time bomb such that it would detonate automatically, not upon my firing, but today, just about now, when the payroll comes out missing my social security number, long after my departure. To activate the sequence, I didn't even have to touch a library computer or be anywhere around. Just wait and let things take their course. Even better, while Helms may strongly suspect what happened to make all the files go haywire, he'll be totally unable to prove anything, because my clever little secondary sequence will see to it that nothing connects me with anything that happened. Charges can't be made to stick on mere suspicion, can they?

I was so cool that day when Helms came over to me with that look of triumph in his eye. When I preceded him into his office, there were the library's two biggest security guards, standing there on either side of his desk like flankers protecting a quarterback. Obviously, the goons were there to react if I made any trouble. Trouble? *Moi?* Oh, it was beautiful! Helms was worried that I might decide to go violent on him and maybe launch myself over his big wooden desk at his fat throat and try to strangle him with his own necktie—not that it wouldn't have been a really good idea, of course. But he got the first of many surprises then, because I was the model of decorum and professional behavior when he gave me the bad news, and he must have felt foolish for bringing those two big bruisers into his inner sanctum to witness it all. No, Helms's jaw dropped when I smiled in parting and said, "Have a nice day!" And when the guards—under orders—escorted me and my box of belongings out of the building, I surprised them, too, by telling them how much I'd enjoyed working with them. What a moment: priceless!

About the sequence? My best work, and so easy: some planning, a few minutes at my terminal some weeks ago, after hours and over the past few weeks. After that my creation just lay dormant in the electronic innards of the library's mainframe computer. But today, any minute now, when the payroll program triggers it, *boom!* Clean sweepdown, fore and aft. No more information on the library's computer. My only regret is not being there now to eavesdrop on their frantic attempts to explain their sudden disaster to city hall. That'd be fascinating to hear. Totally. My program has been just lying there waiting. And now, because today is payday, all the library's electronic records—every bit and byte—will suddenly disappear for good, because the payroll is minus my employee number.

Two minutes, now.

Think of all of the computers in that place wiped clean! Some glitch or virus or something, they'll guess, getting past the firewalls and other safeguards. They'll try to reboot and scratch their heads and mutter when they can't recover any of their files. A fatal crash, the new systems guy will call it, and he'll be right about that. They'll try to fix it but when they can't restore the system, it'll turn into a nightmare. The files won't just be temporarily inaccessible, as they hoped; they'll be gone for good. All the files—*everything:* payroll, circulation, holdings, budget, and ordering—wiped clean as though a huge, powerful magnet had passed over the library's computers and stolen all the information, leaving nothing in its wake but empty hard drives and blank screens. Truly a catastrophe.

How big of a catastrophe you ask? Here's the bottom line: the automated catalog will be inoperable, the payroll and circulation files will be gone (with no record of who has borrowed what or when it's due), and worst of all, there will be no way to ascertain billing information (whom the library owes and how much). I figure they're going to have to contact each of the dozens of their book and materials vendors and ask, "Excuse me. How much do we owe you?" How could this have happened, people will ask. And who allowed it to happen? Some ghastly accident or an intentional act of sabotage?

No one will know for certain, but heads will roll. And Helms will be the fall guy and prime suspect.

Naturally, Helms will think of me, my recent dismissal and my obviously antipathy for him. Naturally, I'll become his prime candidate. Well, let him suspect whatever he likes. I hope he does. Without evidence, his theory won't get very far down at city hall. They'll have the police look for me under my old name and social security number, of course, but even if they ever do find me, let them try to prove anything.

Talk about a perfect crime? This is it.

After all, even if they track me down from my fingerprints or DNA or something, I can prove that I was here today all day, at my new job in Pecan Grove, almost 2000 miles away, when the attacking program self-activated in Sumnerville this morning. It's so beautiful! I only wish I could tell somebody about this. Maybe someday I'll be able to proclaim my astounding deeds to the world, but for now, I'm just going to lie low and enjoy my achievement by myself.

So here I am in Pecan Grove, off to a new start in a new library, under a new name. Amazing how easy it is to buy a complete set of new identity papers! Your basic piece of cake! Forget my old name. I'm Mic Barron now, with all the background and skills I need for the job I just got. But back in Sumnerville, that library is going to be an asylum run by the inmates for a long time. Without the online materials catalog, no one can use the library to look up a book or journal, get a holdings reference, access their e-mail, consult a search engine, or find out whether a book is in circulation, at the bindery, or on order.

My guess is they'll have to close the main building and probably all their branches indefinitely, during a thorough program analysis and criminal investigation, with staff either laid off or on paid furlough. Nobody will know how long it'll be until they get it all back, or even *if* they'll get it back. Actually, they won't. Some actions are just undoable, after all, like trying to "un-ring" a bell. Matter of fact, even *I* couldn't undo what's just about to happen over in Sumnerville. It's like when you drag a Mac program over to the trash and then empty the trash—that baby's history. Flushed. Gone with the wind. Sayonara. Adios.

How could this have happened, they'll wonder back in Sumnerville. They'll search for answers. Helms will dither about recognizing my hand in it, spouting theories, but he won't be believed, because how could an employee he already fired weeks ago, and who has since disappeared without a trace, be responsible for their tragedy? Anyway, they'll be looking for the guy I used to be, not the one I am now. I mean, conventional wisdom holds that the only way someone can bring down a big computer system single-handedly is by getting inside the building and accessing the master computer, using high-level clearance. Helms will report that he fired me, had me escorted from the premises immediately upon termination, and deleted my clearance immediately—following procedure to the letter, all true.

Poor guy—I almost feel sorry for him. He's going to feel like he got hit by a train. Maybe he'll even have a full-fledged nervous breakdown. Hackproof, he used to call his system. *Hackproof! Ha!* He used to boast that nobody without authorization could get into the system, and a firewall working 24/7 ensured that any unauthorized access would be prevented or detected, trapped, and isolated before the bandit can get past the computer's defenses and do something evil. Yeah, right.

In that, to an extent, he *was* right, of course. There was no unauthorized access. Nobody broke in, after all. Nobody unauthorized got his hands on the master controls. This saboteur was *inside* the system and already *had* clearance when the fatal code was inserted into the computer. How could they defend against that? Helms will demand that the police search for his chief suspect—lovable *moi*—who hasn't been seen or heard from in Sumnerville since the day he canned me—insisting that I did this, somehow. But where's the proof? Still, he'll always know it was me. Actually, I want him to. Who else had the motive, the means, and the opportunity to screw up the computers so badly? Now there's a question that's going to require an answer soon. Oh, man! Just two minutes now until doomsday.

Time to open the bottle and let the champagne breathe.

I'm looking at my watch, anticipating the exact moment when everything changes for Helms and his co-workers. Sooner or later, old Helms will get the chop. The tragedy happened on his watch, after all, and he's going to be the one held responsible for it. The buck stops in his office . . . as long as it's still *his* office, of course. His days are numbered, you can take that to the bank. I'm even tempted to wait a day or two and then call Helms, identify myself, and ask him, "So, what's new?"

Delicious.

Just a matter of seconds now. The Sumnerville library payroll gets printed out in five-four-three-two-one-*ZERO!*

Woo-hoo!

Time to pour a glass of champagne. (Just one though—still got to work today.) And now, a toast! Here's to old enemies and new friends! Ahhh, poor old Helms! He never learned the sad lesson that there is no perfect security—only different levels of *insecurity,* but he'll learn after today, oh, yes! He'll remember now. On the unemployment lines, he's going to think of that often, I should imagine. I figure he'll be lucky to find a decent job in another library, after taking the fall for this fiasco. In fact, if I were Helms, about now, I'd stop thinking about the library's plans for recovering its electronic files and begin practicing a new work-related line: "You want fries with that sandwich, sir?"

Another touch of the bubbly, sir? Why, yes, thank you so much. Don't mind if I do.

Questions for Discussion

1. What, if anything, might the Sumnerville Library have done beforehand to prevent a trusted employee from carrying out such a scheme of vengeance?

2. What part, if any, did Helms play in contributing to the situation at hand, and how would you, as director, deal with him in the aftermath of this disaster?

3. What can the Pecan Grove Public Library do in the future to protect itself from the malicious actions of a trusted employee who has all of the access codes?

Case 3

An Offer You Can't Refuse

Joy Nees, mayor of Pecan Grove, to Ann Cameron Bowman, library director, by telephone

Good morning! I'm really glad it's Friday, aren't you? This has been a hell of a week! Well, let me tell you why I've called. It's a matter of some delicacy, so I hope you're alone in your office. Are you? Good. Yeah, I'll wait while you close the door.

Well, to begin with, I don't mind saying that I love being in politics, and serving this city as mayor is a dream come true for a person like me. There are so many advantages to being at the top of this pyramid of command that I can't begin to tell you what they all are. However, there's a downside, too, and that's the problem. When you're a prominent politician, people come to you with their hats in their hands and make requests, but they're not really requests, you follow? I mean, behind many offers is an implied threat, and behind every expression of support is evidence that they're going to be asking me to do something for them, soon, in return.

Remember *The Godfather?* The original one, you know: Marlon Brando as Don Corleone? Remember the opening sequence, when it's his daughter's wedding day, and by tradition, on that day, the Godfather receives requests for favors from his people, and he's expected to grant all reasonable requests in honor of the occasion. Yeah, that scene. There's the little man who owns a funeral parlor, who wants his daughter avenged for a brutal assault. Well, if you remember it as vividly as I do, you will also remember that, in agreeing to have his daughter's attackers sorted out, the don also warns that one day he may request a favor of his own, and that he will expect that it will be granted without hesitation.

Well, that's a good analogy to the situation I have now. Some people were very instrumental in getting me elected two years ago. Mr. and Mrs. Bertram Lee, you know them? Know *of* them, I see. Well, the Lees did a lot for me in fundraising and getting out the vote. And now, they want a little favor in return. Right—an offer I can't refuse. And it pains me to remind you that I was the one who hired you and saw to it that you receive a more-than-adequate salary for your efforts on behalf of our excellent city library. So, it's embarrassing to say this, but I figure you owe me. Yeah, I know, an offer *you* can't refuse, this time. That's the way it goes. Quid pro quo. But wait until you hear what I'm asking—it's such a small matter that you might have done it without all this buildup. But I wanted to emphasize how important it is to me to see that it gets done.

What kind of favor am I asking? Not much, a very small matter, actually. All I'm asking is that you move one of your employees from one job to another, that's all. Nobody gets fired, nobody's demoted. Everybody's pay stays the same.

Yeah, you're right. I admit it. The request is easy. But the devil is in the details. Ann, I'm normally loath to intrude in personnel matters in your library system, and I think of myself as a laid-back, laissez-faire, sort of manager. But pressure has been brought to bear on me, and so I promised it would be discussed with you.

Specifically, I'm talking about Tommy Lee, who serves as your downtown library's mailroom clerk. He's the only son of Mr. and Mrs. R. Bertram Lee, who happen to be prominent citizens of Pecan Grove, as you know, and, I don't mind adding, substantial donors to my political war chest. Yes, I know, politics can be a dirty game, and the problem with accepting money from supporters is often that it comes with hidden strings attached. Anyway, I want to accommodate Mr. and Mrs. Lee who are concerned for the safety of their son, Tommy. So I promised I'd speak to you about it and then leave the matter to your best judgment.

Tommy Lee is a young man who finished high school with mid-level grades last year and is now taking a year or two off to "find himself" while he decides whether to continue with his education. In the meantime, you will remember, I trust, that I recommended him strongly for the job of mailroom clerk and messenger for the downtown library. This recommendation was based on my personal acquaintance with the young man, and the fact that his parents wanted to get him a job downtown, where he would enter the world of work and receive a paycheck for his efforts. Tommy went to work for your library last summer, and as far as I know, his evaluations have been favorable. He's not afraid of hard work and has an engaging personality that has won him a number of friends in the library system. He goes about his daily duties cheerfully, opening the mail, sorting it, routing or bringing it to staff at their workstations, and helping with the unpacking of book boxes and other containers containing library materials.

He says that he was happy in his job before September of last year, but then, suddenly, the world changed forever, at least as far as daily life in America is concerned. The drumbeat of frightening news stories concerning the transmission of toxic and life-threatening substances to various public figures via the mails has caused him a lot of concern. And it's not just hysteria, as you know: some have already died of Anthrax inhalation or been infected with the less serious but still potentially life-threatening skin form of Anthrax. There is even talk of smallpox being unleashed on citizens by terrorists, domestic or foreign, but so far, thankfully, no outbreak of that type has been reported.

But forget smallpox. Anthrax is real, it is devastating, and it is frequently delivered by persons unknown via the mail to their intended targets. As a matter of fact, while I personally have not received any letters (or at least no one in city hall has yet tested positive for anthrax spores) I think it is fair to say that we are all more cautious about what we do. The simple act of opening our mail can lead to sickness and death. Still, if we are reasonably prudent, the government assures us that we will come through this dark period in the nation's history with flying colors. We will refuse, as a people, to succumb to fear, which is one of the principal objectives of the terrorists who are sending those toxic substances around.

Which brings me back to Tommy, who is, as I said, the only and beloved son of some of the most influential people in town and personal friends of mine. Now the Lees watch the news and read the papers just like everybody else. And when they became aware that some mad and vicious people were sending letters full of Anthrax through the mails to people they want to infect, they became alarmed. I'm sure you are aware that Tommy's job description requires him to sort mail and to be the general intake person for all the packages the library receives every day of the year. This puts him at high risk for coming into contact with whatever is on or in the envelopes, packages, or containers he routinely handles.

I don't think he wanted to do it, but his parents bullied him into going to his personnel head at your library—a Mr. Bozeman, I believe—and requesting a transfer out of the mailroom to a safer job. His reasons were pretty compelling: He does not wish to die as a victim of airborne or impregnated substances on the mail he handles. Unfortunately, Tommy reported to his parents that evening that Mr. Bozeman refused his request. He said that no Anthrax evidence had yet turned up in Pecan Grove and that moving Tommy out of the mailroom job would mean putting someone else at risk. To soften the blow, Bozeman offered that the library would purchase a supply of disposable surgical masks and surgical gloves to help Tommy ward off anything that might be on the letters he handles or boxes he opens every day.

The bottom line, Tommy was told, was that no one would voluntarily exchange places with him, and no one should be asked to do so.

Now, I haven't actually talked to Tommy about this, personally, and I don't think I really need to, but his parents call me frequently, asking if there's anything I can do for him. They'd be calling you all the time, as well, but I made them promise that they wouldn't bother you. So I'm running interference for them; as I said, they're friends of mine, they're very helpful in fundraising, but I also think it's the right thing to do. Mrs. Lee, in particular, tells me that for months she's been having frequent nightmares involving her Tommy and something nasty in one of the letters he has to open every day.

But she should see this problem from my perspective: I've got a quarter of a million people living in my city, and I feel responsible for their safety and welfare. What that means is that I can hardly watch the news anymore because every time I do and I find out that somebody new has been infected with the Anthrax bacillus, I get anxiety attacks. That's no exaggeration, by the way. I'm under the care of a therapist over this, and it's probably only because of the wonderful drug I'm on that I can discuss this with you so calmly.

Well, I won't chatter on about my personal problems, but I'll just let you go with a personal request. I'm asking you—as a friend and as your boss—to intercede with your Mr. Bozeman in personnel and arrange for Tommy Lee to be transferred to some other job within his abilities. I don't really care what, although I understand that he has considerable computer skills, based on his parents' reports that he spends huge amounts of his free time playing some sort of interactive game on his PC. The details of the transfer I'll leave to you, but I think it's important that Tommy keep working for the library. Maybe you could transfer him someplace else in the system.

Do this for me, Ann, and you will have accomplished several feats at once. First, you'll reduce my anxiety level a bit, because these irritating but influential people will get off my back when their Tommy is out of harm's way. Anyway, they're not asking this out of selfishness or greed, like some of my constituents do when they come to me for favors. They're just acting out of deep love for their son. Second, Tommy sounds like a smart and flexible enough young man to be able to do a good job wherever he happens to be working. So why not reassign him to make his parents happy? Finally, I firmly believe in quid pro quo, so if you do me this favor . . . well, all I can say is that I'll owe you one.

A big one.

I can't define any further the extent of my gratitude now, but you'll recognize it when you see it. Do this for me (and for my friends and their Tommy) and you just might find me able to open a few doors in the budget process next year, if you know what I mean? What? Bozeman? Heavens, no! No reprisals. He was just doing his job, but I'm sure you can use your powers of persuasion to make him see the light, am I correct? Look, we're both busy people with important jobs, so I'm not going to take up any more of your time. I'll leave it in your capable hands now. It's just a little favor I'm asking, but it's not a small matter to me, or I wouldn't be making a special point of asking it of you. Tell you what. Take some time to mull this over, but I hope to hear from you by Monday morning about what you decide. I know it'll be the right thing. My best to your husband and the kids! Talk to you again soon. Ciao!

Questions for Discussion

1.   What precautions should mailroom employees in libraries take to avoid contact with hazardous substances?

2.   As director, how would you respond to the mayor's request?

3.   As director, what would you say to the personnel specialist to justify overruling his decision?

Case 4

"Borrowing" Privileges

Mike Early, security guard, to Mary Rhoades, head of reference, in the central library's break room

You know, sometimes, I think I'm psychic. No, don't laugh. I just seem to know, sometimes, what's going to happen next. Now, I don't expect to get my own TV show as one of those infomercial psychics or anything like that; but, in my opinion, I've got a form of ESP. They talk about stuff like that all the time on TV, you know, the sixth sense, like somebody knows the instant that a relative dies, or people get this funny feeling when the phone rings, and they know who it's going to be. But whatever I've got, I figure I have more of it than your average person.

And I figure that's what makes me a good security guard. I can usually tell when people are up to something. So, is that ESP? Like with so many things, I guess, it all depends. I'm skeptical about ESP, but I try to keep an open mind about it. There are so many crooks and bogus prophets and con artists out there advertising themselves as psychics that I can't credit the idea that some people can actually tell when something is going to happen ahead of time. I'm no mind reader; I'm just an apt student of human behavior.

Yeah, I'm good at that. I can check people out, size them up, and, more times than not, figure out what they're going to do next. Where did it come from, my gift? Well, it's not genetic, so I prefer to think that I learned what I know about human behavior—not in college or university—but in the school of life. How does it work? I don't really understand it, myself. I just keep my eyes open and have learned to interpret what I see. The payoff is that I can identify problem patrons, even when they look like everybody else, just by looking. I just know what to look for. No magic about it.

It also helps that I'm a really big guy—even though I'm getting on in years and haven't really been in shape for the last 20. Sometimes my size has been helpful—one look at me coming up on them, and threatening people tend to back down. I have another gift, as well—what the sisters back at my parochial high school called the gift of mimicry. I can watch another person and pick up their traits. For instance? All right: Clint Eastwood. You know him, right? His movies? There was one in particular, one of the "Dirty Harry" movies he starred in maybe 25 years ago that still gets a lot of play on late-night television. Anyway, it was the one where he pointed a gun at a criminal and said, "Go ahead, make my day!" with the most terrifying glare I've ever seen on a nice looking guy. Yeah, Eastwood can go from a gentle grin to that steely look in a second, and whoever he's looking at that way looks scared enough to wet his pants.

So I've practiced my Eastwood look over the years, especially as my face got more wrinkled and weather-beaten. I've pretty much perfected it and used it to pretty good effect over the years. Avoided a lot of difficult situations just by turning my laser beams on some delinquent or tough guy who thinks he's bad. No, I don't have to say, "Make my day," but they get the idea. I don't mean to brag, but a lot of guys back down, even some less than half my age.

But you know the boss lady, Ann, bless her. She says that while she can appreciate the uses of my stern expressions and demeanor, she expects that there should be very little call for me to use them in the library. "After all," she says, "intimidation and threatening looks may be part of the bag of tricks of a bouncer in a nightclub or bar, but this is a public library. I'm sure you can see the differences between your job as a library security guard and being a bouncer." Sometimes, I wonder, though. Maybe she's right about that, but she's also wrong, in a way. True, maybe 99 percent of the problems I run up against in my daily work don't require any bouncer tactics, but there's that other one percent, like what happened this morning.

There's this young guy who comes in three or four days a week and makes right for the Reference area. You can usually see him over there in the back of the room where we keep the law reference books, with several of them stacked all around his place at one of the tables and his battered briefcase bulging with legal pads and pages of notes. What's he look like? Well, have you ever seen a weasel? Like that, sort of, with bright little eyes (even behind those thick lenses he wears), a small wiry frame, and a nervous, darting manner. He's been here so much lately that I've started thinking of him as "The Weasel," although I really ought to knock it off with giving our problem patrons nicknames, even privately. Someday, I might slip and use one of them in the wrong company, and that could be bad.

But forgive me if I refer to him as the Weasel. Until I read the police report, I never knew his actual name, and given the way he behaved today, I think the name I hung on him is very appropriate, even if it's not exactly a compliment. So anyway, today, from about quarter past nine on, this Weasel is in his usual spot, writing down stuff in one of those notebooks he keeps in that briefcase and muttering to himself as he does. I've seen him doing that so often lately that I didn't think anything special. In fact, I'm so used to seeing him there that he's practically a part of the furniture. On occasion, I'll catch his eye and give him, not the Eastwood look, but an "I'm watching you" look, just to keep him aware that he's under observation. Because, as I say, I have a sixth sense, sometimes, and this guy was wrong. I could almost smell it.

Now one thing I've observed is that when the Weasel gets up and scuttles out the front door at lunchtime, he walks fast, keeps his head down, and swings his briefcase, which tells me that it's pretty light because it's easy to swing from one arm, even for a little weasely guy like him. See what I mean about powers of observation? My ESP? No big trick. Just observation.

Today, however, things were different, not so much in what he did as he moved toward the door but different in . . . I don't know . . . call it feeling. Yeah, that sixth sense I was telling you about was sending alarm bells up and down my brain stem, even though everything else about the guy looked pretty normal. But at about noon, I was standing facing the front doors, looking at everybody coming and going. Today was typical—too early for the student crowd, mostly the usual: retired people, homemakers, and a few business types. No kids at that hour, except on Saturdays and school holidays. The usual suspects, you might say. I try to make eye contact when I can. So this morning, I'm smiling my friendly grandfatherly smile at people, trying to go for the expression that says, "Hey there! Welcome to the library. Glad you're here! Come on in and set a spell!" Less-welcoming looks, I usually save for after school, in case some of the local gangbangers duck into the library for any reason, such as homework assignments. When I see them all tricked out in their gang jackets, they get the "I'm watching you" look, letting them know that Eastwood is always ready. Helps keep order, I figure.

So there I am, standing next to the circulation desk and using my powers of observation. And that's when my sixth sense tells me that there's something wrong, or different, anyway, about the Weasel today. He's scuttling out the door as he always does, looking down at his scuffed sneakers. Nothing unusual there. And, as always, he's got his battered brown briefcase at his side. But suddenly, I realize that that's *it!* The briefcase is bigger, bulgier, and from the look of it, weighing him down so badly that he has to change arms halfway between the Reference area and the front door. Like I told you, previously, that briefcase seemed to be light, swinging easily from his puny little arm. But not today. No, today, the Weasel, on his way to the front door, seemed to be struggling, as though his briefcase was suddenly very heavy.

Naturally, my suspicions were aroused, so I angled over and intercepted him about 10 feet from front door. I just stood in front of the little guy, careful not to look threatening or accusing. Instead, I decided to go for friendly and helpful. Remember I said I had the gift of mimicry? Well, my grandfather brought the family over here from Ireland, and when I remember him, I like to think I can still imitate a brogue. So I decided, since we'd never spoken before, to give the Weasel a shot of my Paddy routine: "Well, now, me son, top o' the morning' to ye, and would ye like us to give you a hand carrying that heavy parcel to your car, then?" Despite my certainty that this guy was up to something, I went for bluff good cheer, smiling broadly.

The Weasel looked up, startled. We'd never said a word to each other before. He looked just plain nervous, his no-color eyes swimming behind those thick glasses of his. Finally, he found his voice. "Uh, no thanks," he mumbled. A thin line of perspiration broke out on his forehead. He tried to side-step me and walk to the door. But I blocked his escape route simply by standing between him and the door. "Oh, come on, fella! Give over. That case looks pretty heavy, and I could do with a bit of exercise just now. As it happens, I'm just slipping round back for a smoke and to get some air, so allow me to relieve you of your heavy burden there and walk you to your car or the bus stop or anywhere you choose."

Looking panicky now, the Weasel raised his voice. "I said *no!*" he shouted, waving his arms in agitation, which caused the old briefcase to slip out of his sweaty hand and fall to the floor. Unluckily for him, the ancient, rust-spotted brass clasp broke open, scattering the contents of the case on the floor around us. Looking down, I could see three or four legal size notebooks, what I took to be a lunch bag, and about a dozen pencils and pens. But the largest item that spilled out of the briefcase was a red-bound book, a familiar looking, massive volume. It had only just fit inside the case so that it could only be closed when squatting down. The title on the spine (along with its reference call number) read *Black's Law Dictionary*. I slowly rose to my full height and smiled rather grimly down at the shivering Weasel, still in character as a bemused Irish cop. "Oh, ho! And what would this be, then? One of our reference books, perhaps, boyo? One of the books that clearly never leaves the building and is plainly stamped as such? Now, how the devil did that find its way into your case, I'm wondering!"

"Um . . ." was all he could manage, unable to meet my eyes. At that point, my sixth sense showed me what he was thinking. He was wondering if he should leave his case and barrel out the door. He was probably wondering how an overweight and getting-on-in-years guy like me could catch a quick little weasel like himself. So that's why I reached out and gently but firmly took hold of his arm. His sleeve, actually, but I clamped down just hard enough that I could feel his scrawny arm.

Now, I also know what *you're* thinking, along about now, Mary. You're thinking that library staff aren't allowed to manhandle the customers, and you'd be right. I know full well that physical contact—except in certain situations—is forbidden. Now, there's a definite difference between what I do and the job of a bouncer at one of those raucous bars down on Main Street. I'm not supposed to touch anybody. Lawsuits, and that, you know. But I figured that this was one of those special situations, and I acted accordingly. Tightening my grip on this guy's sleeve, just in case he was still thinking about making a run for it, I whispered as softly as I could, so as not to alert any more people than necessary to what was going on. I breathed into his ear, still playing the Irish cop, "Come along quietly with me, boyo; that's right, no fuss, and we'll have a wee chat about all this, upstairs."

Thus far, the kid hadn't made any real mistakes. All right, he'd tried to rip off the library—and, therefore, the community and the taxpayers—of a very expensive and useful component of the reference collection, but now, having passed through terror, he decided to go for outrage instead. He resisted me, as best he could, trying to disengage his arm, and screamed, "Fascist! Let go of me!" He looked wildly around the room at all the people who were startled from whatever they'd been doing, like one of those old stockbroker commercials, you know the ones? It's a party, maybe, and everybody's eating and laughing it up and talking small talk, when one guy in a tuxedo says to another, "Well, my broker is E. F. Hutton, and he says . . ." and everybody freezes in the hopes of hearing what Hutton has to say on the matter. Well, it was like that.

The kid kept trying to pull away from me, all the while trying to inform spectators of what a gross miscarriage of justice was being visited on his innocent self. "You're all witnesses that this big thug attacked me and accused me of something I didn't do!" he said. "Now he's forcing me to go upstairs with him. Look carefully at my face. Not a mark on it, right? Just remember that in case there are mysterious lumps or bruises on it later, all right?"

Suddenly, I'm aware of how this might look to someone who didn't know what was going down. Here's me, tall, wide bodied and powerfully built and still well muscled, even if I'm going to fat, holding the arm of this puny little guy, who must stand about five foot six, tops, and weigh no more than 140 pounds. And he's playing to his "audience," making all that noise about being repressed by a vicious bully, and we have a publicity disaster in the making! Of course, I considered taking my own case public by holding up the big red book that was sitting on the floor and announcing to everybody in the room that my actions were justified by the fact that the Weasel has just been apprehended trying to steal it. But I decided that that was probably not a good idea, so I just stood there, contemplating my next move, not about to let go of the struggling Weasel. Mind you, I was careful not to hurt him, but the temptation to tighten my grip was very strong.

At that moment, Mike Chitwood, the associate director of the library, hearing our row, came trotting down the stairs and rushed right over to us. Motioning for us to get out of the main entryway, Mike looked first at the Weasel and then up at me. The kid started to say something, but Mike motioned for him to hold his tongue. "Perhaps we'd all be better off if we discussed this—just the three of us—in the privacy of my office," he suggested, although clearly, it was not a mere suggestion. "This way, gentlemen!" He motioned for us to precede him up the stairs. I stooped, picked up the book, watched while the young man collected the contents of his briefcase, and accompanied him upstairs, my hand still lightly but firmly clenched around his skinny arm. Fortunately for all concerned, the kid said nothing on the way up. One more time was all he had to call me a fascist, a goon, or a Nazi, and I might've . . . well, I don't know what I might have done, but I didn't see any reason to let him insult me. After all, he was a crook, caught redhanded; I was just doing my job, rather well, if I do say so myself.

Once we were seated around the conference table, Mike got down to business. He asked me first to tell him what had just happened, so I did. As I spoke, the Weasel looked at everything in the room but me, and I was afraid to look at him, lest I decide to leap across the table and bash him one for all the insults he'd shouted. Anyway, I gave a straightforward recitation of the facts. Then Mike turned to the Weasel, whose story was, of course, that he had no idea how the book got into his bag, and that I had no right to detain him or assault him.

"Assault you?" I said, probably too loudly. "Nobody assaulted you, son, and you know it. All I did was to prevent you from stealing one of our books. Trust me, son, if I'd actually assaulted you, you wouldn't be sitting here now chatting about it." And I couldn't resist; I gave him a shot of Clint Eastwood when Mike was looking away. He said to the kid: "Look, I want to find a satisfactory resolution to this unfortunate little incident, and I'm giving you a chance. Either tell us how that book came to be in your briefcase or I'll have no choice but to call the police and let them sort it out, so what's your pleasure?"

Finally, the Weasel gave it up. You could see him slump in his chair, like a balloon leaking air. Looking down at the conference table, he mumbled, "Well, maybe I did sort of happen to stick that book into my briefcase, yeah. But it was an accident. I mean, I wasn't stealing it. I don't need to steal a book, you know. I have an inheritance. I could buy my own copy. But stealing? No! See, I'm in first-year law at the local university, and I'm sure you'll believe how competitive that is. Like, the first day of classes, this senior prof walks in, welcomes us to law school, and then tells us that everybody should take a good, close look at the person to our right and the one to our left. Why? Because, he says, that there's a very good chance that of the three of us, two aren't going to be there to graduate. Think of that! Two out of three will wash out! And then think that there are maybe 200 students in our entering class, all wanting to use *Black's Law Dictionary* at the same time over at the law library. But here? Well, here I always find *Black's* in its place on the shelf whenever I come in, and nobody ever is, like, breathing down my neck to hurry me up. So I thought if I could just, you know, take the thing home and, like, memorize it or something, during these first two or three critical months, I'd be pretty much guaranteed to get decent grades.

You see, it's really important that I do well in law school, and flunking out is not an option for me. My grandfather was a graduate of the place, and so was my dad. Now it's my turn, and I mustn't screw up. So when this guard of yours says I was stealing this dictionary? I know that's what it looks like, but, no, see, I was just, you know, like, borrowing it temporarily. But you gotta believe me. I totally intended to bring it back at the end of the term! Honest! Besides, there's an honor code at the university and they take it seriously. So if what happened downstairs just now gets out, not only will my family never speak to me again, but they'll probably dismiss me from law school, so please! I'm begging you! Let me go and I promise that I will never, uh, borrow any of your books again without permission. I swear it!"

Well, Mike, thought this over and actually went for it. Yeah, to my astonishment and anger, he asked, "Then we have your solemn promise that you'll never try to make off with any of our materials again?" And the Weasel—I'm not making this up—put his hand across his heart (assuming he has one) and said, "I promise, so help me God! You have my word!"

I'd had enough of this. "Oh, come on, now!" I blurted. "Don't tell me that you buy this guy's act! I know guys like this. They have larceny in their soul. You can't honestly believe that he's never going to take another book. Tell me you're not that naive!"

Mike turned to the kid. "Young man, you know what you stand to lose if you try anything like this again, don't you?" He glared at the Weasel with his own, watered down, version of Eastwood. The Weasel just nodded. "And you won't pursue the matter of any alleged "assault" any further?"

"What assault?" asked the little thug, beaming innocently.

"But you can't . . .," I started to object, but Mike cut me off.

"I think we're finished, here. Young man, you are free to go. But one more incident of this kind, and the consequences . . ." He left the end of that sentence hanging in midair. Looking like he'd just won the state lottery, the Weasel rose from his chair.

"Thanks a lot!" he said. "I won't let you down, I promise!" He walked quickly out of the room. Any faster, he would have left skid marks on the linoleum. After he left, I couldn't think of anything to say that wouldn't get me suspended or even fired for insubordination. What's to say, anyway? I know Mike went easy on him, and he knows it, too; but it was his decision. Administrators get paid to decide things like that. That's why they get paid the big bucks, I figure. For two or three minutes, Mike and I sat silently. Finally, he broke the silence.

"We'll speak of this matter later, when we've both had a chance to reflect on it. For now, you have your duties, so you'd best return to them. One warning, though: When you see that young man in here, you may watch him closely, but I expect you to treat him with the same courtesy as you do all the rest of our visitors, is that understood," Mike implored. I shrugged, feeling tired, sullen, and defeated.

"Understood," I said.

"So as you leave, would you please take *Black's*, here," he pointed to the big red book at the heart of all this excitement, "and replace it in its customary place?" I lifted the book, and, as I reached the door, he added one final thing. "Listen, I understand how you feel and actually agree with you about getting tough on book thieves, but no matter what the provocation—unless bodily harm is in the offing—you just can't manhandle the customers. I guess we're going to need to talk about some anger management for you, eventually, but that can wait. That's all. Thanks for your alert detective skills. I appreciate that, without your quick work, we'd be out one important reference tool, at least until Christmas break comes, over at the university."

I nodded my head, acknowledging the compliment, and left, thinking about the way things are and how I wish they could be. So were my actions worth criticizing? I don't know. I'll have to sit down and think about that some more. But I can tell you this: if it'd been up to me, that Weasel would be banned from the library for life, and possibly, just possibly, with a little tune-up around his face to remind him of his adventures today. Thinking these thoughts, I trudged back into the Reference room and stuck *Black's* back in its hole on the shelving against the wall. So, tell me: What happened to justice in this world?

Questions for Discussion

1. Was the guard justified in using physical contact to detain the young man from leaving the building with a suspected stolen item in his briefcase? What if he'd been wrong?

2. Under what circumstances would it be appropriate to prosecute library patrons for "shoplifting" library materials?

3. Was the "deal" that the associate director made with the young man an appropriate action?

Case 5

An Ill Wind

Michael Chitwood, associate director, to Cindy Cutting, reporter for *The Pecan Grove Observer*, in a telephone interview

Lawsuit? Oh, I don't think it'll ever come to that. Or at least I hope not. But I guess you want my side of the story, so here it is: This all happened yesterday. You know how this time of year, maybe twice a week, they break into television programming to announce a weather advisory or bulletin, and it's usually a false alarm for most people in our viewing area? A few sprinkles, a thunderstorm, maybe even hailstones every once in a while, but nothing serious. Usually, when they call for a "tornado watch," a watch is all it is: the greatest thing that almost happened. Just because they issue a warning, it doesn't necessarily mean that we're going to get clobbered with damaging storms, or even necessarily that we'll see a single drop of rain.

So when yesterday's forecast called for the potential of severe storms in the area, I didn't really pay much attention, because we get advisories like that all the time. In fact, most of our viewing area was supposed to have partly cloudy skies, with little to worry about in terms of bad weather. Anyway, the advisory was for a watch, and there's a big difference between a tornado watch and a "tornado warning." Most folks are so used to them that they shake their heads and go on with their lives. Who really thought that one of those freak things would hit our library? Or that I would be named defendant in a lawsuit over my actions? Not me, I'll tell you that.

But tornados are quirky things, as you know. One might touch down, take out a house, then cross the street and total a second one, and then lift up into the clouds again, leaving the other houses on that block more or less untouched. Maybe a kid's bicycle gets picked up from a lawn and thrown back down in another yard a mile away. Who knows why one house is untouched, and the neighbor's house gets reduced to matchwood, bricks, and rubble?

Anyway, yesterday morning, I had heard the warning but I just filed it away under information to keep in mind and promptly forgot about it. I just figured that if there were any kind of serious weather scare, there'd be plenty of time to get ready for it. You know, sirens and alarms going off; dark, threatening clouds, heavy rains, thunder and lightning getting closer and louder, and more of those bulletins. But this time, I guess the fates had a great big nasty surprise in store for our library; we're just glad it didn't end in disaster. Anyway, when I pulled into the main library's staff parking lot at about eight-thirty yesterday morning, it was warm and humid, with thick cloud cover; but that's not unusual on a summer's day here in this part of the world. And once I was in the library, I had a huge number of items on my "to do" list, all screaming for attention at the same time, and I forgot about what was happening outside. Until lunchtime, anyway.

At one o'clock, I had lunch at a nearby restaurant; when I walked outside, I thought, uh-oh, we're in for it. How so? The air was full of the usual oppressive humidity, but there wasn't a speck of breeze and the sky was—I don't know—a funny color. What color? Hard to say. Sort of orange and tinged with shades of green, maybe. Not an ordinary sky, that much I can tell you. Still, I was alert to the fact that something could develop in the next couple of hours. As I walked back to the library, I listened, but I couldn't hear any thunder. Then? I guess it was about three o'clock, I became aware of thunder, audible even over the noise of the library's air-conditioning system. I couldn't tell whether the thunder was approaching, receding, or what.

Just then our administrative assistant, who keeps a radio on her desk, came bustling out of her office, and I knew something was up. She said, "I just heard on the radio that a tornado they're describing as potentially severe with very high winds just touched down about a mile south of the airport, and the weather service says it's headed this way." Uhh, how shall I put this? What I said is something you can't print in your newspaper. Here's a hint, though: it's a single word, and it's what a lot of people say when they receive sudden, surprising, bad, or frightening news. Just then, the sound of an air-raid siren came waxing and waning as it revolved around its perch on top of the First National Bank building. That's when I realized that we were all possibly in danger. So I closed my eyes, took several deep breaths, and decided it was time to make the emergency announcement over the PA system, still in the process of deciding what I would do after that, and in what order.

Normally, Sam, our library's security officer, handles such situations, but just by luck, he was spending his three-week vacation in Nigeria visiting his family, which left me in charge of his duties. Still, I'm no rookie: I knew what had to be done. Our library system has this main building downtown and four branches, and our security responsibility covers all of them. So before anything else, I telephoned all four branches to tell them what they had probably figured out for themselves: a tornado alert was in force for the city for the next hour or two, and they should follow standard emergency procedure.

Some libraries up north have basements, I know. That must be nice. One trouble with this part of the country is that almost nobody has a base-ment—houses and other buildings are typically built on concrete slabs. There's seldom a hole to crawl into when being above ground suddenly be-comes risky; not surprisingly, none of our five library buildings has a base-ment or cellar. Too bad, too, because a basement would have come in handy yesterday when that tornado came bearing down on us. But there was no time for wishing—I had to deal with the situation and assist in every way possible to see to it that nobody got hurt if or when the big wind hit. That's when I made the standard emergency announcement over the PA system, trying to keep any hint of panic out of my voice. What does it say? Let me read it to you:

> May I have your attention, please? The National Weather Service advises us that a confirmed tornado has been sighted and is now moving in the direction of the library building. We are therefore required to evacuate the building immediately. Everyone please move quickly but carefully to the main exit at once and remain calm. I repeat: Remain calm. File out of the building in an orderly fashion. Staff members will be posted at the exit to assist anyone needing help. Once outside, do not attempt to return to the library until the "all clear" has sounded. Thank you.

I guess that announcement says it all, conveying the urgency of the situa-tion without alarming people unduly. After I read it, I rushed downstairs and looked around the Adult Services area. Of course, a lot of folks had already gone home—gittin' while the gittin' was good. But maybe 18 people, scat-tered at various desks and tables, and perhaps 6 more over by the computer terminals, their faces all showing varying degrees of alarm, confusion, and fear, were still in the room. I just hoped that nobody was in the restrooms, because I couldn't be bothered to investigate the stalls given the crisis. Out-side, the rain seemed to intensify, while heavy thunderclaps were slamming down from all points of the compass at the same time. Was I scared? Well, yeah, but in control. But my heart was racing like crazy—I remember that.

My first priority, I figured, was crowd control; so trying for a confident smile, I raised my voice and addressed them all. "Folks," I said, "you heard the announcement. The library is now closed, and we all have to leave the building immediately for our own safety. So if you'll just follow me." Most of them needed no persuasion. They walked or ran outside and darted across the walkway to the adjacent parking lot. Not everybody, though. There's always one, isn't there?

"But I don't understand," said one large woman of about 50, sitting at a reading table. "Why can't we just stay inside where we're dry and protected? Wouldn't we be safer and better off in here than taking our chances out there with all that rain, wind, lightning, and who knows what else?"

"Sorry, ma'am," I said. "Orders are orders. Ours is not to reason why. Anyway, we don't really have any choice. This is an emergency, and emergencies require everyone's complete compliance. Now, please gather up your belongings and head on out the door. After I lock all the doors, I'll be right behind you, as soon as I check to see that everyone has left the building. So, please . . ." I gestured unmistakably to the front door, through which lightning flashes looked almost continuous.

Most of the people I'd spoken to had already hurried through the door, although understandably, nobody looked enthusiastic about going out there in that kind of weather. I saw one guy open his umbrella, but within seconds the wind whipped it out of his hands, up and away. Not an encouraging sight, admittedly, which must be why the woman I'd been talking to refused to budge. She'd seen it, too. She just stayed in the chair she'd been occupying, and stared at me fixedly, her face a mask of frightened but stubborn determination. "No way am I going out in that!" she said. I must admit I couldn't really blame her. Who could? Out of the corner of my field of vision, I could see a few last staff members rushing through the door and dodging through the rain as they struggled to get to the parking lot and the possible safety of their cars.

But the woman was still refusing to budge, and debate was not a viable option. "Lady, *please?*" I screamed, out of exasperation because the wind had escalated to a freight train roar. "There's no time for this! We're out of time! I have to ask you to evacuate the building now, like everybody else! We're the only two left, and I have a wife and children who need me, so give me a break! Make it easy on both us. Let's get out of here, while there's still time!" Outside, the roar of the wind was getting louder and louder. I could tell that she could hear it, too. But she stayed seated, her face a mixture of defiance and terror.

"Not going anywhere," was all she said. At that point I was so terrified and furious at the same time, that instinct must have taken over. So I reached out and grabbed her arm and hauled her up to her feet. I know I'm not supposed to touch the patrons, and certainly never manhandle them, but I didn't stop to reason it out. I just grabbed her nearest arm and yanked on it.

"I don't have time to argue with you," I shouted, "so either you head out that door *now,* or I swear, I'm going to drag . . ." But I never got to complete that sentence (probably just as well, because I wasn't sure that I could actually make good my threat to drag a large woman all the way to and through the front door). Because just then, two of the six big floor-to-ceiling picture windows on the west side of the library blew in at the same time with a crashing roar. Thank God for safety glass is all I can say, because instead of thousands of jagged shards, those huge windows fell to the floor into millions of tiny pieces.

Now, the woman forgot all about staying put, threw herself into my arms, wrapped me in a big, perfumed bear hug, and held on for dear life (literally), while what seemed like enough water to sink the *Titanic* poured into the building through the large, rectangular holes where windows had been just seconds before. Clearly, she needed no further persuading of the seriousness of our predicament. Without further protest, she clung to my neck, moaning softly, as we hobbled (like gawky contestants in a three-legged race) around the circulation desk, and into the back room, where there are fewer—and much smaller—windows. Anyway, those windows faced east, away from the storm and tornado.

Once we were in the back, I steered the woman over to a chair, where she slumped, weeping softly. I could see her lips moving—saying a prayer, perhaps—but before I could do anything else, I became aware that the tornado seemed to be lifting and the winds howling around the building were subsiding quickly. Lo and behold, five minutes later, the winds had died and the rain had quit. Another minute and I could see through the back windows that the thunder and lightning were rumbling and muttering off to the east, and the big storm was just about over. When it seemed quiet enough, the woman shot me a murderous look and ran out the front door; she didn't return.

When I got back to my office and picked up the telephone to call around to the branches for preliminary damage reports, I wasn't all that surprised to find that the phones were all dead. Fortunately, no one was hurt and nothing serious happened at any of the branches; what had happened right here downtown was bad enough. The library reopened later in the afternoon with only what you could call "moderate" damage to windows, carpeting, and some books, but no injuries or loss of life. The city sent some guys around this morning with plywood to stick in the window emplacements, and some glass workers are scheduled to come around and reinstall those windows soon. When will that happen? I don't know. Tomorrow, if there's a rush on it; otherwise, Monday at the latest.

We did sustain some loss, of course. Maybe 400 books—including, unfortunately, some rather expensive reference titles—were damaged from the inrush of water, and some of them will have to be discarded and replaced. Also, all the public access terminals had to be rebooted and restarted. But it could have been a lot worse. All scheduled staff got the following morning off with pay, and, at noon, we had a staff meeting of all hands. We delayed reopening the building until two o'clock, which might have made a few citizens unhappy, but it was necessary. We had to do a visual inspection of the building and discuss the recovery process with all of our employees.

And that brings me to the lawsuit. Or threatened lawsuit, anyway. I'm hoping it won't come to that. I mean, the woman—yes, Mrs. Barnes—is correct that I yanked her up out of her chair, but assault? Under the circumstances, I don't see how an honest attempt to save someone's life could be construed as assault, do you? I mean, think what might have happened to her if I'd just, you know, run like mad and left her there! Maybe it's true what they say, "No good deed goes unpunished," you think?

Personally, I don't think she's got any kind of case against me. She's alive and safe and sound, after all, and I was just doing my best to follow procedure, so where's the assault? After all, we can replace or restore damaged books, and we've already arranged to replace the windows. By tomorrow, all the computers should be restored to full operation. But Mrs. Barnes could have been killed—I hope she realizes that. Yeah, we have differing accounts of what happened yesterday, and I know you need to cover both sides, but I swear that I'm telling you the truth.

You know what I hope? Next time there's some kind of emergency, our designated security officer will be on the premises and will take charge, and all I'll have to do is leave the building, like everybody else. Until then, I'm going to keep on plugging for a detailed policy document that covers tornados, because the next time, we may not be so lucky. I may even volunteer to write the policy myself. After all, the life I save could well be my own! And you can tell your readers that I'm not worried about any lawsuit—my conscience is clear on that matter. But about yesterday, like I said, the weather report called for rain, and only a 50 percent chance of thunderstorms. Who knew?

Questions for Discussion

1. How can a library best prepare for weather emergencies?

2. Does an emergency, such as severe weather, justify physical contact with library patrons?

3. Should the library's associate director be sued for assault in this case? Would you, as director, testify on his behalf?

Case 6

Guard, Off Guard

Kyle Bozeman, human resources, to Michael Chitwood, associate director, in Chitwood's office

Yesterday, for the first time ever, I had to fire someone, or more correctly, I recommended that someone be fired, and my recommendation was approved by the director. And while I'm not all that happy about it, I figure it had to be done. Besides, firing people is an occasional part of the job, and my decision was endorsed, so my conscience is clear. Mostly, anyway. Let me tell you the circumstances, and see if you agree or disagree with my decision. You know I value your opinions, Mike, and I know you'll give it to me straight.

Well, first, in case you didn't know, I'd better tell you who I had to sack. The employee is T.A. Sanders, whom, you'll remember, we hired as a third security guard on a part-time basis last fall. We shifted money around to respond to the need for an increased security presence, especially in the evenings. Hiring her was the most acceptable response to the rising number of purse-snatchings, minor altercations, and petty crimes reported in the building. We were also hoping that if a guard were standing there watching, fewer library materials would leave the building by unauthorized means.

Anyway, the personnel options we considered for solving the need for an enhanced security posture in our library were

- Hire an off-duty police officer to moonlight in the library building in the evenings and Saturdays
- Hire another full-time security officer.
- Hire a part-time security guard to work evenings only.

The first option had its definite appeal, because a uniformed officer of the law, sporting a nightstick and a sidearm would, we thought, cause juvenile delinquents and others bent on crime or mischief to reconsider their plans. This option was, however, deep-sixed, when we called the police station and attempted to price the hourly rate for such an officer. Needless to say, what the cops were asking was well beyond our budget.

The second option—hiring another full-time security officer—was just not a workable option either. When we did the numbers, figuring in staff salary and the usual benefits package, that too was rejected. The basic appeal of the third option lay in the fact that we pay part-time help as independent contractors, meaning that their hourly wage is all we have to pay out; no benefits. By city rules (whether it's fair or not), an employee working fewer than 20 hours per week is considered part-time. Basically, given the recessionary times we live in, and the fact that the taxpayers are disinclined to pony up more money for libraries, this option was all we could afford.

So, you may remember that I put an advertisement in the classified section of *The Pecan Grove Observer* two weeks in a row, and only two candidates showed up. The first person I interviewed was completely unsuited for the job. As I questioned him, it became clear that he was a truck driver hoping to earn a little extra cash, with no training or aptitude for such problems as dealing with difficult people, crowd control, emergency evacuation, and the like.

The other applicant for the job, however, was T.A. Sanders, a mature, likable, and self-possessed woman who had spent three years in the Army stationed in Germany as a member of the military police. This impressed me—as well as Matt, who sat in on the interviews—because hiring T.A. would mean minimal training in the basics of security. T.A., being female, also appealed to us because we figured that a woman might be able to handle or defuse certain situations better than a male guard. Besides, hiring her satisfied certain of the city's affirmative action goals, and that was another bonus. So, she was hired on the spot.

Now, T.A. is a nice enough woman—personality never took a part in my decision. In fact, maybe she's too nice, and that's her whole problem. By that, I mean that she's the kind of person who walks around the building and says "Good afternoon" or "Good evening" to just about everybody she encounters. A real people person, which is kind of refreshing, because frankly our security chief and the regular guards, Matt and Mike, are very large and tough looking, however warm and friendly they might be in casual conversation. You've seen T.A. around and probably talked with her. She looks diminutive standing next to Matt, because he's about six foot seven and wide bodied, and she stands maybe five foot three, with a sturdy but compact build.

At first, we were all pleased with her work, especially with the commendable way she smiled at people (Matt and Mike are nice guys, but they do tend to glower, especially at teenagers who look like trouble to them). I also appreciated the way she didn't seem to take herself too seriously as she went about her day. She had a kind word for everybody.

But in the last couple of months . . . well, I don't like spies or informers, but when you're in my position, it happens sometimes that staff members come to me privately and complain about—or at least discuss—fellow employees. I try to keep an "open door" policy, so that people can walk through my door, close it—if they're planning to discuss anything sensitive—and speak freely about anything that's bothering them. So people know they can come to me and tell me things, in complete confidentiality.

I always investigate complaints to see if they're legitimate or just born of animosity or resentment. After all, you can't expect everyone on a library staff to get along perfectly. I figure that a library staff is like a large family, then there are always going to be some relatives who you love to be around, a bunch of them you tolerate, and a few . . . well, let's just say that you don't mind it too much when they don't show up at family functions, if you know what I mean.

Well, here's the set-up. When we went from two security guards to three for the downtown library building, we imagined that since there would be 25 percent more hours of security coverage, we could expect something like 25 percent more security. Matt and Mike would work daytime hours, mostly, and T.A. would help us out in the evenings, when security problems are usually more frequent. So after T.A. began working evenings, Matt and Mike started coming in early and leaving at five o'clock.

When we got T.A., she was assigned evenings, coming in at five Monday through Thursday and working until closing at nine. She would stay on an extra hour until ten to go round the building, check all the doors, make sure that everyone had left the building, and generally make herself useful. We were delighted to have T.A. join the staff, and her sturdy presence in the evenings was reassuring to staff and patrons, alike.

Then . . . well, I don't want to say who told me this, but I started hearing reports that T.A. was spending too much time at the circulation desk, in deep conversation with the clerk or librarian on duty and not paying due attention to the rest of her job. She was expected to take frequent walking tours of the various rooms of the library and the stack areas. Now, I admit that it is still possible to do some security duties without actually leaving a seat behind the circ desk, because the desk commands a reasonably wide-angle view of much of the building. From a position behind the desk, you can see more than half of the Adult Services area (which includes the Internet area), and a corresponding chunk of the Children's and Young Adult area. And while that may sound pretty good, remember that it is not possible to see the other half of those rooms, and certainly nothing going on in the carrels and aisles of the stack area in the back.

My source told me that T.A. would typically report to work just before five, get her situation report and instructions from Matt or Mike, and, after they left, take up her post behind the desk, where she would engage in loquacious conversation with whomever was working. When I asked my source what T.A. and the clerks talked about at the desk, I was told that it was nothing inappropriate but just the sort of chit chat that goes on between friends and acquaintances . . . details of their lives, past histories, television programs they had watched, dinners they had eaten in restaurants, and the like.

One staff member told me that T.A. had "bent her ear" for half an hour one evening concerning the preparation of stuffed mushrooms and had seemed to resent being interrupted when a patron approached the desk to ask questions concerning borrowing privileges and how one gets a library card.

Another source told me that T.A.—who was expected to get up off her stool every so often and take a leisurely, but highly visible, tour of the building—seemed to flout the rules repeatedly, only bothering to take her walkabouts at five, when one of the full-time guards was still around and likely to see her, and again just a few moments before nine, after the closing announcement over the public address system and the flashing of the lights. Between a few minutes after five and a few minutes before nine, however, T.A. parked herself on a stool next to the circulation clerk and schmoozed for hours, looking up only if something within easy view of her stool happened.

After getting a series of similar complaints, from both staff members not involved in these chats and the circulation clerks themselves, I decided that I would investigate personally, before actually talking to T.A. about her problem behavior and possible dereliction of duty. So last evening, after bidding her and the rest of the night shift good night and walking out the front door and around to my car, I didn't go home. Instead, I took myself out to a fast-food joint, went back to the library, and let myself quietly in the back door. Then I walked through the darkened back room of the Technical Services area as quietly as I could and peered out at the circulation desk. There was T.A., seated on a stool, cheek by jowl with Mo Davis, our circulation clerk, and deep in conversation.

Feeling a bit sneaky, I stood in the shadows and watched for 10 minutes, and sure enough, T.A. didn't arise even once from her stool. Well, I said to myself, I'll just give her the benefit of the doubt. Maybe she's just completed one of her assigned tours of the premises. So I stood quietly back there and watched for another 25 minutes. Neither Mo nor T.A. moved during that time, although Mo seemed to be doing her work, checking out books for patrons, and once directing a young teenager to a terminal with a magazine index on it. But T.A., as I said, didn't move. Not even once did she get off that stool!

I thought about my various options: confronting her then and there; greeting her the next day with a printed reprimand, then talking it over with the boss or you; or just figuring, well, if nobody seems to have a problem and there's no emergency, maybe there's nothing wrong with her just sitting there. I mean, even just sitting there, she's still a conspicuous security presence, displayed front and center, and maybe that's enough.

Then without ever letting either woman know I'd been there, I quietly retreated from my place of concealment, sneaked out the back door, and drove home.

So, this morning I went to see Ann about the problem, and, after she listened to my report, she agreed that when T.A. comes in tonight, I should call her in and firmly but gently send her packing. After all, just sitting in one place was not what we hired her for.

So when T.A. appeared a few moments before five o'clock, I stopped her and asked her if she had time to chat, summoning her into my office where I closed the door behind us. Once inside, I came right to the point, telling her what I had been told and had personally observed. To ease into the topic, I said that I knew that her job in this busy place was stressful and that sometimes she must find her duties to be almost overwhelming. "Tell me about it," she said, laconically.

When I told her what I'd been told (and personally observed) she didn't seem to have any comment at all. She just sat there. I waited. I thought she might explain her behavior, or provide enough mitigating circumstances to get me to change my mind. But instead of saying that she was sorry, or asking for another chance, or promising to do better in the future, she snarled, "Do you encourage employees to spy on each other! Come on, gimme a break! I can't be everywhere at once, can I?" Apparently, she's got a real attitude problem, this girl.

When I patiently (at least I think I *sounded* patient) explained that all available evidence seemed to suggest that she typically parked her rump on a stool behind the circ desk after her first evening round and then never got up again (except maybe for a bathroom break) until just before closing time almost four hours later. I waited to see what she'd say to that. What she said was, "What is this, an ambush?"

I was a bit flustered by the challenging tone of that question, but I blandly said, "No, T.A., we're just talking about your work habits and whether you're living up to your job description, that's all."

"What about my work habits?" she asked in what writers call a truculent tone.

"Well, it's been reported that you spend most of your shift, four evenings a week, sitting behind the circulation desk, chatting with whoever is on duty and doing precious little else on your checklist of assignments."

"Who says?"

"Never mind that. Just tell me if it's true."

"Certainly not! I always make my rounds, just like it says in my job description, and before I go home, I go all around the building and try each of the 42 doors in this place, just to make sure that they're securely locked."

"Well," I said, not really wanting to have to mention this next part, "last evening I stood where I could see the desk out front, and I personally observed that between approximately 6:15 and almost 7:00 P.M., you sat next to Mo Davis chatting, and never once in all that time did you come out from behind the desk and conduct your appointed rounds."

T.A.'s face now had become an alarming shade of crimson. "Wait a minute! Are you saying that you . . . spied on me?" There was nothing to do but acknowledge the fact.

"Yes," I said.

"So, like a little sneak, you hid yourself and peeped out to catch me doing something I shouldn't?"

"How else does management find out whether employees are doing what they're supposed to be doing?" I asked in return. "I mean, if you ask, they'll exaggerate, in many cases, and we can't exactly catch 'em on *Candid Camera*, but it is instructive, sometimes, to catch people in the act of being themselves."

Another thought now struck her: "Hold on. You didn't just, like, decide to stay late and hide in the shadows back in Technical Services. No, somebody else must have squealed on me, ratted me out, and I want to know who did it. Somebody with a grudge, I'll bet. I demand to confront that person. At least, tell me who it is, and exactly what was said about me!"

"My sources have to remain confidential, I'm sure you understand."

"Well, don't I have the right to confront my accuser? Isn't that what our legal system is all about? Aren't I innocent until proven guilty?" She had a point, but I hurried on.

"This isn't about guilt or innocence, T.A. It's about doing your job, and frankly, I observed you just sitting there, so it's not about tattletales. I saw you. And what I have to conclude from what I saw and have been told is that you're not performing your duties the way your job description plainly specifies, nor are you doing what you were trained to do when you first came here."

She made a gesture halfway between dismissal and disgust, emitting a growl that sounded like, "Awwrrrr!" Then, a new thought struck her. "So what happens now," she asked. I hated to say it, but that's what the conversation was all about.

"What happens now is that we have to let you go. Since you're not doing what we hired you to do, and given that you're still well within the probationary period prescribed by the city's civil service policies, we are terminating your employment as of this Friday. I'm sorry, but with all the petty crime and purse-snatchings going on in this building, especially in the evenings, we cannot afford to have our security guard staying in one spot for hours and devoting her time and attention to conversation instead of her duties."

"And don't I get a second chance? Surely, there are always chances for a new beginning. What if I say that I didn't understand what the job entailed but now, after this conversation, I do?"

"Sorry," I said. "Our decision is final. As of the end of the week, you no longer work here. You have the right, if you choose, to appeal this to the downtown civil service office, but I don't plan to change my mind. I am told that your behavior has been going on almost since the start of your time with us, and now, I'm afraid you're only promising to mend your ways so you won't get fired. But it's too late for second chances, T.A. I like you personally, but as of Friday, consider yourself fired. I've seen to it that you get two weeks' severance pay folded into your final paycheck, which, under the circumstances, I think is extremely generous."

T.A. just sat there for a while, glaring at me. Finally, she stood up, called me a name I won't repeat, and strode furiously out of my office. A few moments later, I was informed that she had decided to leave the building on the spot, rather than work her final shift.

So that's my story. How do I feel about this unfortunate incident? Not so hot, actually. In the first place, I hate confrontation, and I didn't enjoy having to give a fellow employee the bad news of her dismissal today. In the second place, we're back to square one in terms of security in the evenings. Until we can get someone new to work nights, it looks like either Matt or Mike is going to be rearranging his life to cover us from five to nine. And finally, I am still trying to persuade myself that I did the right thing, even though I'm pretty sure I did. I don't know, maybe T.A. deserved a second chance.

Maybe it's wrong to practice what the books on personnel management call "unobtrusive observation," what others might call "spying on people." But I did what I did for the good of both the library and its patrons. Look at it this way: What if something ghastly had taken place out in the stacks—which is maybe 100 steps and around several corners from the well-lighted public area—while T.A. was chirping away with Mo or somebody about stuffing mushrooms and serving them with a mixture of wild rice and orzo?

Well, you're right. Might as well recognize it now, I guess. Administration means, sometimes, making decisions that hurt other people; decisions you're not entirely comfortable with. It comes with the territory. Still, you've been at this a lot longer than I have: So tell me, did I do the right thing?

Questions for Discussion

1.   Is the "unobtrusive observation" method of checking up on employees fair and ethical?

2.   Do you think, under the circumstances mentioned in this case, that Kyle should have given T.A. another chance?

3.   How would you, as Kyle, now modify your staff policy and procedures manual to stress the importance of adhering to job descriptions?

Case 7

A Harmless Eccentric

Andy Michlin, reference librarian, to the Systemwide Reference Group, at its monthly group meeting

My turn? Well, um, yeah, I do have something to share with the group today. Although I wouldn't exactly classify my problem with some others we've talked about, like a gunman taking hostages, a man who exposes himself to women, or that freak who used to come in here and just walk up to children and start touching them while humming to himself. Those are clear-cut cases of threatening behavior, and I think we're all on the same page about what to do when one of them shows up: call security or the cops, then try to get everybody else away from these wackadoos, if at all possible.

But the problem I had yesterday was different because it involves what you might call eccentric behavior on the part a harmless old man—harmless except that his behavior could keep people from coming to the library. That's what makes it interesting: The usual rules of what to do about threatening behavior don't apply. Or do they? Well, that's what these meetings are about, right? So let me explain, and we can discuss it as a group and perhaps formulate a plan for future action.

Today was a quiet day in the reference department, just the way I like it. Everything was normal, and my two-hour desk shift was going along without incident. Some patrons telephoned or came to me at the reference desk with questions, which I answered (for a change) without any undue searching or labor. It's amazing what you can find out with an Internet-equipped terminal sitting next to your elbow on the desk, don't you think?

I mean, consider the "old days." People would ask a question: first, I'd negotiate it carefully until I was reasonably sure that both of us were in agreement as to what the question was, and then I'd take a minute to develop a logical search strategy, or plan of attack. That usually consisted of deciding which books, indexes, and other reference tools I would consult and in what order. Sometimes, I'd use one of the online search services to answer questions, but that was a chancy method of looking for information because those services tended to require careful formatting and input—with Boolean search operators, word order, and command structure—and each one was different from the others.

Another reason was simply that online searching in commercial databases is comparatively expensive, and no one has to be reminded about how much we have to watch our expenditures and ration unnecessary budget items. The worst part of the commercial search services was that you paid for the search, whether it yielded anything useful or not.

But yesterday morning went downhill quite rapidly, as far as my day at the desk was concerned. It all seemed innocent enough at the start. At about eleven thirty, I was sitting at the desk, checking some review media, trying to choose what to purchase for the library concerning the greenhouse effect, global warming, and all that. Then from behind me, I heard a female voice say, timidly, "Excuse me, sir?" I turned expectantly, thinking, ah, another customer. Great! I was about to fall asleep here. Now I'll have something to do that'll carry me up to lunchtime.

I'm always happier—and the day goes by much quicker—when I'm searching for information, especially when I find what I'm looking for. Plus, I learn something new, almost every time I go searching on the Web. This middle-aged woman didn't seem seriously upset or anything, but she was nervous about something, I could tell. I'm pretty good at gentling and settling down nervous people, so I gave her a warm, interested smile.

"Good morning, ma'am. Something I can help you with?"

"Um, yes," she said. "Listen! Can you hear that?" I hadn't noticed anything out of the ordinary. I have pretty good ears, but I guess when I'm really concentrating on something, I tend to tune out background noise. So now I focused my mind (and ears) on what I could hear. And then I heard it.

Laughter. Peals of delighted, uproarious laughter. That's what I heard. From the sound of it, it was a man, literally roaring with amusement at something. I got up from the reference desk and took a look to discover the source of all that hoarse laughter and noticed an old man convulsed in mirth, while everybody else in the room had fallen dead silent. Looking reassuringly at the woman standing beside my desk, I asked her to wait at the desk while I investigated. She nodded in agreement. So I walked in the direction of the laughter and here's what I saw:

The people in the reading room were staring in wonderment, concern, or fascination at a reading table where a balding, elderly man was hunched over something he was reading. Almost without pause, he was breaking out into fresh gales of mirth and merriment. Well, it seemed pretty obvious to me as to what I had to do about this guy. So I went over to him, caught his eye, and asked him if he would mind holding it down, because he was annoying and upsetting others in the room.

Too weary from his hilarity to speak, he just nodded in what I took to be a friendly manner. As I stood there, curiosity got the better of me. What, I wondered, could he be reading that was cracking him up into so many helpless fits of guffaws, roars, and giggles? I know we stock a respectable number of comedy books; I have even enjoyed taking some of them home and reading them myself. You all know me: If there's a funny joke (clean or the other kind), I want to remember it, and probably tell it to others. Naturally, I was curious to know what this old guy was reading, so I could make a mental note to read it after he was finished with it.

But when I glanced down and peered at the book open to a double page in front of him, guess what he was reading! Go ahead, guess! A comic monologue? No. Some of George Carlin's one-liners? Nope. Not even close. Give up? None of y'all would guess what was so funny that I thought this old party was going to have a heart attack right there at the table, so I'm just going to tell you. It was the phone book. That's what I said: *a telephone directory*! Go figure.

Turns out, it wasn't even the local phone book, although I doubt that mattered much to this weird old guy. No, in front of him was the residential directory for the city of Wilmington and New Hanover County, North Carolina, which had him laughing so hard that tears kept leaking out of his eyes and dripping onto the pages in front of him. I've visited Wilmington, and as it happens, it's a nice resort and university city on the Atlantic coast, and it's possible that some aspects of the place may be amusing. But there's nothing so flat-out funny that anybody should begin cackling hysterically over the names of the residents, arranged alphabetically. And yet, there he was, laughing, all the same.

He couldn't seem to stop, and all around me, people were staring. I figured that it was time to intervene because it was obvious that his behavior was no longer a private matter but was causing concern and consternation to maybe 20 other people. So I stood over the old man and said exactly the same words the woman said to me only a few minutes earlier.

"Excuse me, sir!" I said. He glanced up, and I could see that he had laughed so hard and long that not only his eyes (behind thick lenses) but also his nose was running freely. For a moment, he looked at me as a sleeper might look at an unexpected visitor who had just roused him from a dream.

"Uhhh?" he asked, with a hitching sigh.

"Sir," I said, with elaborate politeness and patience, "it would appear that your laughter is so loud that it's disturbing other people in the room, so I'm wondering if you could manage to keep it down a bit?"

Still looking at me in a sort of unfocused way, the old man stabbed downward with a blunt fingertip at the page in front of him. Then he looked down to see the name next to his finger. "Wonder who we have here?" he said, then he moved his lips a moment and let out a whoop of amusement at the name he'd found. I think he was trying to say the name printed on the page in those tiny, bold little letters, but he couldn't really get out any coherent words. Clearly, though, he was highly amused by the name he had found, because he dissolved into fresh peals of laughter, even louder than before. I just stood there with a confused grin on my face, as he laughed so hard—you should have been there—and slammed his palm on the table three or four times, for emphasis. Then he moved his finger a bit lower on the page, which occasioned new laughter.

Well, this was a new one on me. What was I supposed to do about this guy? I mean, in my job, I've had to tell loudmouth boys that if they don't quit shouting, they're outta here, and they've listened to me and believed me. And I've certainly had to deal with my share of weirdos—who hasn't? This is a public library, and after all, we get 'em all, eventually. But this guy was just laughing. And laughing, as long as that's as far as someone goes in the direction of acting out, isn't really against the rules. How could it be? So I stood there for a while on one foot first, and then on the other, watching as the old guy returned to his reading and laughing. Once, he even gave me an amused look and said, "Listen to this one! Can you believe it?" He tried to pronounce some ethnic name, failed miserably, and reacted to his own attempt by breaking once again into ear-splitting peals of laughter, and he was off and running again.

Well, I stood there knowing that I had to do something, but I was indecisive as to what the correct course of action might be. I know I should have been firm and assertive, but here's what I was thinking: the world can be a depressing place. There's terrorism and turmoil and killing, and consumer confidence is bottoming out. And my personal life isn't exactly paradise on earth, either. But here's this tired looking, scrawny, used-up old man, not only keeping his sunny side up, but kicking up a storm of laughter, which, as everybody knows, is good for the soul. And suddenly, I was smiling. I can't explain it, but at that moment, I felt energized, optimistic, and—I don't know—good to be alive! So I grinned and decided that he wasn't doing anything really wrong, but then remembering the other people around, I said, "Please, sir! Just hold it down, okay?"

"Sure, sure," he gasped, looking at me with kindly, leaking eyes as he wiped his moistened glasses with a large dirty red handkerchief. "Sorry for the fuss, son!" And he returned his gaze to the Wilmington white pages once again, finally seeming to master his mirth, or perhaps just resting. Did you ever laugh for maybe 10 minutes? Well, it's hard work. I'll tell you that. Almost like sneezing over and over. It can be really exhausting. This guy must have been twice my age, and I thought this must be putting a strain on his heart. So I turned slowly and walked in the direction of the few people remaining in the room, who were speaking together in low voices and pointing past me at the old man with the phone book in front of him.

"That dude's crazy!" said one young man wearing black from neck to toe. "Why you let him come in here and yuk it up and bother everybody else?" I guess he had a good point, but I explained, in a low voice, that I'd talked things over with the elderly gentleman and that he'd agreed to subdue his noise from then on, so he wouldn't be bothering anyone else any further. He seemed to accept that, so I walked back to my neglected reference desk and was pleased to note that no further peals of laughter were emanating from the back room. At least for a while. But then, new laughter rang out, and, while I was sitting there, figuring out what I ought to do next about it, I saw that the young man in black was striding purposefully over to my desk. When he reached me, he sounded seriously exasperated: "Let me ask you something."

"Certainly, go ahead," I said.

"Why don't you do something about that guy?" he seethed. "He's crazy, and crazy people belong in an asylum or hospital and not here in the library with regular folks. They need help, sure, but the rest of us need to be protected against whatever they might decide to do. Am I right or wrong?"

Privately, I agree with such sentiments, but I decided not to say so. I guessed where he was going with this, though, and I was nervous about falling into a logical trap where I'd have to do something I didn't want to do. "And . . .?" I asked cautiously.

"And now we got us a genuine crazy person back there. You heard him. Old dude be cracking up over the telephone book! The *telephone* book! What so funny about that? Ain't nothing funny about the telephone book, man! Nothing at all. So I figure, if he thinks that's funny, he must be crazy, and even though he's little and old, he could be dangerous. Anyway, I came here to study today, and I can't get no studying done when some old whack job be carrying on like that!"

"Tell me, what would you like me to do about him, sir?" I asked, hoping that I wouldn't hear any bad news.

"Do? That's an easy one! Do your job. Throw his skinny butt out of here. One old man can't be making it so nobody else can read or concentrate, or even think, in that room. Why you think just about everybody else in that room is either gone home or someplace else in this building?" He stopped for a moment, during which we both were aware of the continuous laughter reaching our ears. "Enough talk, man!" he commanded. "Throw him out of here, or I do it for you. Crazy like he is, he don't belong downtown alone without a keeper. Now, do it! Otherwise, it's gonna be *my* problem!" Glaring down at me, he crossed his arms defiantly across his chest and waited to see what I was going to say.

"Look," I began. "I hear you, and I understand what you want me to do, but it's not as easy as you seem to think it is, sir. For one thing, he's not really breaking any laws or rules under which we operate, and for another . . ." Uselessly, I found myself wishing it were late in the afternoon or in the evening, or that one of the big guards was nearby to deal with this problem. The maniacal laughter continued.

Obviously, the young man had had enough. With a final glare at me, he turned to leave, saying, "Well, forget this place! I'm going to find me a quieter place to study. I ain't ever coming back in here! And I ain't the only one who feels that way. But I tell you what: you going to lose a lot of customers if you don't start doin' what's right." He walked out of the room toward the exit door, followed by the woman who had originally brought the old man's laughter to my attention and several others.

As he headed for the front door, he turned and gave me his exit line: "The only difference between this place and Bughouse Square, that I can see, is that you got warmer seats!" Yeah, just do what's right, I sighed to myself, as I watched him walk out. Just that easy. But I just couldn't bring myself to go back and deal harshly with that old man, even if he had literally cleared the reading room of all the other patrons. He was so harmless, you know what I mean? When my shift ended at noon, I explained the situation to Mary and left it in her hands as to what to do.

So here's my question: Did I wimp out, or what? I want to know what the rest of y'all would have done. I mean, you can't just let somebody rave on over his phone book, if it means chasing everybody else within earshot away, can you? But rousting a harmless old man and throwing him out for finding bizarre amusement in library materials? I just couldn't do it.

Funny thing, isn't it? I deal better and more effectively, by and large, with clear and present danger than I do with nuisances and annoying people. But a nuisance that loses us customers isn't really just a harmless nuisance, is it? Any ideas?

Questions for Discussion

1. Under what circumstances does nuisance behavior warrant expulsion from the library?

2. As Andy, would you have thrown the man out for laughing aloud because it was annoying or alarming to everybody else around him?

3. Would you have just allowed the laughing man to stay and continue doing what he was doing?

Case 8

Breaking Up Is Hard to Do

Mary Rhoades, head of reference to Kyle Bozeman, human resources, during lunch at a nearby restaurant

The trouble with turnover in our library staff is not so much that good people leave—that happens everywhere. The real trouble is that when you have to replace them, the new employees come with problems. It's just that some people we hire have emotional baggage that they carry around with them, and, of course, they don't tell you about it during the job interview. We're not even allowed to ask personal questions. And that's the way it should be. After all, it's nobody's business what your private life is like. But when someone new comes aboard, it's a crapshoot as to whether that person has a messy personal life that's going to interfere with his or her work or even a potentially dangerous situation that could result in tragedy if nothing is done about it. My new reference librarian, Nancy, is a case in point.

You'll recall that Nancy Bratcher came to us from another library all the way across the country. She had interviewed extremely well and her references, her academic grades, and her letters of recommendation were all first rate. I also liked her sunny personality and the way she smiled (with what looked like genuine pleasure) when I spoke to her about the job. So it was a no-brainer as to which of the three candidates I wanted, and, fortunately, the boss and the rest of the personnel committee agreed with me.

Nancy was hired as a Librarian II and assigned to me in Reference two months ago. She was just what I was looking for: warm, approachable, knowledgeable, well read, eager to share, and technologically proficient; and she knew a lot about search engines and Web sites and all that stuff. In short, she was ideal, and I took to her immediately, both personally and professionally. In fact, if it doesn't sound like bragging, she reminded me of myself at her age; she showed great promise.

That said, I had no way of knowing about her private troubles, even though I'd listened carefully during the entire day of interviews and at lunch, to see what she said about her family. All I could glean from her remarks was that she had a husband. No children were mentioned, but that might have been because she didn't think such details of her life outside the library were germane. I was, naturally, curious as to why she had moved to our city, but when I asked a general question along those lines, she didn't offer too many specifics. As I recall, she merely responded, "Oh, well, it just seemed like a good time for a change of scenery," and that was that. I didn't pursue the matter. None of my business, actually.

From day one, I decided that hiring Nancy was an unqualified triumph. After a bit of orientation, I showed her around, introduced her to everyone (both staff and the public) that I could, and then let her get her feet wet, answering telephone inquiries and handling walk-in traffic at our busy reference desk. I was delighted with the way she handled herself. As a matter of fact, if I weren't just a few years away from retirement, I might even fear for my own job because she just glittered as she did her work. We got along famously, and, after a day or so, it seemed as if we'd known each other forever (I know it sounds like a cliché, but there it is). Even better, staff members kept coming over to me and telling me that they thought Nancy was a real find, and all I could do was agree.

Then, somewhere in the middle of the afternoon during her third week here, I first glimpsed some of the troubles that lurked beneath the surface of an apparently self-confident, delightful, and untroubled young woman. I happened to be walking behind the reference desk, when the phone rang. Nancy picked it up and chirped, "Pecan Grove Public Library, Reference Department, Ms. Bratcher speaking. How may I help you?" But then, well, I'm not an expert on body language, but I could see her back suddenly tense when the caller spoke to her. She turned in the chair, cast a nervous, wary glance back at me, and I heard her say (in a terrified little voice) "How did you find me?" Faintly, I could hear a buzzing in the earpiece she was holding to her head, obviously a deep-voiced, male voice. She listened for a bit longer. Then she raised her voice. "Please leave me alone," she said, halfway between a prayer and a shout, obviously fighting for control of herself, and then abruptly hung up the telephone.

At that point, I was torn between two courses of action: interrogating her about what had just happened or ignoring it. I mean, slamming the phone down on a caller is not normal behavior, and it is certainly not condoned unless the circumstances really warrant it. So I settled for a compromise: "What was that," I asked her, "obscene call?"

Nancy gave me a peculiar look but took a minute to ponder how best to answer me. "I guess you could say that," she finally said, clearly not wanting to elaborate. "It doesn't matter."

"I get those sometimes," I commiserated. "They creep me out, but I try not to let the perverts and weirdos know that they're scaring me. We can fight back, you know: The police want to be notified whenever we get obscene or threatening calls. They have ways of identifying who is calling and from where. Want to give them a call?"

"*No!* Will you please butt out?" said Nancy, so loudly that I was startled. For the first time, I could see how stressed and unnerved she was by that caller. Several patrons in the area lifted their heads from their books and magazines and looked over with interest. Then she softened and said, "Sorry I shouted. No. Thanks, Mary, but I can handle it. I've got it all under control."

"You sure about that?" I asked, skeptically. This girl brought out all my maternal instincts, and I felt concern for her.

"Quite sure, thank you." Her smile was wide—too wide—to be convincing. She was trying to sell me on the idea that it was nothing. There was nothing else to say, so I gave her a lingering look of concern and left for the back room, where I was putting together a big end-of-year reference order and running out of time to do it.

The next day, the same thing happened, at about the same time. And again on the next. By the third call, Nancy didn't even speak to the caller—she just slammed the telephone down. I could see how unnerved she was, so by the time Thursday afternoon rolled around, I offered to take all incoming calls between two thirty and three, and she gratefully accepted my offer. Sure enough, at exactly 2:38 P.M. by my watch, the phone rang. But when the caller heard my voice, there was only silence on the other end. Well, not exactly silence. I could hear sounds. A radio was playing softly in background, and some faint but ragged breathing, but no one spoke. I repeated my standard greeting, but still nothing happened. So after waiting and listening a bit longer, I hung up softly. Then, at 3:00 P.M., I turned phone duty back to Nancy. When the phone rang a few minutes later, she picked it up and gave the standard greeting. She listened for just 30 seconds or so, hung up, then dissolved into racking sobs right there at the desk. I guess you could say she fell apart. When she could speak more calmly, she said, "Mary, would you please take over for me? I need a few moments to myself." And without waiting for me to respond, she rushed out of the room.

I was now convinced that there was no coincidence here; nothing I'd imagined from watching too much TV or anything. Someone—for whatever reason—was scaring the bejabbers out of my new reference librarian, and she was terrified of him, that was plain to see. What to do? What to do? I pondered my options while she was in the back. I decided to find out what I could.

I said, "Nancy, I don't live far from here, and I fix a mean turkey noodle casserole, so I have an invitation for you, and I hope you'll say yes. Tomorrow, when we're done with work, you can come home with me for some dinner, and we can talk and get to know each other better. My husband's out of town for the next few days at a convention in San Francisco (the lucky dog!), and I'd count it as a favor if you'd come over, sample some adequate wine with me, and dig into that casserole and have a talk. What do you say?" She brightened immediately, face flushed with gratitude.

"Thanks, Mary, I'd like that," she said. "What time?"

"Oh, right after work works for me," I responded. "You all right with that?"

"Sounds perfect. But may I bring something? Dessert, perhaps?"

"Just you," I said, smiling. "And as for dessert, there's an ice cream pie in the freezer that'll make a delicious topper for a summer meal. Unless you're watching your weight, of course, and it doesn't look like it from here."

"No," she said, smiling and looking down at her flat stomach. "Dieting is not one of my problems, and I love ice cream."

"Good," I said. "So after work tomorrow, leave your car in the lot and come home with me after work in my car, and stay as long as you'd like. When you're tired or have to go, I'll run you back here. How's that?"

"It's a deal!" she grinned. I grinned right back at her.

Friday, when we closed at five thirty, Nancy came home with me after work. First thing I did was to kick off my shoes, and at my invitation, she did the same. Then I brought out a bottle of potent red wine I'd been saving and opened it. I'd prepared the casserole previously and needed only to top it with a layer of crumbled potato chips and stick it in the oven for half an hour to finish it off. In the meantime, I brought out some munchies in little colored bowls, and while that bottle of wine was doing what connoisseurs call "breathing," I decided to offer my new young friend a conversational (and emotional) lifeline and see if she'd take hold of it.

"Nancy," I began, "I'm very glad you've come to work at the library, and I hope that you and I will become dear, close friends."

"So do I," she said, grabbing a fistful of tiny pretzels from a bowl and crunching them rapidly with her small, even, and very white teeth. "I could use a friend, actually, since I'm new in town, and if you're applying for the job, I promise to fast-track your application. All the members of my former support system are hundreds of miles away, and while that's only a phone call or an e-mail, it's nice to kick back with a friend and just talk."

My turn to grin. "I don't want to tread on your toes or make you uncomfortable," I said, "so, if what I'm about to ask now is none of my business," I went on after taking a deep breath, "just say so, and I'll try not to mention it again."

Nancy said nothing. Her smile began to sag, however, as though some of the air was coming out of a balloon. Probably thinking, "Oh, here it comes!" but then she seemed to shrug and reach a decision. Then she took a sip of wine and said, "No, that's all right. Actually, I could use somebody to talk to. So what is it you want to ask?"

"Well, I don't mean to pry, please understand that. But I am both your friend and your supervisor. It's about those phone calls you've been getting."

"Oh. Those calls." She looked for one moment as though she was going to grab her purse, slip on her shoes, and run out of the apartment. But her indecision passed, and she relaxed and took another sip of her wine. "Just someone I used to know. Nothing, really. I just . . ."

"A former boyfriend?" I offered.

"I wish! Neither former nor boyfriend, actually. More like present husband, at least in the legal sense. We're separated now. I wouldn't mind if I never saw or heard from him again. In fact, I wouldn't be sad if he . . . ." She hesitated, and decided not to finish that sentence.

"Look, we're having a nice evening, here, Mary," she said, looking at me as though evaluating me carefully. "I'm not sure you want to have to deal with the sad and depressing details of another marriage gone sour, do you? I mean, if you'd rather talk about growing roses or finding bargains on clothing, I'll understand."

"I just want to be your friend," I said. "And to help, if I can."

"All right, then. Here's the story in a nutshell: Back where I grew up, I always intended to marry my high school sweetheart, but, I don't know, something was always missing from our relationship. Tom was a great guy—steady, reliable, and predictable. I guess that's the problem because when I met Larry at a party one night when I was out without Tom, Larry seemed to be everything my steady date wasn't: unpredictable, exciting, and maybe even a little dangerous. So when he asked me to go for a motorcycle ride in the moonlight, it was my dream come true." She paused and took another, longer drink of wine. Silently, I refilled her glass. "One thing led to another, and, eventually, over Tom's strenuous objections, and those of my parents, Larry and I got married. Without going into too much detail, I'll say that decision was the worst mistake of my life. See, in the moonlight, when a big, handsome, hunky guy puts his strong arms around you and tells you how beautiful you are, it's hard to think clearly or to resist.

"So we were married in a small, civil ceremony. But not long after we got married, I became aware that Larry had changed. Like he'd been wearing a mask, and now he wasn't. Sound familiar? I'll bet there are enough women with stories like mine to fill a stadium. Yeah, he changed, all right, but not for the better. Instead of asking me, he started telling me, and instead of discussing things with me, he issued directives and orders. And once or twice, when I stood up to him and defied his orders, he . . ." Her voice trailed off. She didn't want to say the next part, so I took an educated guess.

". . . got physical?," I said. "He hit you or twisted your arm to coerce you physically into doing what he wanted."

"How did you know?" Nancy looked startled, staring at me like I was a clairvoyant who had just predicted her future. "Have you been there, too?"

"No, thankfully. Not me. But it seemed like a natural enough conclusion to the sentence you left hanging. My husband is the dearest and gentlest man in the world, fortunately. But I've heard stories like yours too many times and read about them even more. So, what did you do?"

"Do? About what?"

"When Larry struck you or knocked you down. What did you do?"

"Not much. Cried, mostly. I sure couldn't give back what I received. Larry's an ex-football–interior lineman and weighs even more now that he did in his playing days. Whereas, look at me." I solemnly checked out her petite and trim figure, fighting down a twinge of envy. "I weigh 100 pounds with my clothes on. How am I going to get up off the floor and hit him back? He'd have totaled me if I ever fought back. Or maybe even killed me. I know it!"

"But you couldn't just sit there and take it," I said, thinking that my husband, Owen, might hit me once—twice if he was quick about it—and then we'd be dealing with each other only through our attorneys.

"Couldn't I? Well, I did. I just took it. Larry whacked me dozens of times in our two years of marriage, or pinched me. Hard. I think he enjoyed pinching me. Other times, he'd push me down or slam me into a wall. Later on, he'd calm down. Then, the day after, he'd be sorry, and he'd be all loving and tender, at least for a while. Flowers. Fancy dinners. Did you ever see the play *A Streetcar Named Desire?*"

I nodded. I know the play well. *Stelllllla!* Stanley Kowalski. Blanche du Bois. Oh, yeah. The classic movie version, with Marlon Brando, back before he swelled up to monstrous proportions. The image of Stanley, down on his knees, to Stella in the pouring rain flooded my mind. "Know it well!" I mused.

"Well, that was our life. Every so often, he'd do something horrible. Then, later, he was all, 'I'm sorry, baby. It'll never happen again. I promise.' And for a few days or weeks, he'd actually be gentle and loving again and I'd forget, or try to forget. But sooner or later, I'd do something to irritate or enrage him, and he'd turn into a beast again. The funny thing was that he blamed his outbursts on me!"

"Sounds like Larry needs help," I offered. "You know: professional help?"

"Yeah, right, help," agreed Nancy, with a trace of a grin. "I asked a few times for him to go into couples therapy with me or to see someone just by himself for anger management, but the thought of exposing our dirty laundry to another person made him resentful and extremely negative. Well, after the last time, about a month ago, I just . . . left. I had it all planned out, actually. I waited until Larry was at work, packed some clothes, filled my Mazda with as much of my stuff as it could hold, and drove away.

"My plan was to lose myself and start over, in a new town with a new job, and never have to see Larry's furious face again. That's what brought me here—two thousand miles away from my old life with an angry man. But now I see that you can't really disappear. Stupid plan. Like those people the FBI fits out with a new identity in its witness relocation program. I read that most of 'em get found eventually anyway. Well, I got found. How naive I was to think that Larry wouldn't find me! With private detectives and do-it-yourself Internet sleuthing, it's probably a snap. But the last few weeks have been wonderful because I could live without being afraid and leave work without wondering if I was going to get clobbered when I got home. So I moved here and applied for the position in Reference at the library, and you know the rest.

"Basically, my insanely jealous jerk of an ex has been stalking me ever since the separation. And now, he's coming for me. For a while, I'd thought I'd given him the slip. But it's happened. Larry's tracked me down; he knows where I work and probably even where I live. When he calls, he keeps saying that we belong together. And you know what else he says? Every time he calls, he says, 'I'm coming for you, baby!' Some story, huh?"

"The police!" I said, expressing a half-formed thought. "Why don't you call the police? They'd deal with Larry. Stalking is illegal in this state, and if what he's doing doesn't fit the definition of stalking you, then I don't know what does."

"Well," Nancy said, "he's still my husband, and despite everything, I couldn't bear the thought of getting him thrown into jail or him losing his job."

"What?" I blurted. Her concern for him was appalling. "Nancy," I offered, "sometimes, it just comes down to him or you. And if I were you, I'd make sure it was you who walked away from your train wreck of a marriage."

"I agree," she said. "That's why I moved all the way out here to Pecan Grove. But I'm scared and confused. So, you want to be my friend? Tell me what to do! But it can't be anything that might lead to getting Larry arrested. I need you to promise me that you won't call the cops about this or do anything else that might lead to trouble for Larry. Promise me."

"Nancy," I said, after a deep breath, "I can't." All sorts of visions of their reunion, leaving this poor young woman injured—or worse—were crowding my mind.

"*Promise me!*" she insisted, her eyes intently boring into mine.

I threw up my hands in surrender. "All right," I sighed. "I promise."

And that's the way we left it. I can't do what I think needs doing, because I promised I wouldn't. Was that a stupid thing to promise, or what?

Questions for Discussion

1. As Nancy's on-the-job superior and her friend, how would you counsel her about her situation?

2. As Nancy's work supervisor, what would you do about her situation?

3. Under what circumstances would you break your promise and contact the police about Nancy's problem?

Case 9

No Time for This @#$%&!

Darrell Day, managing partner, Sullivan and Rosen, P.C., Pecan Grove office, to the Honorable Michael Willis, Pecan Grove city court judge, in chambers

A thief? Me? You've got to be kidding, Your Honor! Look at me: Do I look like a thief to you? No, I didn't think so. Know what I pay for my suits? Probably more than that guard's weekly take-home pay; maybe even a biweekly paycheck. Sorry if I'm being plain spoken, but it offends me to be called something I'm not, and that's why I'm speaking this way. I assure you, while I am many things, I am no thief, and I resent fiercely being called one. Give me a minute here . . . to collect my thoughts. Thanks.

Ahh, listen, Your Honor, I'm sorry for what I said a few minutes ago. I was hot about the accusation, but now that I'm calmed down, I'll tell you exactly what happened. And I greatly appreciate having the chance to tell you what happened here in chambers and not in open court where anyone with nothing to do is free to drop in and hear cases. But now I've regained my composure, and I'm ready to tell you what happened yesterday; and please try to keep an open mind, will you? I mean, I really hope you won't blow this thing out of proportion or decide to make an example of me for the benefit of the media or anything. It's not really any big deal. A tempest in the proverbial teapot, is all it is. Nothing has been lost, after all, and I'm being a stand-up citizen, here, by bringing back everything that was taken, so there's no crime, no victim, and no villain in this little drama. Just a big misunderstanding . . . and maybe some bad judgment on my part. But let me tell you what happened yesterday, and then you'll understand. And once you do, I hope you'll see things from my perspective.

So, you and me, we're both professional men, right? You're a judge and I'm a stockbroker, so I'm no schlepper or anything. What I do for a living takes education, training, personality, and brains, like your job. And in my line of work, there are times when split-second decisions can make the difference between profit and loss, between gainers and losers, and like that. I guess you could say that my job requires me to think quickly on my feet. That's how I kept my job when a lot of the people I used to work with have fallen victim to layoffs and cutbacks and other ramifications of the recent downturn in the markets. I tell you this not to brag about how important I am, but rather to explain why timing is everything, and delay (especially if it's avoidable) is unacceptable.

What? Right. I *am* getting to the point. Just let me tell this my way, please! So like I was saying, in my job, I have to make snap decisions and I have an instinct for making the correct ones, usually. But the price tag is that sometimes I get impatient. Yeah, because timing is everything, I tend to go bananas when snags interrupt the flow, like when I get caught in traffic, or have to wait in a slow-moving bank teller line, or get stuck on hold waiting for a client. And if you understand that, then maybe you'll understand what happened yesterday.

Yesterday about, oh, two o'clock, as a brief extension of my lunch hour, I hotfooted it over to the public library downtown, in search of a couple of books that I had read about on the Internet. They were reviewed as "a must for day traders" and "a concise guide to stock picking" respectively. Now, I suppose I might well have bought those books online and had them delivered by next-day shipping, but I really didn't need to own them. I just wanted to look them over and see if there was anything in them that I didn't know or that I could use to improve my prospect list or hit rate, all in the interest of better serving my clientele.

I go to the downtown library all the time, and I've got to say that my batting average, when it comes to finding the books I want isn't so great, actually. Probably about one success in three coming away with the book I want in hand, but it's only a couple of blocks from my office to the library, and I can use the exercise, so I decided to walk over there to try to find those books.

This time, I got lucky. Well, halfway lucky. One of the books I wanted was in, and available to be checked out for a three-week period. So I grabbed it off the shelf and got in the check-out line, figuring that even though there were maybe six people ahead of me, it wouldn't take long to get my transaction done and I'd be in my chair in plenty of time for the closing numbers from Wall Street. But it didn't work out that way. If it had, we wouldn't be having this conversation, with me attempting to void or plea bargain away my conviction for a misdemeanor. But it didn't. Work that way, I mean. You know that part of Murphy's Law that not only do things go wrong, but they go wrong at the worst possible time? Truer words were never spoken, I guarantee.

Your Honor, try to visualize what I'm telling you. Here's me, waiting in line—fidgeting around, because that's just the way I'm wired—but waiting, like any other library patron to charge out my book in the prescribed manner. And I count: I'm number seven in line. Ahead of me are six other people: a teenager, female, cute looking, with an armload of books; a drab housewife-type checking out what looked like a novel; a long-haired punk with multiple piercings, tattoos, and the whole nine yards—what he was checking out I couldn't imagine; another woman, with a couple of what looked like how-to titles; a teenaged boy in a Dallas Cowboys jacket, clutching a couple of medium-sized books, and just ahead of me, a little old man with only wisps of white hair left on his spotted dome. So here's me, in seventh place, jittering around, looking at my watch. Hey, time is money, you know what I'm saying? All right, already, impatience is one of my faults. So sue me.

Now, yeah, I was impatient, but not really rude, you know? I mean, inside, I'm shouting, "Move it, move it, *move it*!!" But I'm not a nasty guy. It's not my nature to be rude, even if time's a-wasting. So I don't say anything out loud. All I allow myself is an occasional sigh, or I mutter things like, "*Jeez!*" and of course, I'm trying to catch the eye of the check-out clerk, but she never looks my way. So I wait.

But after about 10 minutes, I'm only up to number four in line. Seems like everybody's transaction is much more complicated than just, "Here's my book, here's my card, charge it out for me, thanks, see ya." Finally, I say to myself, this is taking too long! Way too long, because the closing numbers from Wall Street are going to flash across my office computer screen any minute now, and I'm going to miss 'em. But I kept waiting and hoping. After what seemed like hours, there's just one person ahead of me: the little old man.

I could see that he's wearing hearing aids and walks with a cane, but what I don't expect is that the hearing aids aren't doing him a lick of good. So, he's asking the clerk a whole bunch of questions. Seems like everything he wants to know requires a long response, and even though I can hear what she said clearly enough, evidently, he can't, because he keeps asking her to repeat herself, saying "Eh?" and "Come again?"

So that's when I say, "Yeah, right. Like I'm supposed to spend my whole lunch hour waiting in your stupid check-out line! Like my daughter says, '*As if!*' " And with that, I got out of line and left the library—or tried to leave, anyway. I never meant to break the law. I just had to leave. Figured we'd sort it all out later, when I came back. How was I supposed to know about the alarm system they've got over there? Anyway, if you were as busy as me, what would you have done?

Your Honor, I see you're looking at your watch and I hear you sighing. What? Someplace you have to be soon? Yeah, I hear you. Me, too, actually. A busy schedule, like yourself. Closing numbers, and all that, back at the office. I'm sorry to waste any more of your time. So yeah, I guess I'm guilty as charged.

Technically, I admit I took the book and just broke for the exit without actually checking it out. I figured I'd already put 20 minutes of my life into waiting around, and besides, what was the big deal? I'm no thief, as I told you—you believe that, don't you, Your Honor? The kind of money I make, I could buy dozens of copies of the book I borrowed yesterday, so why would I bother to steal it? I just couldn't wait another minute. And I planned to make good on it on my way home from work, even if I had to pay some inconsequential fine for the library's inconvenience.

But then that security gate locked (because the book tripped the library's alarm system), a loud siren went off, and everybody was looking at me. I was confronted by that big old guard, the one with the face of a bulldog and a disposition to match. Well, like I said, I was already in a state of high anxiety, so when that guard refused to let me pass, I guess I said a few unfortunate things. He demanded to see my identification and then issued me a ticket for a court appearance for what he called an attempt to steal library property. And so here I am, as ordered.

But look at the circumstances: First, I didn't steal anything—the book is safely back in the library; second, I always intended to return the book, and where's the larceny in that; third, I am an account executive with a respected brokerage house, and nobody's idea of a sneak thief; and fourth, I was subjected to acute embarrassment when the gate jammed and the alarm bell went off, causing everyone to see me and draw their own unfortunate conclusions.

To top it all off, that security guard treated me like a common thief. I'm toying with the idea of calling my lawyer and suing him and his library for defamation of character; but I probably won't. Like I said, what's the big deal? It's just a library book, not the Hope Diamond I tried make off with. I mean, we're not talking about an armored car robbery here. I checked. That book costs $24 retail, and sells for even less on Amazon.com. I offered to buy it from the library and pay for it on the spot, plus any reasonable fine.

So, Your Honor, I hope you aren't going to cause me any more embarrassment for a silly misunderstanding that never would have occurred if the library had had both of their circulation machines manned during the busy lunch hour.

Of course, I'll pay the fine. But please, I'm asking you, don't release my name to the court stenographer, because I know how stuff like that has a way of ending up on police blotters, and in the newspaper on a slow news day. I could maybe lose my job over this. Let me skate just this one time—and I promise, I swear—that I'll never try to make off with a library book again. In fact, I've figured out how to use the library and not have such a problem ever again. I'll visit the library in the early morning, when stock trading is slow on all three exchanges and over the counter, and borrow my books then. Mornings are the best time for guys like me. There are days when I've been in there early when you could maybe throw a grenade in the library and nobody would get killed—or even hurt—when it went off.

Thanks for your consideration, Your Honor. What? Oh, sure. Yeah, I'll call the clerk of court in the morning to learn my fate. And abide by it, too. That goes without saying. I'm a law-abiding citizen, after all, and always have been. Just remember, please, that I am no thief. Call me impatient, call me abrupt, I can accept that. But I'd never steal library property, and so . . . uh, if you could maybe get the library to offer me a public apology?

What? Oh, sure, right. Bad idea. But I figured it was worth a shot. Doesn't hurt to ask, does it? So thanks for your time, Judge. I know you got things to do, and so do I. Money to be made out there. Do this for me, Your Honor and I'll owe you one.

What? No! Not at all. Not a bribe. No way would I try that. Just a sincere expression of gratitude, is all. And by the way, if you could ever use the services of an astute and experienced money manager and highly successful stock picker, then here, let me give you one of my cards.

Questions for Discussion

1. What alternative options might a patron have besides trying to leave the library with a book without checking it out?

2. How can libraries guard against other people trying to do what he did?

3. Critique the argument that removing a book from a library without following procedure is no big deal.

Case 10

It Rhymes with *Witch*

Karen Klaus, circulation clerk, to Ann Cameron Bowman, library director, in the director's office

Ann! You wanted to talk to me? Here I am. My side of the story? Right. Well, here goes nothing.

Please understand: I pride myself on getting along with just about everybody. That's part of the reason why I think I'm an effective circulation clerk. I'm good at my job and well suited to it. You may remember that I've been selected system employee of the month three times in the five years I've worked here, and I think that speaks for itself. Anyway, you know that this library, as a public facility, welcomes a cross-section of people every day. So it's natural that not all of them are going to be especially nice. Some of them, in fact, have serious amounts of what my son calls "attitude" and a few might even be psychotic, although don't ask me to define that term. And that's my point: definition.

It's not easy to define "verbal abuse," either. Seems to me, one person's verbal abuse may be another person's colorful language, or a constitutionally protected form of self-expression, but when somebody directs strong, unpleasant, and insulting words at me, that's where I draw the line. I say that's verbal abuse, and I won't have it. I heard more than enough of it just now when that man started using the kind of foul language I haven't heard since my late husband's navy days, and directed at me!

So that's the reason I turned and walked away from the circulation desk. Call it abandoning my post if you like, but I'd do it again, in a heartbeat. This guy had been in my face for a long time, giving me so much attitude that I reached a point when I just said enough, already, and walked away from the desk, retreating to the back room where he couldn't follow me or yell at me anymore. He used some really derogatory words, and I don't think that I should have to listen to that. Yes, I'm aware that he's lodged a formal complaint about my alleged impertinence, disrespect, and rudeness, and wants me punished, or even fired, but I still think that I did the right thing, and I hope you'll back me up on my actions.

Look, the way I see it, I had a few options: I could have just stood there mutely and taken all the verbal abuse this angry jerk wanted to shout at me until he tired of it; or I could have given it back as good as I was getting it, and believe me, when it comes to cuss words, I know some doozies (see, my late husband was a 20-year navy man, and you can imagine what kind of colorful expressions I've heard in my time, just hanging around with Harold and his buddies when they got together and had a few drinks).

But the problem with that option was that there were witnesses present, and I can just imagine how it would have looked for me to be exchanging insults with that guy in front of everybody. I also thought of picking up a couple of the books in front of me and sailing them at his head like frisbees, but I know that would have cost me my job. Anyway, I'm generally under pretty good control. My final option was to walk away from that angry jerk and duck into the back—to end the conflict and to collect what was left of my shattered composure. So that's just what I did.

Oh, I suppose I could have chosen to remain passive when he screamed insults at me until he got hoarse and stopped shouting, or until he left, but I wasn't up for that. Besides, dozens of people were nearby or within earshot when he went off on me, and it didn't seem like something you'd want to prolong. So I removed myself, and he eventually quieted down. I still think it was the best thing to do.

Of course, I could have picked up the phone and called the cops, since there was no security guard on duty at the time, but I judged that the situation wasn't going to result in violence—most guys who scream aren't going to start coming over the counter or pull guns or anything. It's just a rule of thumb, mind you, but in my 60 years of living, I've found it to hold true most of the time. It'd be nice if there'd been a big, beefy security guard handy, but it was the middle of the morning when it all happened, and Matt wasn't around. And about calling the police? Our instructions are not to summon them for small-potatoes stuff like flashers and loiterers and shouters or people who swear. I mean, if someone's safety is being physically threatened, then sure, every staff member is instructed to call the police, but for stuff like an angry man blowing off steam at me? I'm supposed to be capable of handling that situation myself.

So that's how I handled it. I walked away. Wasn't I right to do that? How did it start? Well, let me think . . . oh, yes: *Value Line*. When *Value Line* comes in every Wednesday morning, it attracts a lot of interest, to say the least. Some of our patrons seem to line up, or just mill around, waiting for a chance to get their grubby hands on it before anyone else does. Sometimes, some guy will take a look at the page of recommendations, give out a hoot or snort of excitement, and go running out of here like he's double parked or something. Must be going to one of the stock brokerages a block or two away, I don't know. But yesterday, about five minutes after I put the *Value Line* out in the reading room with the other newspapers, that's when the disturbance broke out.

How did it start? Well, I wasn't an eyewitness, so I couldn't say exactly how, but suddenly there was a lot of noise and commotion, and cursing, coming from the direction of the reading area for periodicals. When I got there, I saw two old men fighting over the latest *Value Line* and snarling to beat the band. One of them had it clutched in his hand, and the other one kept trying to snatch it away. They were squared off like prizefighters and seemingly about to start duking it out. As far as I could see, no blows were landed, but I remember hoping that there wasn't going to be a tug of war because that would not have done much for the *Value Line*, I can tell you that. Anyway, the man holding the newspaper grinned in triumph and started waving it at the other guy, saying (and I'm not making this up) "Naah, nahhnahhnaaaaah naah!" just like a little kid.

The other old party—a very large man—didn't take that lying down. He went over to the daily newspapers, which are all slotted on sticks, and he grabbed one of those newspaper sticks—paper and all—and started swinging it at the first man, who by then, had sat down to read *Value Line*. By this time, the big one seemed enraged.

We can't have that kind of behavior in our library, now can we? So I intervened. Or tried to anyway. I tried to spread sweet reason around to take the place of anger, selfishness, and childish behavior. It doesn't always work with kids, but I figured it was worth a try with a couple of adults. It turns out I was wrong about that, but I had to do something, right? So with a sweet smile on my face, I walked over to the combatants and asked them what the problem was.

"I had it first!" quavered the one sitting down. His name? I didn't get it. But you've probably seen him. Little guy. Wears a stained brown homburg, rain or shine. Comes in here all the time. I recognized him. I think he lives in a senior home a few blocks south of here. The other one—African-American, and big and beefy for all his 75 or so years—said something I won't repeat here, but it was one of those expressions that shows disbelief at what someone else has said. You know, bull—! You get the picture.

After he said that, the big guy tried again to snatch *Value Line* off the table where the little guy had it spread out. But the little man was quick, and whisked it away with a flourish, just missing some young woman who had walked over to see what was going on. Well, I said to myself, enough of this.

I've learned not to mess around with this sort of thing. I just call the police, tell the troublemakers what I've done, and try to contain the situation until the authorities arrive. Usually, after problem patrons hear that the police are on the way, they don't stick around for their arrival. They're almost always gone by the time the first uniform walks through the door.

So I walked over and stood like a referee between these two furious old men, wondering what I'd do if one of them took a swing at the other—or at me. They were both breathing hard, and I said the first thing I could think that might help the situation: "Can't y'all just share? Take turns, or something?" Picture the situation: two grumpy old men, puffing out their chests like cavemen squabbling over a fallen musk ox, and so angry they both looked as though they were about to have a heart attack. Personally, I don't know how adults could squabble like preschool kids over something so trivial.

"Turns? Sure," said the little guy, "works for me. Turns are fine. But me, first, because I was first to get to this *Value Line*, here. When I'm done with it, it's his turn, and I don't care what he does with it. But I had it first, so make him get away from me, and let me read it in peace, all right?" I turned to the big guy, hopeful, but he wasn't having any of my sharing plan.

"*You* had it first? That's a lowdown dirty lie!" he roared. He turned to me. "I had it first, and this little twerp snatched it right out of my hands. And if he doesn't give it over right now, I'm going upside his head with my fist, or maybe just put one end of this stick," he brandished the newspaper he was holding, "where the sun don't never shine."

Uh-oh, I thought. So much for creative solutions. Time for a decision. I turned to the larger man. "Look, sir, let's be reasonable, here. I can't say which of y'all actually got to *Value Line* first, but since this gentleman has it now, why not just go look at something else for . . . shall we say 15 minutes? I'm sure that when he's finished with it, he'll gladly let you have your turn, isn't that right?" I turned to the seated man for confirmation.

"Maybe, maybe not," he said in a sort of sing-song, taunting way. "The way I'm feeling now, I may just read it cover to cover—very slowly—and then set it on fire, or take it home with me to line the bottom of my birdcage."

"One more word out of your ugly little mouth and . . ." thankfully, the big man left the rest of that sentence unsaid and made no further move to use his impromptu weapon, but there was always that chance.

As assertively as I could, I said, "Then it's decided, all right? This gentleman, I gestured to the seated little man, will use *Value Line* first, for 15 minutes, and when he's finished, it'll be your turn. Now enough of this childish anger! We have a workable solution to the problem, right?" I peered up into the perspiring face of the larger man. "And next week, sir, if you're here when the new issue comes in, I'll see to it that it's your go first. I promise. Now be reasonable, can you do that? No fighting, no biting, hear? Take turns!" I looked sharply at each one, then turned and walked briskly back to my desk, fearing another outbreak of hostilities.

And wonder of wonders, the truce seemed to hold. The big guy, muttered something about "15 minutes and not a damn second longer" and stalked off to the men's room. Meanwhile, little guy started to read *Value Line,* taking occasional notes in a grubby and well-thumbed notebook that he took from a pocket in his frayed jacket. Feeling worn out but satisfied, I returned to my duties, wondering if I'd missed my calling, and should've been some sort of labor arbitrator or something like that.

But the temporary truce was just that. Temporary. Ten minutes later, the big guy was standing in front of me, shaking with rage. "What you did before wasn't right, Missy!" he said, wagging a thick finger across the counter at me.

"Sorry you feel that way, sir," I responded. "But an occasional part of my job is to make decisions that help keep order in here, and I made the best one I could."

"It isn't right and it isn't fair," he said, glaring at me. "Matter of fact, I'm mad as hell and I'm not going to take it anymore. Know what you are, Missy? You're a bigot. These aren't the old days of Jim Crow, you hear me? Bigots like you can't get away with that stuff, as you're about to find out!" Well, I was stunned. A bigot? Was he talking about *me*? No one has ever called me that. I've been called many things, but a bigot? Not hardly. Talk about unfair! That one really hurt.

"Sir," I said, politely, when I could speak, "I assure you that my decision was not based on discrimination but about who had it first." But he wasn't really listening.

"No, I've run into your kind before, and I know a bigot when I meet one, and that's you. Maybe you didn't call me any racial names, but I know what you did, you . . ." What he called me then was even more horrible, unfair, and ugly. It's something that rhymes with *witch*. Like I said when I first started this job, I can accept a certain amount of rough language, without getting all prudish and shocked at a dirty joke or if someone makes a sexual reference. But when he called me that, I just turned and walked away. Away from the desk, from the problem, and from him. I think most people would have done the same. It was so unfair!

Not only that, but he added as I fled, "I pay your salary, Missy! You work for me! But not for much longer. When I'm finished with you, the only time you'll spend here in this library is to look for another job in the morning paper's classified section!" I estimate that maybe 35 other people heard this rude and insulting man saying what he did. So I think I made the right choice by turning around and heading to the back, before I clocked this guy with my date-due stamp or anything else close to hand.

"Come back here, Missy!" I could hear him shouting as I kept walking away. "Don't you turn your back on me, ——— !"He used that same word again! "I'm talking to you! We're not finished, here!" I just kept walking until I was behind the partition and out of his line of sight. The last thing I heard him say was, to someone else on the staff who must have come over, "All right, that's it! I want to speak to the director. Now!" I ran into the bathroom, where I had to fight down my anger and nausea. That always happens to me when I get shocked. I sat down in a stall and did some heavy breathing until I calmed down. Ten minutes later, when I came out, I wasn't surprised to hear that he'd been up here in your office, and that you wanted to speak to me alone in your office, so here I am. Actually, I'm glad you summoned me, because I wanted to present my side to set the record straight.

What happens now? I don't want to lose my job over this but I've reviewed everything I did in my mind, and I still don't think that abandoning my duties or my behavior in those circumstances was wrong. Oh, he expects an apology? Well, he can just keep on expecting. Please don't ask me to apologize to that man, because I don't think he deserves one. Not for calling me a bigot and that other name. No way am I apologizing! In fact, he should be apologizing to *me*, but I know that there's a fat chance of that. My mother taught me to be a lady in all circumstances, but pardon the indelicacy: If he comes over to me again and starts in about an apology, I'm going to tell him I got his apology right *here*, if you know what I mean. Right here!

Questions for Discussion

1. Did the clerk handle the conflict between the two patrons well? What are some other possible solutions?

2. What should be the role of library guards when tempers flare and abusive language is uttered? What if no security guards are on duty?

3. If you, as director, supported the clerk over the patron, how far would you be willing to go to fight the angry patron's lawsuit, if one is brought against the library?

Case 11

Security Is Everybody's Job

Robin Lewis, branch head, Lake Highlands Branch, to Pat Sanchez, city manager, in Pat's office

I shouldn't even be here today, but you asked me to come in, and I do feel bad about the tone of that newspaper story. I feel as crummy as I look, actually. Yeah, I think it's just a cold. The flu brings fever with it, doesn't it? My nose keeps running and my throat is sore, but so far, no fever. I just hope I don't give it to you. I'll just sit over here while we talk, and when I'm done here, I'm going straight home to bed to sleep this off. Decongestants have really clogged up my brain so I doubt that I'd be much good at work today, if I went back in. But I know that you need information, so I'll try to reconstruct what happened yesterday that led to that unfortunate quote in the newspaper.

You know that saying they have in public relations, that all publicity is good publicity? Well, that's not always true. Sometimes, in fact, it's flat wrong. At least, that's what I think after yesterday afternoon. I thought a chance to be interviewed by a newspaper reporter might lead to some good publicity for the library, but it doesn't seem to have worked out that way. I should have pointed to my throat, made a face, written the word *laryngitis* on a pad of paper, and then shown that reporter out. But I went ahead with the interview, as you know. Who's sorry now?

Right off the bat, she asked me about security in my branch. The question just came out of left field and landed in my lap, especially difficult since I was starting to come down with something, you know what I mean? When she asked me that, I said the first thing that popped into my mind just to get her to go away as soon as possible and leave me to suffer alone in my office. If I'd felt in tip-top condition and had time to consider what I was saying—and the ramifications—I would've said something else, or at least put a different emphasis on my words, or asked her to come back another day.

Why did I say it? Well, it was raining most of the morning, a cold, hard rain. The expressway wasn't flooded, but it was bumper-to-bumper traffic with slow-moving cars full of irritable drivers. So it took me 20 minutes longer than usual to drive to my branch, which put me in a bad mood already. And then, after sniffling and coughing all morning, I broke a nail. See? This one. I spend a lot of time and money on my fingernails, and when one of them just snaps off, it does nothing to improve my mood, knowing that I'm going to spend the rest of the day with nine long, well-shaped nails and one filed-down nub. I don't know, every so often, I snap one off. Maybe I should take extra calcium, you think?

So all that's by way of framing my mood when my front desk clerk phoned back to my office to tell me that a reporter for *The Pecan Grove Observer* was waiting out front and wanted to have some time with me. I figured it could be good publicity for my branch, so I went out to the front lobby to greet her. The reporter turned out to be a nice enough young woman; maybe just too aggressive in pursuing a story. But she caught me off guard, and I forgot to run everything I said past my internal censor and editor, the way I do when I have my wits about me. Wish I had that moment back, but I don't. Can't "un-ring" a bell, can you?

So I'm sitting in my office across the table from this cub reporter, wishing I could just go home and go to sleep, but no. I'm being interviewed and cross-examined about library safety, while I'm going through a whole box of tissues, dealing with my sniffles. And here's this pink-cheeked junior reporter looking for a story. She flips open a little notebook, looks at it, then asks me whether I feel responsible for the crimes that have been committed recently in and around my branch library. *Responsible* for those crimes? I want to grab her by the lapels of her perky little blouse and scream, "Why should *I* feel responsible!" but of course I don't. She's just doing her job, after all, and besides, I didn't have the energy to scream. I just felt wasted.

Oh, the article? I wish I could say it's a pack of lies, but taking statements out of context, everything I said is, unfortunately, reported accurately enough. I know what she's referring to. As you know, the Lake Highlands Branch lies about seven miles from the downtown library and serves residents on the north side of the city. Ours is basically a neighborhood of single-family, well-kept houses, but with some gated communities for wealthier people too.

What this means is that my branch has always enjoyed a lower crime rate than either the downtown library or any of the other branches. In fact, our area has enjoyed the lowest crime rate in the whole metropolitan area for most of the 15 years I've lived in Pecan Grove and worked for this system. Very few calls to the police come from my branch, except maybe a few about a purse snatching or a pickpocket.

And it *is* nice at the end of the day to walk out of the building I work in to my car, in the dark, without worrying that someone is going to jump me—unlike my colleagues in the other branches.

But things have changed recently in Lake Highlands; the crime rate out our way has skyrocketed recently. I guess that's why she wanted to interview me, to get my take on the unexpected crime wave in my branch's vicinity Why the crime wave? Several factors, like a spike in unemployment, for instance, together with the reported use—and even sale—of illegal drugs like crack cocaine, ecstasy, and speed in the vicinity of our library. Anyway, for various reasons, crime is way up, and the library incident rate has risen in response.

Thankfully, most of the crime we experience, even now, around my branch isn't heavy-duty stuff, like rape, murder, and strong-arm robbery. We're a library, not a bank, after all, and frankly, there isn't that much worth stealing for drug addicts who need ready cash. But still, if you compare the figures for this year to corresponding figures for last year, what jumps out at you is that crime is on the rise, even in and around our quiet branch. Crime is on the upswing all over the city. And the city is responding by putting more cops on the street and in squad cars.

The city has also suggested to uniformed patrol officers in the area that they swing by my branch every once in a while during their rounds and show themselves, as a deterrent to criminals bent on mischief. That way they know if they get caught trying anything, they might well find themselves spending time in jail. But that's only about police presence, commendable as it is.

What I really want is to restore the budget line for a security guard at my branch, a guy who doesn't have to come *by* the library because he's already there. Not long ago there were five guards on the payroll at the downtown building and at least one uniformed guard working at each of the regional branches of the library system, including mine. But that was then; this is now. Deep cuts in the library's budget have caused cutbacks in what you people here at city hall call "inessential services." The result? As of today, there are two full-time guards downtown, one out at Lakewood (because that's in a rough part of town), and for us here at Lake Highlands and the other branches? No security guards at all.

When we lost even the part-time services of our last security guard, I protested, of course. I wrote memos to the director and sent e-mails to human resources here at city hall to point out the vulnerability of people—patrons and staff alike—to who knows what if we had no police protection and no security guards, whatsoever. What happened? Nothing. Well, I did get a memo from human resources thanking me for my note, commiserating with my concerns, and expressing regret that there wasn't enough money to go around. Your HR chief wrote that difficult decisions had become necessary because a new austerity budget had dictated cuts in programs and services, and we were all just going to have to soldier on bravely without certain things. When conditions improved, the memo promised, the city would take another look at those cuts. Yeah, right.

The bottom line is that our branch, as of last year, is, in effect, defenseless. Our longtime guard was pensioned off, moved to Florida, and he was never replaced. Nowadays, despite the rising crime rate, no security guard patrols Lake Highlands. At least ol' Frankie was there to keep an eye on things, even if he was nobody's idea of Robocop.

So, like I said, when I questioned our situation, I was told, look, we're all in the same boat. Deal with it. With any luck, in a few months, the budget will come back to previous levels (or higher, even) and you, your staff, and your patrons will once again be protected by security. Blah, blah, blah.

But yesterday? Well, that young reporter who drove over to my branch in all that rain to interview me about public safety in the library, and what we're doing about it, I guess she got under my skin. As I said, I was already having this awful day suffering from this bad cold, and there were still five hours to go before my shift ended, and that's when I had to sit down and try to "explain" the recent crime wave to this kid reporter. Can you see why I forgot to be careful about what I said?

First, though, I gave her the company line about self-reliance and making do. I mean, this nosy kid reporter came around asking questions, and when she observed that she didn't see any uniformed security, like she had seen downtown, I just said the first thing that popped into my head. Unfortunately, it wasn't the right thing to say, but what was I supposed to do, agree with her? I don't think so. So in response to her question about the lack of security presence in our branch, I got a little sarcastic, maybe. What I said what was, "We're *all* security officers, here, honey."

Of course, I admit that calling her "honey" was a mistake—I could see it in her face immediately. I'm willing to apologize for it. But this reporter looked, like, maybe 19, and just so smug with her preppy little outfit, so when she leaned forward and hit me with that question, I lost it for a second and said the wrong thing, I admit. Calling her "honey" was out of line, even if I was thinking of some much stronger terms, believe me!

But I sort of *did* apologize. My exact words? I don't know. Give me a moment. Well, I think I said, "Sorry about that. I'm getting a cold, and I'm having a bad day here." Not much for contrition, maybe, but it was all I could muster at the time. She seemed to nod her understanding, though, and asked her next question. Who knew what she was thinking? But did she ease up on me a little bit? No way! She said, "When I go downtown to the main library, I see a very big security guard walking around in a uniform and he's got a communicator, which makes me feel safer. How come you don't have any security here, in this dangerous neighborhood?"

"Dangerous neighborhood?" I asked, feeling surprised, probably too loudly and between clenched teeth. I didn't want to let that remark go un-challenged. But I did let it go. Instead, I patiently explained why we had no security guard. The real answer is that the main library gets most of the patronage, so it gets most of the funds—for security and just about every-thing else. We out here in the distant provinces get what's left over.

Well, after about five more minutes of this back and forth, I was *willing* this kid reporter to just get up and walk out of my office before I threw her out bodily. But I didn't. Still, I figured she'd take a hint, because as the in-terview wore on, all she got was mostly name, rank, and serial number to the rest of her questions. Yeah, I know she was just doing her job, and I'm sorry I was snotty with her, but just then, she was making it extremely hard for me to do mine.

Finally, she flipped the notebook shut, got up, thanked me, and walked out, leaving me depressed but grateful that I hadn't killed her or called her any of those rude names I was thinking. Then, since I had a busy day going, I did my best to forget the half hour we'd spent talking in my office. Today, of course, the *Observer* ran that feature story in which my comment became a headline, "We're all security guards here, honey!" in the metropolitan sec-tion, as part of a series on public safety in Pecan Grove. Uh oh, I said to my-self, when I saw that feature. Guess it's going to hit the fan now. That turned out to be an easy prophecy because your call to me, asking me to come to your office, came less than half an hour later.

Damage control? I'm glad you asked me that. You bet I'm interested in damage control! Since most of the newspaper's subscribers have by now read what I said, I'm plenty concerned about the aftermath, on two fronts. To cer-tain members of this community, I'm afraid that my comment that we're all security staff here may look like a notification that we're undefended and are easy pickings. And calling that reporter "honey" and having everybody see that in the paper? That article makes me look like a total b——! I guess that's payback for my disrespect.

So that's my story. I'm really sorry if I caused a ruckus, and I want to help minimize the fallout from my ill-considered remarks if I can. The first thing I've decided to do is to call that reporter and apologize and try to make her see my warm, fuzzy side. Maybe I'll offer to buy her lunch one day or wash her car or something. Beyond that? I'm willing to help undo the problem I created. Just tell me what to do, and I'm all over it.

Finally, though, I want to say that if the city expects librarians to work in an environment without the protection of security guards, I think we ought to get hazard pay and be provided with crash helmets, bulletproof vests, and stun guns. An exaggeration? Maybe, but not all that much of one. Look at the crime statistics and you decide.

Well, if that's all, I just want to repeat that I'm very sorry for giving the library a black eye yesterday, and I want to do what I can to make up for it. Thanks for listening. And oh yeah, one last question: which is right, feed a cold and starve a fever, or is it the other way around?

Questions for Discussion

1. What can a branch library do to improve security without extra cost?

2. As Robin, what would you now do to try to mend fences with the reporter and her newspaper? With the community? The library administration?

3. As the library director, would you take any disciplinary action against Robin for her remarks to the reporter?

Case 12

Just Like at the Airport

Mike Early, security guard, to Cindy Cutting, reporter for *The Pecan Grove Observer*, in an interview

I suppose it looked like a big windfall for the library, solving a serious problem that's been growing every year, and at the same time not costing us a red cent. I'm talking about that surplus metal detector that was donated to the library by the airport authority, but like a lot of "free" merchandise, it turned out to be a double-edged sword. We found out that there's a lot of truth in that old saying that you ought to be careful what you wish for, because you just might get it.

The problem began last year when Ann Cameron Bowman, our director, spoke to one of your other reporters about the library, its role in the community, and all that propaganda. Toward the end of the interview, the reporter asked what some of the problems we faced were, and what we were doing about them. After mentioning the continuing problem of money, our number two problem, she said, was security. Hey, I'm a security guard, so I don't have to be sold on the truth of what she said. My only question, if they'd asked me, would have been whether to make security our number one problem, instead of money, but I guess they're related, aren't they?

Ann said that crime of various sorts was an ongoing problem for the library. Over the past year, we caught maybe a dozen young kids bringing handguns, switchblade knives, and other potentially lethal objects into the building. Dealing with such people, she said, was high on her list of priorities. She actually used the airport as a point of comparison. If you try to bring a weapon through the checkpoint and into the gate area at the airport, and it gets discovered or detected, you could get arrested, fined, and do jail time—even if you don't take it out or point it at anyone. But in the library, we have no way of knowing who's bring in or carrying what. We're just as concerned with the safety and welfare of our staff and patrons as are the people who work in and protect airports, except we don't have those electronic screening gates.

77

See, at the airport, it's a federal crime to carry a concealed weapon without authorization. No tolerance. Big fines. Disturbingly, some people still get through, of course, like that guy who had six or seven knives and a stun gun, last year at O'Hare in Chicago. But walk into my library and the rules pretty much tie my hands as to how much I can do to discourage the "bad element" from bringing weapons in. I can't frisk people, for example. Not even supposed to touch anybody.

And Ann mentioned—maybe she shouldn't have, but she did—that an astonishing collection of weapons had been taken from library visitors over the years, ranging from bayonets to live grenades, handguns, nunchucks, and once, even, a garroting wire, like the one they used in the *Godfather* to strangle people. Probably not the cleverest thing she's ever said, in my opinion, listing all those weapons. Oh, I know what she meant to emphasize: that guards like me are vigilant and are trying to prevent, deter, or deal effectively with the occasional punk who comes in "strapped" or packing a weapon under his clothing.

But she did point out a problem: We're not even authorized to ask anyone to empty his pockets or lift his shirt, and we can't pat down anyone for weapons. So people can come in armed to the teeth, and we have no way of knowing.

Ann's interview brought results, though. I guess it was two days later that the head of the airport authority called her and told her that in the wake of recent terrorist activities, the Pecan Grove Airport had just taken delivery on a number of gleaming new, ultra-sensitive metal detectors for use in the terminals, leaving them free to dispose of the old ones as they saw fit.

Somehow, it occurred to somebody who'd read Ann's remarks that the library might want to get one of those castoffs, which were perfectly good devices, just superseded. If Ann said yes, this guy said he would be happy to deliver one of them that afternoon and arrange for a free two-hour training session for the personnel who would be running it. He said he couldn't supply or pay for operation and maintenance, but if the library would assume responsibility, he would donate the machine.

The machine arrived the next week, consisting of two major parts. You've seen them at airports, so you know what they're like. There's a long conveyor belt, where people's bags and other carry-on items are X-rayed so that a technician can see what's inside. At first, we liked that idea, because then we guards wouldn't have to search belongings manually. I could tell you about some of the disgusting stuff I've found in patrons' bags, but I don't want to get you sick. Also, we could get rid of those coin-operated lockers out in the vestibule. The other part of the apparatus was a pass-through gate for people, designed to beep when somebody carried anything metallic through it.

Of course, that presented other problems. What about the differences among the gates? In my own traveling experiences, I've found that some days I trigger a beep just from my belt buckle, and other times, I just throw my ring of keys into a little basket and sail on through.

But every so often, they catch somebody carrying actual weapons past the metal detector. And who knows? Nobody wants a hijacked plane. Especially nowadays. So those things are useful, however annoying and hit-or-miss the procedure might be.

But what nobody seemed to think about is that such security entails expenses of its own. Suppose the alarm beeps when someone walks through the gate. Somebody's got to take that person aside and run a wand over him or her to try to locate the cause. Yeah, the airport donated the wand, too. So there's another problem, right there: additional personnel to scan the carry-on bags, deal with people who set off the alarm, and direct them to the wand guy or gal. And that's every minute the library is open to the public. Where is that kind of money supposed to come from?

Well, we did the best we could. A staff member, usually a circulation clerk, was assigned to door security, while Matt or I patrolled the interior of the building. So, that one staff member would greet incoming patrons, direct them to send their bags down the conveyor belt, run around to the screen to check their belongings for bad things, and then, if there's a beep, run over, grab the wand, and pass it over their bodies. That's a lot of work. It keeps you running, I'll tell you that.

Even though there are whole hours when nobody comes in at all, we can get upwards of a hundred visitors an hour at peak times. But it's not as bad as at the airport, especially on weekends and holidays, when thousands of people pass through the terminal's security in a single hour.

When the system was installed, and a couple of the circulation clerks were trained, I felt pretty good about it, because it made my job easier. Now I didn't have to watch people when they come in anymore, and I could pay more attention to them once they're inside. I just kept an eye on everybody, you know? Get up to no good in "my house" and I'll descend on you like a ton of bricks, is what I like to project with my expression. Most of the criminal element have learned that I mean business, and they'd best not break the rules of conduct, because if they do, they're going to have to deal with me. They don't want that.

I mean, I'm not allowed to beat on 'em, but if the situation warrants it, I have permission to grab 'em by the collar or sleeve and see 'em to the door and outside. Haven't had to do it often, but I'm ready for anything. Anything . . . except a gun, I suppose. That's why I was in favor of that metal detector gizmo. It sounds off when it senses guns, knives, and other weapons, unless they're made out of plastic or ceramic or something. Once the machine sounds off, I can either make 'em leave, or get on the phone and call the cops. Got several friends on the force, and they pay attention when I call because they know I'm not just getting hyper over something small. Guns are serious business, so I don't mess around.

But that's the ironic part about what happened. It wasn't some punk or thug that caused the recent ruckus. No, it was a city councilwoman who came to the library yesterday to get a book she needed. The councilwoman is ordinary looking, maybe 50, with sharp eyes and a ready smile. She's done a lot for this community over the years and nobody wants to irritate her. Big library booster. Always gets my vote.

So yesterday, this councilwoman walks in here, carrying a briefcase, and the clerk on duty does her job, saying, "Good morning, ma'am. Welcome to the library. If you'd be so good as to put your briefcase and purse on the conveyor belt and walk through the gate, which won't take but a second, you'll be on your way."

The councilwoman, however, decided to get confrontational. "What's all this? When did this get here?" she said, eyeing the new machine at the entrance. I walked over and said, "Good morning. It's new: a gift from the airport authority. Now, ma'am, if you'll just please place your bag on the belt and step through . . . ."

She glared up at me. "I'll do no such thing! I'm your elected city councilwoman. Are you implying that you want to put me through this thing because I might be contemplating the commission of a crime?"

"No, ma'am," I said, keeping a respectful tone, "Not at all. But those are the rules and they apply to everybody, with no exceptions. Just like at airports all over America, we've installed this metal detector for everybody's protection. So please . . ." Following procedure and orders, I asked her to send her purse through the scanner, empty her pockets, and step through the gate where our clerk was waiting. That was the last straw, I guess, because she demanded in a loud angry voice that someone call the library director immediately to explain this outrage. Politicians, you know. Think they're above the law.

The clerk made the call, and a minute later, Mrs. Bowman, our director, came downstairs and walked over to her. The annoyed woman asked Ann, belligerently, "What's up with the metal detector at the front door? This isn't Metro airport, you know." Ann didn't cave in under this sort of blustering, though, and I was proud of her for that. In a calm, assertive voice, she said, "No, it's not, but it *is* a public place, and those who come here deserve the same protection as those who travel by air, don't you think?"

The councilwoman said that this was a different thing, altogether. She said that she understood that if somebody brings a bomb on an airplane, or commandeers one with box cutters or whatever, hundreds or thousands of lives could be lost. But the library? She gave a little laugh, saying, "Who's going to be bringing a bomb to a library?"

Ann had a ready answer for that one too. She cited an incident that occurred at the main Salt Lake City public library building[1] some years ago, when a deranged man with sticks of dynamite strapped to his body threatened to blow the whole place up and everybody in it. Fortunately, he was killed by authorities before he could do any damage, but he *was* a real threat.

"Besides," said Ann, pointing at our "stop-loss" gate, "we've had this other gate here at the exit for years, and you didn't have a problem with that." The stop-loss gate indicates when somebody is trying to make off with books or other materials that haven't been charged out. "What's your problem with this additional bit of technology?"

The politician didn't back down. She said that there's a difference between checking people who want to leave and checking people who are trying to enter. She added that she could see the merits of stopping juvenile delinquents from bringing their arsenals inside but didn't like the idea of using airport technology in the library. "Besides," she asked, "how often do you hear about things like that Salt Lake City problem?"

"That's the point!" Ann said. "We don't want it to happen ever again in any library—especially not here in ours. I think it's a good idea to have this equipment that detects when people enter our building with guns and knives. In fact, I'd welcome a chance to get additional machines like this for our four branch libraries without any expense on our part."

Well, the councilwoman would have none of that. "It's intrusive to saddle honest citizens with such inspections," she said. "More to the point, it's unnecessary. And let's not forget the various privacy concerns. At the next city council meeting, I'm going to urge that the council recommend the removal of this device as soon as possible. People want transparent access to public facilities, not intrusive searches of themselves and their possessions. That's what distinguishes this free country from the rest. There's already too much intrusion on our private lives, and I'm going to put a stop to it at this library."

She pointed a finger at Ann. "I'll be back. In the meantime, you might want to give some thought to returning this monstrosity to the airport, or if they won't take it off your hands, then maybe you should see how much it will fetch on e-Bay. Good day!"

As she stormed off, Ann and I stood sadly, side by side, and watched her leave. We knew that we had not heard the last of that councilwoman and her campaign to eradicate the new security machines. Ann said something softly to me as she smiled wearily and trudged back up the stairs. I can't be sure, but I think it sounded like, "Why me?"

For details of the Salt Lake City incident mentioned in this case, see "Bomber Holds Librarian and Patrons Hostage at Utah PL," *Library Journal,* 1 April 1994, p. 17.

Questions for Discussion

1. How, if at all, is library security different from airport security?

2. As director, would you have accepted the airport's gift? Would you have implemented it in the same way?

3. Is some abridgment of individual freedom necessary to achieve heightened security?

Case 13

Noonchook Boy

Patricia Ridley, circulation clerk to Cindy Cutting, reporter for *The Pecan Grove Observer*, in a telephone interview

In all me years, I've never been interviewed for a newspaper write-up before, so forgive me if I'm a bit nervous, and that. You want to know about our Noonchook Boy? I'll tell you what I can. Oh, the way I talk? You could tell from me accent that I'm not from around here. Noothing gets past you, eh? Actually, I coom from Yorkshire, a county of northern England, and beg pardon if you already knew where Yorkshire is, but so many of you bloody Yanks don't know booger-all about geography. In me opinion, it's a crime and a shame that every little English schoolchild learns ever so much more about your country in school than a child over here in the states ever learns about their own.

I mean, when me children coom home with their friends, I soomtimes ask their mates a few questions, as a sort of an experiment, like, joost to see what they know or oonderstand about England, so similar to your country in so many ways and yet so different. Anyway, the typical school child roond here knows summat about Loondon and maybe has heard of Manchester and Liverpool, but if you asked them to stick pins in a blank map of the British Isles to show where those cities actually are, well . . . I'm just saying that it seems a bloody shame to me that American children are so ignorant of places across the pond, that's all.

But you're not here to talk about international awareness, are you? No, you want me, I know, to tell about that unfortunate incident including that misguided yoong lad the other day, and what happened when he began fiddling aboot with those martial arts things roond his neck. I didn't know what they were called a few days ago, but I do now, and I'll never forget that weird word: noonchooks. Oh, you didn't? Well, not to worry: neither did I, oontil recently, but I suppose I'd seen them used in those martial arts films that are playing at the cinema and on the telly—you know the ones? Films with yoong Asian men and women leaping in the air, delivering smart kicks and poonches to their adversaries, and ootherwise doing things you might expect to see at the ballet. But let me joost bash on with it and tell you what I saw.

The lad is a nice looking yoong man, I moost say. Very clean-cut and mooscular, with long and very straight black hair and extremely well-defined mooscles sticking oot of the sleeves of that vest he wears instead of a proper shirt. No, I don't know his name. While I'm on the circ desk I try to be friendly to everyone who walks through the front door, and polite in me charge-out and other transactions with our patrons. But I don't ask people's names, unless I need that information for getting them fitted out with library cards, or sooch.

This lad cooms in here three or four times a week, wearing what seems to be the same kit each time: blue jeans, that vest with no shirt oonderneath, a tattoo on his arm, and a black sort of rag roond his forehead, to keep the long hair oot of his eyes, I imagine. Roond his neck, almost like a sort of necklace, he always has a set of . . . well, now I know they're called noonchooks. They have two handles and between them, a length of metal chain.

Oontil yesterday, he never took them off his neck, so I took little notice, not really. Whenever he passed me desk, though, he would flash me this radiant grin. Perfect white teeth, he has. And that smile just brightened oop me day. Oh, no, he's half me age and I'm married with children, besides; but still, a girl notices handsome smiles, doosn't she? Too many of the folk we get in here are cross, cranky, groompy, and the like.

What? Any trouble? That loovely young Asian lad with the noonchoocks round his neck? Not at all. First time I saw him, I thought, Well! Here's a bloke who's been watching too many late-night Kung Fu films. But he never did anything frightening before, not a bit of that. No, no trooble until yesterday. I mean, aye, I always noticed that steel necklace he had roond his neck, but he never did anything with it but let it hang there—like the woman in the circus who carries a python roond her neck, have you ever seen her? Fearsome-looking brute it is, too, with a triangular head this big, but when she's wearing it, it seems content just to, you know, hang aroond her neck and just look at people. So yes, this lad had been bringing in what seemed to be a weapon, if you want to look at it that way, for some time.

But it never occurred to me to be alarmed by that, because he never used it. I reckon it was just part of him, like this pin with the Union Jack I wear every day is part of me. I never really gave it mooch thought. As I say, he didn't seem dangerous, quite the contrary. I was always quite glad to see him, and you might say that I enjoyed having him stop in for a trip roond the building, or, on occasion, to borrow a book, or take a drink from the boobbler (what you lot call a water cooler) over there in the corner.

I'm not soft, you know, and I know you want me to get doon to cases and tell you what I saw. Well, it was yesterday, I'm not sure of the time, but it was probably soomewhere between three and five (what we called tea time at the library I worked in back in me home town). And there was noothing amiss as I could see: the usual assortment of patrons and the odd staff member on view from me majestic perch at the circ desk.

Now this Noonchook Boy (yes, I know he has a name, but I joost think of him that way) walked in, grinned at me, gave me a slight bow and nod, and continued on his way oot into the stacks. But the three-to-five shift is a busy time for me, so after returning his silent greeting, I put him oot of me mind.

Oh, aye! I'm almost sure of it, anyway. He had them with him, draped roond his neck as usual. After moonths of seeing him come in like that, I doobt that anyone remarked on the bloody things anymore. They were just part of his uniform, the way a blue shirt with epaulets are part of a policeman's kit. And once he headed off oot into the stacks, I put him out of me mind. But when I heard all the shouting cooming from oot there, I decided to see what all the row and fooss was aboot.

Here's what I saw when I got there: a man I'd never seen before—or didn't recognize, anyway—was lying on the floor, moaning and holding his knee. What? Oh. Left knee. How do I remember that? I remember distinctly that he was lying on his right side and holding his trooser leg oop. His face was contorted in obvious pain. I suppose he was cursing, too, but I wasn't listening carefully to what he said—me concern was with the poor injured knee.

He was moaning soomthing amazing. I suppose if you'd had your kneecap whacked by a set of them noonchooks, you'd be moaning as well. It bloody well hurts to have your knee banged up. Once, as a girl in Yorkshire, I had one of mine strook a glancing blow by a passing lorry and I'll not soon forget how much that hurt.

When I looked up from the man rolling aroond on the floor clootching his knee, I saw our Noonchook Boy, standing over the unfortunate man with the sticks held high and the chain hanging between them, looking ready for further business at a moment's notice. He was glaring down at the man on the floor, although he didn't say a word, but he seemed to be daring the oother man to get up and coom and get another blow for his offenses. Well, enoogh of this standing aboot, gawking, I said to meself.

I spent a moment trying to figure out which one of these blokes I should be talking to first. Then I came oot with a line I learned from half of the police dramas they show on the BBC, back home. I said, "What's all this, then?" addressing me remarks to both men, Noonchook Boy an' the one writhing on the floor.

The bloke on the floor was wearing a suit, I could see now, but one that had seen better days, what with frayed cuffs, and all. He was the first to pipe up: "I was just minding my own business," he said, between groans of pain, "when this refugee from a bad Kung Fu movie attacked me for no good reason at all!" He moaned piteously, and added, "I think he broke my knee." Actually, what he said was one word longer, but I'm not aboot to tell you the word he put between "my" and "knee"—that wouldn't be proper.

Then, pointing oop, he said the other fellow had whacked him a good one with those "fighting sticks" and the stout metal chain had slammed into his kneecap, probably boosting it. Finally, he moottered soomthing aboot suing everyone in sight, including our library, for letting foreign criminal elements wander oonchallenged with death-dealing weapons wherever they wished in the building.

That was me first clue that this could be troobble for us all. I looked up at Noonchook Boy, who was no longer looking like a cobra poised to strike again with those sticks and chains of his. "And what have you got to say for yourself, then?" I asked him. To my astonishment, the yoong man coom back with perfect English, soonding like just any other Yank from Texas or somewhere. Well, I was astonished. I guess I'd assumed that because of the way he looked, he was going to sound like he was froom China or Japan or Korea or one of those places. But no—he sounded American enough—mooch more American than me, coom to that.

"This man lies," he said, as the noonchooks went back roond his neck so he could gesture with his hands. "I was minding my own business, as I do every day when I come in here—you've seen that for yourself, dear lady. But this man came walking up to me and called me a racial name."

"Oh, my!" I said, not knowing what else to say. But he wasn't finished. "Dear lady, please understand that my discipline and training have equipped me to withstand and ignore virtually all taunts, jibes, and ethnic slurs that one encounters in the course of going round this city. In fact," he said, looking coldly down at the writhing man at his feet, "I am really quite disappointed in myself for letting an idiot like this defeat my self-control."

"Idiot?" shouted the man on the floor, struggling to rise. "I'll show you who the idiot is, you . . ." I think, if you doon't mind, I'll leave out the rest of what he was shouting. Fortunately for him, the bloke was halfway oop when he screamed in pain and fell back onto the floor, where he once again was clootching his damaged knee and crooning to it softly.

"Here!" I said, quietly, to Noonchook Boy. "There's little to be served by passing insults, joost because he did it first, you know." The yoong man gave me a little bow of acknowledgment and agreed, but didn't seem to be able to resist throwing in a last comment.

"Idiots will always say idiotic things," he said, cutting his eyes downward so I wouldn't miss his meaning. Fat chance of that. To his credit, though, the lad did offer to help his adversary get oop, but the nasty brute ungraciously spurned his offer, moottering something dark aboot payback and vengeance, and the like.

I turned to the small crowd that had gathered to see what all the fooss was about. "Anyone else see this happen?" I asked. Everyone joost shook their heads.

Well, I'd seen enough to know that there was not going to be any more combat joost then. The older man was, after all, going to need an ambulance and soom medical care in a hospital, I figured, and the lad no longer seemed to be in the mood for getting physical. Joost then, Michael, our security guard, arrived in time to sort everything out and send the gawkers and bystanders on their way, giving me the chance to walk back to the telephone on me work desk and call 911, the way we're drilled to do in emergencies and accidents. And the incident was over.

Except it wasn't really over. It'd be nice to say that it was, but it wasn't. Plainly, we couldn't joost put paid to this oonhappy incident without consequences. Not really. Because what had happened left hanging a coople of delicate questions concerning such things as liability, prevention of violent incidents, when to call the bobbies, and the like. Well, that's me report. I suppose I'm partly responsible for all the fooss and feathers because I could have prevented the confrontation somehow by making the lad remove those noonchooks, but I did nowt aboot it.

Final thoughts? Well, yeah. Soomtimes, I think I should've stayed home in England, like me broothers, Harry, Nigel, and Clive. They all have steady, ooncoomplicated jobs driving trooks (although we call them lorries on the other side of the pond) and seem happy as can be. Now, there's talk that the man our Noonchook Boy assaulted is bringing charges, and I've got to appear as star witness for the prosecution. I'm not looking forward to it, and that. I doon't suppose I could joost get called home or summat . . . like a family emergency, or that?

Questions for Discussion

1. What should be standard procedure with regard to offensive and defensive weapons carried into a library building by patrons?

2. As Patricia, what would you have said or done at the time of the incident, after you'd heard the conflicting stories of the two men?

3. If this matter goes to court, what is Patricia's responsibility with regard to what she heard and saw?

Case 14 _____

In Loco Parentis

April Engel, children's librarian, to Scott Lucas, patrolman for the Pecan Grove Police Department

Officer, I'm a children's librarian, but don't get the idea that just because I read stories to tots and sometimes sing and dance and wear funny costumes and weird hats that I'm not keeping my mind in the game. If anyone's accusing me of laxity in protecting the kids who come in here, I deny it heatedly. Even while I'm horsing around to amuse—and hopefully, to educate—the kids who troop in here every day, I keep my eyes moving. Especially when anybody who isn't a kid—or doesn't belong—walks into this department. I mean, just because I deal every day in Barney, Sesame Street, and Dr. Seuss stories, I still know that it's a mean old world outside, so we're told to try to watch everybody who comes in.

But you can't watch everybody all the time, know what I mean? See, we're short on staff here in Children's just as they are in all the other departments. Try as I might, I can't keep an eye on everybody or ask questions of people who seem out of place. Not our job, really, to maintain surveillance on everyone who comes in here anyway, and we're spread too thin to even try.

Once in a while, we get people in here who are *not* visiting the children's room just to look at books or puppets or the pictures on the walls, if you get my drift. It happens. Every so often, some guy who likes children—I mean really *likes* them—enters our area with who-knows-what in mind. Perverts, pedophiles, and guys who like to look at little children come in here unchallenged, especially if they look normal—whatever that means—and are well dressed.

Anybody who looks like he might be there to mess with any of my kids? I'm not afraid to walk right up and challenge him. Done it lots of times. And while I'm always polite, they quickly get the idea that I don't appreciate their hanging around here, and that it'd be best if they went someplace else.

But this much is true: I did allow that man to get away with that little girl in his arms this morning. I admit it. Just sat there and watched it happen. Here are the details: I'm sitting in that chair, reading a story to maybe a dozen kids circled around me on the floor. Then I hear a little voice call out, "Daddy!" Suddenly, this really big guy rushes in and grabs up a kid. He shouts to me, "It's all right, I'm her father!" and runs out again. Tell me: What was I supposed to do about it? I did notice that the little girl was smiling and buried her face in his neck. She called him "Daddy," after all, and I thought, "Well, that's all right. If he's her father, he has every right to pick her up or take her out of here. Sounded reasonable to me. How was I supposed to know what was going on?

I'm sorry. Let me try to tell this in sequence. It all started this morning at story hour. Now, we can never be sure how many kids are going to show up—sometimes with their parents and sometimes without—for story hour, but we plan for about 20 of them, typically. Usually there are more in winter and fewer in summer, when people are traveling, or just away, to escape this city's brutal heat. So I'm trying to control and amuse and entertain maybe 18 children—some with what appears to be a touch of ADD. What's that? Oh, sorry. ADD stands for attention deficit disorder. We use the acronym so often that we hardly ever bother to say it in full. Anyway, as I was saying, some of the kids that come in here can't seem to concentrate, and then I have to be reading a story and watching for kids fighting or wandering off at the same time. Multitasking, with a vengeance.

The kids started showing up around nine this morning, and some of their parents gave me specific instructions as to what to watch out for. I do my best to see to it that their special needs are taken care of. Most of the ones we get here are housebroken, which is one less thing to worry about, thank goodness. So with all those parents talking to me, I suppose it's possible that somebody's mommy might have told me how little Judy was not to be released to anyone else but her, but I can't always make sure that things go according to everybody's timetable, you know? This library is not a for-profit daycare center, where we know who comes, where they live, and who they are to be released to, which is, of course, a larger problem.

So anyway, around nine thirty or maybe a few minutes later, I sat everybody down in a semicircle and began to read picture books, showing the illustrations around. It was a fairly quiet day—no fighting, no biting, and nobody bursting into tears. Everybody seemed to be having a good time.

Various parents came back into the room and claimed their little ones, and I do remember the little girl—Judy, cute little thing—shouting, "Daddy!" and throwing herself eagerly into the arms of that big guy and leaving with him. How was I supposed to remember—if I was ever told—that Judy was a pawn in some knock-down, drag-out custody battle, and that under no circumstances was I to allow anyone except Judy's mommy to remove her from the premises?

In my own defense, if I had suspected that the guy who came in here to collect little Judy wasn't supposed to have her, I would have been in his face immediately! I may be short, but I'm responsible and assertive enough to challenge anything I think is wrong. But Judy knew the man, obviously was delighted that he was here, and left snuggled securely in his big, brawny arms. So how was that supposed to tip me off that it was a kidnapping in progress? Well, not a kidnapping, maybe, but whatever you call it when the non-custodial parent takes the child away without the knowledge or consent of the custodial one. Is there a term for that?

Anyway, about ten minutes later, all hell breaks loose. I look up—startled—to hear a distraught woman shouting, "Where's Judy?" and "Jooo-dee!" as she ran around the Children's area, panting and sobbing, and into the girls' bathroom, getting more and more frantic as she went. Finally, she rushed over to me. "Excuse me," she said, obviously fighting for composure. "I dropped off my daughter here about two hours ago, and now I can't find her."

When she told me the child's name, alarm bells began ringing in my brain. "Judy," she said. "Judy Martin. She's six years old, about this tall (she held her hand horizontally at the level of her waist). She was wearing a red knit top, blue slacks, and white sneakers. Please tell me you know where she is, before I panic. *Please!*"

I did what I could to calm the woman, but I had a sinking feeling that I'd innocently walked into something where I might be accused of not taking better care of my charges. "I do remember a little girl that fits that description, yes," I admitted. No point in playing dumb, I figured. "And I remember that she left with a man I assumed to be her father. She certainly knew him, and looked glad to see him, anyway."

"No," said the woman, conversationally, at first. Then, after lowering her head into her cupped hands, she said it several times more, only louder and with a lot more emotion. "No! No! *No!*" she wailed, looking up and glaring at me.

"Wasn't he Judy's father?" I asked, suddenly aware that I was in need of covering my posterior, here.

"Biologically, yes, but that's about all. Wait! Describe the man you saw!"

I told her what I could remember of the man: Big and beefy, with a moustache, and some kind of chin beard. Van Dyke? Goatee? One of those. Dark complexion. I also told her I was sure that Judy was fine, because from what I did see, her father seemed gentle and protective of her.

"You *idiot!*" the woman shrilled at me, pointing an accusing finger. "You've let my revenge-minded ex make off with my little girl. Want to know what you've done? You facilitated his kidnapping of my daughter, that's what! Why didn't you check to see who it was she was going off with? Now he has her. Because of your carelessness, they could be two or three states away from here soon, and I'll never see my little Judy again." She dissolved into tears, and shrugged off my attempt to comfort her.

"Do you want me to call the police?" I asked.

"What? You haven't called the police, yet? *Duh!* Of *course,* call the police! Have them put out a—what you do call it—an all-points bulletin on my ex-husband. I can give them his name, description, and what kind of car he drives for the police report. But if anything happens to my Judy, dearie, I promise you, I'm going to come after you for aiding and abetting kidnapping, reckless child endangerment, and possibly criminal negligence!"

My day was really going downhill in a hurry. Now I was really alarmed. How was any of that my fault, I wondered. So I called the police emergency number, put the woman on, and let her tell her story. Not knowing what else to do, I just stood there, wringing my hands, wondering how so much trouble could have happened to me so quickly, when all I'd done was read some story books to some kids. "I'm sorry," I told her when she got off the phone, knowing full well how meaningless my words must seem to her. "I'm sure you'll get Judy back. I just know it."

"Know it?" she screamed into my startled face. "Lady, you don't *know* anything! So don't pretend that you do, all right? The police are working the case now, but please don't make any more meaningless noises intended to comfort me when my Judy is gone, and I don't know where!"

"But she's with her father," I threw in. "He seemed loving to me. He wouldn't hurt her, would he?"

"Hurting her physically is not what we're talking about. Ben never was a violent man, despite his size and strength, no. But he's vindictive toward me, and I'll bet he'd keep her just to deny her to me. When we separated, I made him move out, but he didn't go quietly. Now, he's angry and capable enough to do what I've seen on TV. I mean, he might have planned this for weeks, for all I know, and now he's got her, and they're both missing. I saw a movie like that not long ago. Tomorrow, after registering under a fake name at some faraway hotel, maybe he'll change their names and acquire new papers. He may even change her first name. Don't you understand? My daughter is missing, and it's all your fault!"

"*My* fault?" I whispered in an astonished little voice. "I know you're upset, Mrs. Martin—who wouldn't be? But please don't try to blame this whole thing on me. Your husband . . ."

"*Ex*-husband!" she spat.

"Right. Ex-husband. Excuse me. Anyway, if he took her away against the terms of the divorce decree or separation or whatever, then the law will deal with him. But please don't blame it all on me. As you could see, the room was full of children this morning. But if I had any inkling that Judy was being kid . . ."

"Oh, *shut up!*" roared the woman. So I did. Just as well; I'd been babbling anyway. "You don't know what you're talking about," she said, "so just shut up. If this doesn't turn out well, there are going to be consequences for you, I guarantee that! Now why don't you go to the back room and do what it is you do around here, and stay out of my sight!"

Yes, she was rude to me, but under the circumstances, I cut her some slack. Still, I couldn't just leave the floor because she told me to. "Sorry," I said softly. "But I work here. I have duties to perform, and I'll need to be nearby when the police get here."

"If you must, all right," she conceded. "But as for working here? Well, after what you did today—your criminal negligence—I wouldn't count on working here for much longer." That was enough for me. I turned and walked away, over by the stacks where I stared blindly at the books on the top shelf. I'd had enough of her blame and shouting. Seems like everything I'd done and said had turned out wrong, and so I went over there to steady my frazzled nerves, and wait for the police to arrive.

And now, officer, here you are. Some day this is turning into, and it isn't even lunchtime yet. And just for the record, I've been called a lot of things in my 25 years of library service, but "accessory to kidnapping?" That one takes the cake!

Questions for Discussion

1. What—if anything—should the children's librarian have done after watching the man walk out the door with the little girl in his arms?

2. What are the differences between the role of a busy children's librarian and that of a daycare center employee?

3. To what extent do you think the librarian is to blame for Judy's abduction? Where else or with whom else does any share of blame lie?

Case 15

Gulag West

John Boyle, managing editor of *The Pecan Grove Observer*, in an editorial published 5 May 2002, p. 23A

Public Uncomfortable with Library's New Surveillance Security Cameras Create "Chilling Effect" in Visitors' Minds

We don't know whether you're a regular visitor to our city's fine library, or even if you have ever set foot inside, but we think it's important for community residents to know what's been happening down at the library, and how such developments are perceived, at least in this quarter. We are referring specifically to a decision made by the library adminstration—in response to a rather alarming number of books and other materials walking out the door or being otherwise lost, stolen, or strayed—to purchase and install a new camera surveillance system, designed to keep an eye on visitors in the building to deter theft. We also want to share our views on the results of this bold technological move, both good and bad.

To start at the beginning, a recent inventory revealed that the size of the library's collection had shrunk an estimated 13 percent in a single year! To put that figure in perspective, suppose that on this date last year, our library boasted a total of 100,000 books. That would mean that this year, only 87,000 of those books remain on the shelves. And then consider that if this rate of loss or shrinkage were to continue through succeeding years at the same pace, we're looking at just over three-quarters of the original book stock in the third year, and somewhere around two-thirds of the starting total the year after that.

This, of course, suggests that no additions are made to collections each year, even though new books are added all the time, at considerable taxpayer's expense. It should also be factored in that book prices rise steadily every year, wholesalers' discounts have dropped, and we voters—in these uncertain economic times—are mostly disinclined to support a radical increase in funding for the library.

Enough statistics. Last month, the management of the library, correctly deeming such a loss rate to be unacceptable, purchased and installed a sophisticated surveillance camera system in the main building downtown to attempt to stem the tide. Because the library is a free library (meaning not that it is provided without cost but that all are free to enter and partake of its services), a cross-section of the community's residents visits the main building and branches every day. Sadly, among that cross-section, while the vast majority of library visitors are good citizens, well behaved, and ethical, not all of them are. So to keep everybody honest, libraries resort to security measures and safeguards to protect their property.

Surveillance cameras are fine and necessary, in our view, in banks, all-night convenience stores, and other places where money or other valuable things are kept. But in public libraries? We feel that surveillance of people in public places goes too far, smacks of "Big Brother," and should be stamped out. For those unfamiliar with the term, "Big Brother" refers to the kind of ubiquitous governmental surveillance described by British writer George Orwell in his chillingly prophetic novel *1984,* in which everyone was watched almost all the time, and failure to conform to established standards of behavior was punished by torture, brainwashing, and, in some cases, death.

We are not seriously suggesting that installing those cameras down at the library is a first step down that slippery slope toward totalitarianism. However, it does echo systems described in the far-off gulags of Siberia, back when the Soviet Union was still in existence, and, for all we know, even now, in Russia. As one bemused fellow visitor to the library was heard to remark, "Surveillance cameras? Great. Just what we need—Big Brother right here in Pecan Grove!" These words may seem overly dramatic or alarmist exaggeration, but we submit that in these times of government intrusion into private lives, they still have a tang of plausibility.

Suppose the cameras are permitted to continue watching the comings and goings of the building's inhabitants. Then suppose (and don't tell us it couldn't happen here) that the library decided (or was forced) to use its newfound capability to focus not on what people are doing, but rather on what people are reading, and to draw up lists of citizens who are viewed as reading the wrong (i.e., unorthodox) material. And if we accept surveillance of people's tastes in reading, what then? It's just another step down the slippery slope of repression to go from "We're watching over you to keep you safe" to "We're watching you, and we'll get you if we don't like what we see you doing."

Anyway, the library has recently installed several surveillance cameras on swivel mountings: they can move, zoom in on a credit card, and are intended to observe every aspect of library life, except, we fervently hope, that which goes on in the public restrooms. Now, we are not denying that book theft and related crimes are serious concerns in public places, nor are we alleging that there is no need for deterrent measures. But when a visitor to a "free" public library hears a faint whirring coming from near the ceiling and looks up to behold a blinking red light on a camera, whose pitiless, tireless, and unblinking snout tracks and follows them as they move about in the public reading rooms, we strongly feel that it creates exactly the wrong impression. Surveillance, clearly, is both necessary and desirable in prisons and banks, but in a library? Give us a break!

In our "free" library, we view it as counterproductive to freedom to allow surveillance of visitors (and staff) by a soulless robot camera. In fact, the "chilling effect" of the presence of such devices may actually serve to discourage good, honest people from entering and using the library, and that would be a true shame. We maintain that the public library's new surveillance cameras are neither necessary nor desirable, but don't take our word for it. Let's briefly return to statistics to shore up our point.

Last year, the Pecan Grove Public Library reported exactly 38 infractions of the criminal code, despite being open for business a full 351 days. It is possible, of course, that some crimes or misdemeanors went unreported, but the total of 38 reported incidents works out to an average of just over three a month. Hardly a crime wave, wouldn't you agree? And further analysis of library crime reveals that of those 38 incidents reported to the authorities, only *five* were violent or entailed actual or possible threats to human safety. The rest of the incidents phoned in had to do with thieves, pickpockets, and, on a few occasions, "people acting eccentrically" but not, from what we can glean, threateningly. Thus, we may safely conclude that library crime—by any definition—is rare.

In no way does such infrequent incidence of crime justify the existence of those cameras. Therefore, we recommend that the library rely more on guards: large, capable men of serious mien, whose job it is to dissuade and discourage the "bad guys" from using the library building as a base of operations for theft of books and other materials, or from antisocial or delusional acts.

We submit that the library, while it has the obligation to bolster its safety and security posture, was overreacting in installing security cameras with intersecting fields of vision and few "blind spots." The money spent to acquire such technology might (in view of statistics) have been much better spent on more books and videos, giving patrons more choice when they visit the building.

We think, more to the point, that using such cameras to deter library crime is tantamount to opening pecans with a pile driver, or cutting peanut butter and jelly sandwiches with a machete.

Finally, there is the psychological impact of having visitors look up and see those blinking cameras up in the corners of all the public rooms in the place. We Americans relish our privacy, clearly, so what are the privacy implications of installing surveillance cameras? Can you say, "Gulag"?

We urge the library administration to remove all those cameras and peripheral equipment, and return them to sender forthwith. We see no reason to keep them around, not only because they are unnecessary, but because many people feel uneasy around them. Of course, we realize that it will be an item of considerable expense to undo all that has recently been done. Therefore, the library should set up a task force or commission to evaluate the new cameras and all the attendant pros and cons, and take a few weeks to decide on a final course of action.

Let's sum up: In our free country, we believe people should be free of governmental surveillance as long as it is consistent with public safety, and we stand opposed to the library's new camera system because it is unnecessary, restrictive, invasive of public privacy, and an infraction of our right to be left alone.

But as we said before, don't just take our word for it. Get on down to the library and see for yourself. Readers with views on this editorial are invited to send us letters or e-mails (PGO.org) and we'll publish as many as we can.

Questions for Discussion

1. Which is more important: emphasizing personal security in the library building or protecting personal privacy?

2. Do surveillance cameras—accepted in banks, for example—strike the wrong note in library buildings?

3. If you were the library director and wanted to respond to this editorial with a rebuttal, what might you say in defense of keeping the surveillance cameras?

Case 16 _____

Cyrus the Virus

Bryan Pepper, library board president, to the board in a special meeting at Pepper's home

A three-headed computer menace knows as "Nimda" dragged thousands of corporate networks and home PCs to a halt Tuesday, said security experts, who called Nimda one of the most complicated viruses ever to hit. Nimda replicates itself en masse to slow down computer networks and the Internet. It's a cousin to the "Code Red" virus that attacked business networks last month . . . a virus that [writes] over data in popular spreadsheet and word processing programs which could wipe out critical records. Writing malicious software programs isn't that hard, said security experts "After all, teen hackers around the world write such programs all the time . . . and are able to cover their tracks, even across international borders." . . . But the threat is real, and the message is clear: "Nimda" sickens Internet. (*Dallas Morning News*, 19 September 2001, p. 1D)

This special monthly meeting of the library board will come to order. I want to thank you all very much for coming here to my home under unusual conditions of secrecy today, instead of meeting, as is normal, in the library's boardroom. By way of compensation for the inconvenience, a delicious lunch will be served at the conclusion of this meeting, and I hope you'll all stay and enjoy it with me.

Now, there's important stuff to discuss, so just for this meeting, I move we dispense with the usual reading of the minutes, the treasurer's report, and all that jazz. I have two reasons for that request: In the first place, this meeting never *happened,* if you see what I mean, so no record of normal business would be appropriate. And secondly, as I think we will all agree,

99

this Cyrus the Virus problem is serious and we need to deal with it immediately, so let's get right to it, shall we? We're here to speak privately about this problem, and to come up with a plan of action.

Now, as I understand the situation—and someone correct me if I'm misinformed—sometime yesterday, a new and aggressive computer virus somehow found its way into one of the library's public computers via e-mail (or at least that's the best guess of the technical staff) and from that computer, it infected most of the rest by means of a "WORM" program, which replicates itself in open applications. Not *all* of the rest, however, because the quick-thinking Technical Services staff managed to shut down about a dozen of them before the program could spread throughout the system, but quite a few of the library's hard drives were affected.

But, you know, I guess it's fair to say that it could have been a lot worse because the virus didn't permanently disable those computers it got to; what it did do was turn the contents of their hard drives into unreadable mush. Fortunately, it's really not a big problem to reprogram a computer, and, thankfully, we had already taken the precaution of paying extra for the blanket licensing agreement with the company that manufactures the hard drives.

What that means is that Paul Holser, our head of technical services, was able to link all the affected computers to a healthy one and transfer the operating system from the healthy one to each of the ones that had been fried by the virus. End of problem. At least for now.

Just as an aside, I think it's interesting that people compare the spread of a computer virus to more tangible viruses that affect human health, such as influenza, smallpox, or AIDS. The parallel may not be exact, but it's pretty close. People contract viruses from others via physical contact or airborne transmission. Sometimes, a single individual can be responsible for infecting hundreds or even thousands of other people, and they, in turn, infect others, until it becomes an epidemic. Well, it's pretty much the same thing with computer viruses.

Someone seems to have sent a new e-mail around that they're calling Cyrus the Virus (isn't that adorable?), and that program found a way to get past the various checkpoints that we post on incoming messages. Thankfully, however, before it could spread throughout the system via e-mail, the virus was, due to quick thinking and immediate action, located, isolated, and destroyed. Otherwise, it would have become an epidemic of major proportions.

So it appears that we've dodged a dangerous bullet.

This time, anyway.

But we all know there's always the danger of recurrence. A human virus spreading contagion can result in lives lost, lingering illness, millions of dollars in employee downtime, and, sometimes, permanent damage to the bodies or minds of the victims. Computer viruses, on the other hand, may not be deadly in the mortality sense, but they can still disable or "kill" a computer system and turn those powerful machines into mere paperweights and dust catchers, unless someone removes the virus and reprograms the computers, as was done in this case.

To their enormous credit, the library's tech staff acted quickly to contain and prevent the spread of this virus. But we may not be so lucky the next time. Therefore, I have a couple of proposals, and a request, which may be rather startling things to ask, but I'm going to urge that the board approve them, all the same:

First, even though this virus was contained, we need to do whatever it takes to see to it that nothing comparable to Cyrus can ever infect and disable our library's computers again. I am advised by Paul that it is possible for such a virus, even when you think it's eliminated from the system, to leave behind a "trap door," which is a bit of code that makes future access to the program almost effortless.

Against the possibility that some small, harmless-looking bit of code lingers on, deep in the bowels of the computers' operating systems, the tech staff will devote a part of each day to examining the coding of the system (which is an extremely time-consuming and laborious process) and finding—if they're present—any little nasty surprises that the perpetrator may have left behind.

Second, we must find out who got into our computers, *how* they got in, and whether Cyrus was a one-time sneak attack or the vanguard of an ongoing assault on our computers. We need to ensure that Cyrus and all other viruses are prevented from invading all of our library's computers, ever again. Actually, I can tell you now that we do know some information about who did this to us, even if we don't know why they did it.

I see puzzled faces around the table, so perhaps I should explain. Mere hours after we became aware of the incursion into our machines, someone sent the library an anonymous e-mail shortly after the virus was detected. It's my guess that the perpetrator of Cyrus wants to be recognized for genius and is therefore making himself known, without giving up his actual identity. We have turned everything over to the police, of course, and we'll keep you posted on the progress of the ongoing investigation. So, you see, part of the mystery has already been solved.

Now here's my request, and this is extremely important. I need your word that nothing that we've talked about today with regard to the recent virus attack will leave this room. Except for a few trusted members of the library staff, we are the only ones who are privy to this: Is that understood? We need to keep this to ourselves. Trust me that absolute secrecy is paramount. Above all, we must do our utmost to keep the press and the media (and, for that matter, all persons outside of this room and non-Technical Services staff at the library) from finding out about this virus attack.

Why the secrecy, you're probably wondering. There's a very good reason. Some may disagree with me on my stressing that this information not be made public. Some of you may actually be *shocked* at my decision to keep this information from getting out. After all, isn't a public library a public institution? Why should any library information be kept from the public? Well, after I tell you why, I'm confident that you—most of you, anyway—will agree that it's the right thing to do.

First some background: It has come to my attention that other libraries in our state and across this great land of ours have been "hit" by viruses, and, of course, by the thieves (yes, I said thieves!) who design and sneak them into their computers. In one community I read about, news of such an attack was widely promulgated and given a lot of play in the local press. And here are the results: The perpetrator of the virus got a lot of free publicity that described him or her as cunning, clever, brilliant, and a mastermind, instead of as a common criminal, which is, in my view, what should actually be said and written about such people.

And just as the recent troubles regarding suicide bombings and terrorist attacks on this country have caused a crisis of public confidence, so certain people are likely to mistrust the library's ability to keep secrets, if news about Cyrus gets out.

Look around! Watch the evening news! Paranoia is the watchword of the day, and everyone seems to be keeping a wary, suspicious eye on everyone else. Now at first blush, that may sound like a prudent idea—everyone watching everyone else carefully ought to have the net effect of making terrorism more difficult—but a careful reading of the aftermath of similar intrusions into library computers elsewhere reveals that the public is also less likely to trust the public library with their records or their donations.

Bear in mind that one can—if one knows what he's doing—insert a pernicious virus by remote control. Thus, an innocent person might come into the library to access an Internet terminal, decide to check his e-mail, and then go into his Internet service provider to accomplish that task. Now say he enters his user number and secret password— so far, so good. The next step, if you're an AOL user, like me, is that you hear a cheery voice saying, "Welcome! You've got mail!" and you see a colorful screen full of words, pictures, icons, and clickable links.

Next, you open your mail queue with anywhere from one to . . . I dunno . . . hundreds of messages. Now, let me tell you what I do when I view my mail. First off, I open the important stuff: Communication from my daughter away at college, replies to the questions, statements, and jokes sent to me by e-mail. Then I delete all spam, and other unsolicited messages, usually commercial ones involving products and services that someone wants me to buy, but occasionally, shockingly, pornographic solicitations, and the like: "Just click here!"

That's right—I get pornographic ads all the time in my mail queue. How did this happen to me, a happily married man? All you have to do is click on an underlined word and *wham*! There it is. Most of us would never dream of opening such a program, especially in a public library setting, so that's unlikely as a scenario. The ones advertising untold wealth or free money just for clicking? I delete those without reading them. They're not just annoying spam; they're possibly out to rope you into illegal Ponzi schemes, in which you invest money on the promise of multiplying it, and people who take that chance frequently lose it all.

Most of us, as I say, after several years of e-mail as a regular part of our day have become reasonably savvy consumers, knowing instinctively when it's not a good idea to open a clickable link or respond to a question. Most of us, I say. There are always the naive, the tempted, and the reckless, and those people are probably the weakest link in the security chain.

What's really insidious is that an e-mail message might get you to click on it by saying, "Hi," or "In answer to your question . . .," or even, "Nice talking to you again, after all these years." So you bite. Could happen to anybody. You click on an intriguing message to see if you can work out who sent it to you, and you've just—without even being aware of it—opened the door to whomever wants to crawl through it and work whatever mischief the originator of the program has in mind.

Which brings me back to Cyrus and his ilk. We need to keep such devastating electronic attacks from occurring again, so eternal vigilance is going to be necessary. Do these measures present challenges for our library staff? The simple answer is yes, but we *can* and must defend against viruses by installing system firewalls and other defenses against such attacks. But there's always that weakest link out there—the sucker that P.T. Barnum said was born every minute—who says, "Hmm, I'm curious . . . wonder what'd happen if I clicked on this underlined passage here?"

It is also possible that the hackers, themselves, might come to the library, open their own programs, and infect our computers, just out of meanness or that feeling of power they must get when they know they've caused someone else's system to crash and burn. Now, I don't want to make any of us any more paranoid than we already are, but we have to recognize that these people are out there, and we have to deal with the reality of their existence.

Well, enough chatter. I want to get to what I am really worried about now. Here's the bottom line: Once word gets out that a library's security has been breached or compromised, for whatever reason, people may never trust us again to safeguard their information. And very likely, they won't trust us to safeguard their bequests, either. I'm thinking right now of a person of standing in our community who has it in his will that upon his death, his entire collection of archival materials on Teddy Roosevelt should go to the library. He could change his mind, you know, and probably will, if he's worried about the library's ability to safeguard them. Then he might change his will and give that extremely valuable collection, unique in the nation, to a university or museum that "knows how to take better care of it."

As we speak, we're working with the authorities to track down, arrest, and prosecute the perpetrator of this virus, but in the meantime, please! Make sure that the public never learns about how our library got hit, who hit us, and what, specifically, was done to us. That Roosevelt collection I mentioned? It's real, and I can't tell y'all exactly whose it is, but he's promised it to me personally for placement in our library upon his death. Still, I firmly believe that if this philanthropist got worried that this library's security was lax or lackluster, he'd call his lawyer and revise his will in a heartbeat. So it has to remain our little secret. If word of this problem ever gets out, we'll probably be kissing the likelihood of any future rare book donations goodbye.

I'm asking you to place your loyalty to this library and what it means to the community ahead of any slavish adherence to the "openness" policy that normally governs our meetings and our deliberations. I know it's a lot to ask, but if you think about it, I hope you'll agree that sometimes, as in time of war, secrecy trumps openness and full disclosure.

Whoever sent Cyrus the Virus skipping around our library's computers was committing, in a very real sense, an act of war . . . a war that we *must* win. So, now, I move that we keep a tight clamp on information about this Cyrus matter, for the good of everyone concerned. This unfortunate incident was an internal problem, and internal problems of this library should remain just that—internal. Therefore, I urge you, please don't discuss this matter with anyone except one another, the library director, Ann Bowman, and the head of technical services. I wouldn't ask this if I didn't deem it to be of first importance. So, how say you, therefore? Shall we vote?

Questions for Discussion

1. Is it ever appropriate to circumvent openness in order to achieve a specific end?

2. Is Bryan out of line for seeking a cloak of secrecy around the computer virus matter?

3. If you were a member of the library board, and you'd heard Bryan's speech, how would you vote on his "request"?

Case 17 _____

Colors

Steve Fierros, security guard, Lakewood Branch, to Matt DeWaelsche, head of security, via telephone

I tell you, man, it was like a scene out of *West Side Story,* only nobody was singing or dancing. Not even close. You know the movie? There's a song that goes, "When you're a Jet, you're a Jet all the way." Well, that's what caused all the trouble over here recently: gang loyalty and gang hatred. But I guess I knew that when I took the job. It's no piece of cake to be in charge of security at a branch in a tough neighborhood. I'm not saying that life is any easier for you guys downtown, but hey, the west side is dangerous, know what I mean? I don't mean to brag, but I think that without my tough, no-nonsense approach to security out here, the animals would be running the zoo here, in a manner of speaking.

Now just because the newspapers don't carry very many stories about gang warfare in our city, some folks think that local gangs have disappeared or lost membership, but I tell you that's not the case at all. Not in my house, anyway. No, rival gangs are still very big in our area and very protective of their home turf, which they defend vigorously and sometimes violently.

The problem is that this branch sits at the edge of the Dragons' turf and right across the street from the Viceroys' area. See, we're west of Rampart Street, which puts us in the zone the Dragons call their home turf, but if you cross the street you're in Viceroy territory, and they don't take kindly to incursions from the other side of the street.

Funny world, isn't it? I mean, *Romeo and Juliet* was written about 400 years ago (I looked it up is how I know) and still, the same stuff that went on between the Capulets and the Montagues is being played out on our city streets, almost every day. I mean, if it stayed out there on the streets, I wouldn't be so concerned, but too often, members of the gangs bring their conflicts inside my branch. And when those gangs meet up in here, it's

Romeo and Juliet all over again. Only instead of swordplay, these guys carry switchblade knives, hefty chains they wear as belts, and some of them even have guns.

I think it wouldn't have been such a bad situation if the city hadn't closed the Englewood branch a couple of months ago. You remember? The city manager called and told the director that the library's budget needed to be trimmed—quickly—to contain costs. I don't know exactly who it was who decided that the best way to cut costs was to close branches, or who it was who got to decide which branches were targeted for closing. I'm not privy to decisions taken at high levels of administration, and I guess neither are you. Guys like us, we earn our money just standing or walking around and looking so intimidating that most of the kids who are thinking of getting into some kind of trouble see us and then reconsider their plans.

Like you, I've watched all the Clint Eastwood movies that Mike Early recommended—some of them maybe a dozen times—and I've practiced his voice and his icy glare in front of the mirror until I do a pretty good impression of him. You remember: "Go ahead, make my day!" Of course, I never actually get to say stuff like that. That would probably make the young punks and tough guys bust out laughing, rather than wet their pants, which is the idea behind the act. But I give 'em the Eastwood look, and that's sometimes enough to cool them out.

And when I have to speak to them, I rumble threateningly with the best of 'em. I lower my voice about an octave and go for the sound of a car in need of a muffler, and that usually closes the deal. Of course, there are times when it would be nice to have a weapon. My old .38 service revolver, maybe, even unloaded. Not for shooting, but just for show. But the city is adamant on that point. We're not law officers—even though I was an MP in the service for years—and carrying guns, saps, knives, brass knuckles, or even cans of mace is strictly forbidden. So I rely on my size, my facial expressions and body language, and my threatening tone of voice. I don't have to say, "Make my day!" when I'm doing it right. They get the idea.

So where was I? Oh yeah, right, what's been happening since the city closed the Englewood branch. People living on the other side of Rampart fought it, of course, but not that many. I mean, you get a lot more people out on the streets to protest the closing of a city swimming pool than you'd ever see complaining about a closed branch library. Anyway, once the city makes up its mind, protests almost never accomplish anything. So one Friday evening, the Englewood branch just quietly closed its doors for the last time, and most of its staffers were reassigned downtown at the main library.

Now, if you're wearing a suit and sitting in an air-conditioned conference room downtown with a thick carpet on the floor and your own secretary, it might seem logical and reasonable to eliminate a branch by drawing an *X* over it on a library map of Pecan Grove, especially since it's not that far for most residents of the Englewood neighborhood, whom you've just deprived of their branch, to get over here to Lakewood or to go downtown to your big library.

But the suits downtown have no idea of the realities of the situation when they make those decisions. I mean, they're just playing with magic markers and maybe those little colored push pins in figuring out where the cuts ought to be made. I wonder how many of them even know about the Dragons and Viceroys and the long and bloody history those gangs have, and the hatred that's built up between them.

I'm not a sociologist or an expert on gangs, but one thing I can tell you: Young guys form gangs based on where they live, not necessarily on what race or ethnic group they belong to. That's why the guys wearing Dragons and Viceroys jackets look pretty much alike. Both gangs are mixed with Black, Hispanic, White, and Asian members.

So how do they recognize friend or foe? A simple identification scheme: colors. Yeah, I said colors. The clothes they wear. Years ago, they decided—or maybe it just happened without any set plan—that Dragons would wear red, for blood, I think. So then the Viceroys went for blue. Now Dragons parade around in different items of clothing but always something in bright red—shirts, jackets, arm bands, headbands, vests, whatever. The Viceroys (girls as well as guys) do the same thing with blue colors. At least that makes it possible to tell who you're looking at just by checking out the principal color someone is wearing.

Colors. That's what helps me know who's in here, so I shouldn't complain, really. When I'm walking my rounds and I look around the library and see more red than you might see at a Cardinals' or Reds' home game, I know the Dragons are here in force. Although sometimes I figure if I was a Viceroy and wanted to, you know, like, spy on the Dragons, I'd wear a red shirt or something and I might just pass unchallenged through this neighborhood. Unless, of course, someone didn't recognize me or something and started asking me questions. But hey, if they want to play that old game of spy versus spy, that's their problem. It's not about me. My job is just to preserve order in my branch, and I don't care what the kids wear as long as they don't make any trouble and abide by the rules.

Trouble? Take last Tuesday. About four o'clock, I was leaning an elbow against the circulation desk, watching the front door, and making idle chit chat with that dishy Norwegian blonde circulation clerk, Hildagard. I kept looking around, because that's my job. So what did I see? The usual crowd in the building, a few Dragons I knew by face or even by name, mixed in with some women, children, retirees, and other civilians looking up stuff in reference books or sitting at the computer terminals.

The Dragons don't come in every day but when they do come in here, they come in force, and they're usually pretty motivated. I guess even gangbangers have dreams of getting a good job one day and living well, and anyway, they have homework, like the other kids. So Tuesday, I counted maybe seven or eight guys in red, and a few of their girlfriends—some of 'em wearing red "do-rags" wrapped around their heads—but as far as I could tell, they were minding their own business and not doing anything bad.

So I just nodded when we made eye contact and left 'em alone. What? Hassle me? Oh, sure, they say stuff, but I let it pass. I've been called everything from "old folks" to "Deputy Dawg" but the kids seem to tolerate me, and I try to tolerate them, even though I get sick to my stomach at all the tattoos and piercings I have to look at—more every day, it seems.

But then, in walk four guys—big, mean-looking suckers, and all wearing blue! They all had book bags or notebooks with them, too, which seemed appropriate enough, and besides, I knew that the branch on the other side of Rampart street had been closed recently, so they were entitled to find a new library to study in. These guys stood in the central hall, just looking around, scoping out the place.

Naturally, they attracted immediate attention from the Dragons sitting at tables near the back of the reference room. A couple of Dragons stood up and started moseying over toward the newcomers; their expressions didn't look hospitable. I was afraid that a confrontation might take place right here in my branch. So I quickly stepped over to them—getting between the groups—prepared to intervene.

"Now, you boys aren't here to start any trouble, are you?" I asked the guys in blue, careful to keep my voice low and well modulated, but with just a hint of Eastwood that would tell them that I wouldn't tolerate any nonsense.

"No, sir," said one of the kids, smiling disarmingly. "We're just here to study because our own branch got taken away. There a problem with that?"

"No problem for me," I said. "Just see that there *is* no problem."

Then one of the red bunch had to speak up, which I'd been expecting. "What're y'all doing here? This is Dragon country!" The challenging voice belonged to a big, tough looking guy with long, straight black hair whom I'd heard called "Indio." The Viceroys didn't back down, however.

"We got as much right to come here and use this library as you do, man, so just back off and let us alone, and nobody gets hurt," said one of them.

"Oh, sure, you get to come *in* here. It's getting *out* that's going to be a problem, 'less you don't mind leaving in an ambulance." Indio turned to his friends for approval and his crew high-fived and laughed.

This was rapidly getting serious. I couldn't just stand there. "Now, we're not going to have any of that talk in here," I rumbled, giving first one bunch and then the other the full intensity of my Eastwood squint. "These guys have as much right to be here as you and your buddies have, Indio, and I don't want to hear you threaten them again. Is that understood?" I was looking carefully not so much at the faces of the young men but at their bodies, wondering whether any of them (or for all I knew, all of them) were armed.

A security guard's nightmare, as you know, is that some idiots will pull out guns and just start blasting away. That's the stuff that makes the evening news—and innocent bystanders can become collateral damage, too. People trading rounds in a public library is a worst-case scenario, and since I carry no weapon, myself—just a two-way communicator—about the best I can do is to call the cops.

Oh, I could wrestle one of the ringleaders to the ground, maybe, but hey, I'm 65 years old and out of shape, as you know. As Eastwood says in a couple of his movies, "A man's gotta know his own limitations." Besides, I counted five big guys wearing red and four decked out in blue. How likely would it be for me to handle a problem like that, if an actual shooting war did break out? Not much. In fact, I could easily have become the first casualty of the war, and I sure as hell didn't want that.

Things just stayed there like a tableau for a while. Despite my warning, the two groups continued to swap insults and taunts, and the tension was getting stronger by the minute. I had to do something, and do it quickly. But what? Without thinking about it a whole lot—without the luxury of time to think about it, actually—I turned to the Viceroys and said, in my most authoritative voice, "Now, I'm going to have to ask you boys to leave."

"Boys? We ain't boys! Ain't nobody's boys, old man!" one of them spat at me. "Anyway, how you going to make us leave, old dude? There's four of us and just your big fat self, so if you think you can do it, take your best shot." He raised both his arms in a "come on!" gesture. This brought more catcalls and abuse from the Dragons standing behind me, and I hastily turned around and told them to shut up and let me handle it. Then, turning back to the Viceroys, I rasped, "Boy——uh, gentlemen! This is a public building, and there are innocent people here who could get hurt if anything starts, so please—do everybody a favor and just leave.

You might want to know that I play poker once a week with half the cops in the 22d precinct (this is actually true) and all I have to do is make a call, and anybody who throws a punch or anything else is on his way downtown for booking and then maybe looking at a few years downstate for assault." I hit both sides with my tough, sneering look again. "So, what's it going to be?"

They milled around uncertainly for a while. Finally, the big Viceroy spoke up again. "Where we s'pose to go to use a library, man?" he asked, reasonably. "City hall took away the one we had, and we have to go someplace to use the reference books. This is the only other library that we can get to without driving or spending carfare. So let us stay. We won't go near them other turkeys. Just let us stay, all right?"

I knew it was not all right, and I knew equally well that this situation was a powder keg that could explode at any minute, but what the Viceroy kid said made sense. Why *should* they have to leave? After all, it wasn't their fault that the Englewood branch had gone under. Left to their own devices, I'm sure they would rather still be going there for whatever it is they needed libraries for.

So I made another decision, hoping it was a good one. I told the Viceroys to wait where they were. Then, I walked over to Indio and his Dragons and warned them that they were to go nowhere near the Viceroys or they'd have major trouble, big time, adding something I knew was lame about sharing, and even "Can't we all just get along?" Their reaction (laughter, muttering, hard looks at the other bunch) let me know that that dog was never going to hunt.

Seeing a full-fledged confrontation in the making, many of the other library patrons hastily walked around us and scuttled out the door. Lucky them, I thought. I'd like to leave, too. Would I ever! Just go home, knock back a couple of cold ones in front of a baseball game, and forget this place for a while. But I had a job to do, and I take that job seriously.

So I directed each group to a sort of neutral corner and told them the same thing: I would have zero tolerance for violence or even provocation, and they were to ignore each other, to the extent possible. Failure to do that, I reminded them all, would result in the immediate summoning of the police. In the meantime, I'd be watching them all like a hawk. Then, I walked back to my place at the circ desk, where the nervous clerk seemed about ready to rush out of the building, herself.

So far, so good, right? But I heard as I walked away, "What time you leavin' here, old man? Maybe we, you know, sort of see you home, what you think?" I whirled around quickly but couldn't see who had said it, or even from which side the threat had come. Threats, is it? I said to myself. Oh, good. Now I have to watch my own back for trying to keep the peace between two packs of maladjusted delinquents.

For the twenty-third or maybe the seventy-eighth time this month, I wondered whether I had enough money to retire and quit working. Just head for the Gulf coast and sit around and play checkers or dominos or Scrabble® all day, like a lot of other guys my age, and not have to act as a cop, referee, negotiator, and possible target for some angry punks who won't listen to reason.

Nobody bothered me on my way home, but I have to come in here five days a week and there'll be other problems, you can depend on that. Times like this, I find myself wondering what Clint Eastwood would do. So tell me, Matt, Eastwood isn't here but you're the next best thing—what would you do about this gang stuff?

Questions for Discussion

1. What strategies might keep gangs apart in a library or convince them that coexistence within its walls is possible?

2. At what point would you have given up trying the reasonable approach and just called the police?

3. Assuming that funds for reopening the closed branch are not available, what measures might help to ensure the security and safety of all people inside the branch building?

Case 18

Pornucopia

Dee Segrest, technical services clerk (formerly reference clerk) to Mary Rhoades, head of reference, in the staff room

I miss working in Reference, Mary, and I hope you'll arrange it for me to come back to your department and give me my old job back. I've been reassigned, as you know, and I don't think it's fair. Working in Reference was fun, but now that I'm a clerk for Technical Services, I'm bored and frustrated. That's the reason why I think I might have to quit working here entirely.

When I started working in Reference the day after my 16th birthday about a year ago, I was so excited, and I just loved earning a paycheck every week for coming here after school, Monday through Friday, and seeing to the needs of people who wanted to go online, to access their e-mail or to do Internet searches. When I took the job, my job description said that I was expected to see to it that all the computers are operational and showing the "Welcome to the Pecan Grove Public Library" screen when not in use. It was also my job to see to it that the printer alongside each Internet computer was working properly, with ink in the cartridge, and printer paper ready for use. I was told to direct patrons with questions about searching to the reference librarian on duty. That was what my job description said, and I understood it.

But what my job description did *not* say was that I'd be exposed to, and have to put up with, lecherous male patrons who seem to get some sort of special kick out of making young girls look at online pornography. I thought I was going to lose my mind. Mary, I swear I never invited any of those creeps to bother me with their disgusting habits. Repulsive people forced me out of that job I loved in Reference.

But if I have to prepare books in Technical Services for much longer, I might have to quit this place. When I worked for you, I was out front with the customers.

113

Oh, people notice me, of course, as I float around our two dozen or so Internet workstations. Some guys notice me *too much*, if you get what I'm talking about, but I've gotten pretty good at dealing with guys who hit on me. Luckily, one of the security guards is usually somewhere around to come to the rescue if some creep gets aggressive or persistent. That only happened once, but still, it was nice to know that Matt or Mike had my back covered. I was expected to be helpful as regards to logging onto the Net, what do I do when the keyboard locks or the screen freezes, and stuff like that. And I'm not supposed to offer or give any specific reference help. That's the job of the professionals, and I understand and respect that.

One day, when I finish college, I plan to go to library school (or whatever they're calling it by that time) to get my master's degree with an Internet specialization, and maybe I'll even come back here to work as a reference librarian. That'd be totally awesome, although sometimes I think I'd like to go to the West Coast (where the weather is better) and live the California lifestyle.

Anyway, to get specific about why I was transferred out of Reference, let me refresh your memory with a glaring example of what I had to put up with when I worked for you. In the course of walking around among the terminals, I always tried to keep an eye on what people were doing with their Internet time, you know, like maybe who is reading up on poisoning a city's water supply, or who's in one of those hate group chat rooms. Not spying, actually—just being observant. So I kept my eyes open, the way I was supposed to. I had no interest in being some kind of morals cop or anything, skulking around and trying to find out who's looking at naughty sites. Since we don't have filters on our Internet computers, users are free to look at whatever they want. And that's fine with me. Mostly, anyway.

Occasionally, though, I'd walk up behind some guy and see that he was looking at stuff that would gag a maggot, but I tried not to be judgmental. When I caught someone looking at pictures of naked women or stuff that's really gross, I just averted my eyes and moved on. It's a free country. If some guy wants to look at porn, well, my general philosophy about that is, live and let live. Besides, squealing on somebody is bad, except maybe if somebody is using drugs or something and telling their parents would help them get into rehab—that, I could understand, and might even do, if I cared about the friend. But running and telling you or one of the other reference librarians that some man was looking at dirty pictures, well, I wasn't about to rat on the guy. Really none of my business, I figured.

Anyway, I don't see anything wrong with a guy looking at that stuff, as long as that's all he's doing and he keeps his hands out where I can see them, know what I mean? Besides, pornography must be legal and in demand or there wouldn't be so much out there for people to access online, right? To me, those pictures are gross. I've surfed the Net and seen some of the garbage that's available, and I've seen pictures of men by themselves, women by themselves, men and women doing all sorts of things, women together, men together, even people with animals. Yuk! I don't even want to think about that. What I'm saying is that I may be only 17, but I'm not naive anymore, especially after a year working here with the Internet computers. I like to think that I'm no longer easily shocked.

But everybody has a line where they think, "Whoa! This goes too far. This isn't just kinky, this is disgusting!" and last week, *my* line got crossed. That's why I got transferred, and I now spend my hours in the back and away from the public, preparing books for shelving. It's also why I doubt whether I can continue working here. I mean, what that man was looking at was bad enough, but the fact that he wanted to show it to *me* really grossed me out. Totally.

Here's what happened: I was checking out all the terminals when I saw this guy looking at sexually oriented images on the Net. I didn't pay much attention because he didn't look dangerous or anything, and he wasn't doing anything except sitting there quietly at the terminal looking at pictures, which might have been *National Geographic* scenes of Yellowstone, for all I cared. Strictly his business. Suddenly, he turned and noticed me, and the smile on his face was not friendly or sweet, like some guys have when they see a wholesome-looking, 17-year-old girl, dressed in school clothes.

No, what he was doing was leering at me, and I could guess what he was thinking. I mean, I know I'm pretty and have a good figure. I don't mean to brag, but facts are facts, all right? And some men do look at me that way, but so what? I can handle that.

Of course, if there were any little kids around, that'd be different. I mean, if this guy was looking at pornography and some very young kids saw what he was looking at (they'd have to be standing directly behind him to do so, because we have privacy shields on all the unfiltered adult-level computers), that'd be different. We're tolerant of what adults do here at the library as long as it's within the posted rules, but there are laws against exposing young and innocent children to that kind of filth, and if the law was being broken, I'd act.

But there were no kids around in Reference that afternoon. Just me, and I don't think of myself as a kid anymore. So when I realized what this guy was looking at, I took a careful look around and I decided, hey, live and let live, as long as this guy just sits there and looks at images. When he turned and smiled at me, I did smile back, briefly, and then I looked away. I had something to attend to further down the row of computers and I went there. Of course, I didn't forget that man, but since he hadn't done anything else upsetting, I just moved on.

Well, maybe five minutes later, I heard a man's voice say, "Oh, miss?" It was this same guy at terminal number 15, and he was waving his arm. "Oh miss," he said again, real politely, "I seem to be having trouble with this monitor. Could you have a look and help me figure out what's wrong with it?" So I walked over to him. That's what they pay me for: making small problems with our terminals disappear. Not big problems—those are for the technicians—and we have a service contract with a company for the really big ones. But something wrong with a monitor? That's something I can fix, usually, anyway. So, even though I remembered that this was the guy who'd been watching pornography I walked over to him, because, like I said, that's my job.

When I got over to him, he pointed toward his monitor, and by the time I saw what he wanted to show me, it was too late to look away. And there they were—what my father used to call unspeakable practices and unnatural acts, in living color!

Mary, I consider myself a normal teenager. Probably more religious than most, but normal enough. And being normal, I guess, includes being curious about sex, even though I've made a firm decision to save that sort of thing for marriage. So I'm not going to apologize for staring at what was on the screen perhaps a moment longer than I should have. It was just . . . shocking! So vivid, you might say, what those people were doing. Don't ask me for details . . . it's too embarrassing to try to put into words. And it's really embarrassing to tell you that I stared at the screen this creep was showing me for at least 30 seconds, fascinated. Is that wrong?

Anyway, finally, I snapped out of my trance and let out a little "meep" sort of sound, which made this guy laugh. Not just a little giggle but a great big belly laugh. That's when I decided to get out of there. So I did. I was so upset, I went up to the office, told them I was sick and had to leave, and then I just went home and tried to put the whole sorry business out of my mind by watching television all day.

Well, I was pretty shaken up by the experience, so at dinner I told my parents, and the next morning, they called Kyle in Human Resources and requested that I get reassigned to a "safer" job, or I'd have to quit entirely. That's why I work now in Technical Services, so lowlife scum like that can't bother me. But Mary, I want to come back here to my old job and not have to do boring, repetitive work, putting pockets in books, sticking them in protective plastic jackets, property stamping them, and sticking those little magnetic thingies down their spines for the front door gizmo that's supposed to prevent books from being stolen. *Borrr*-ing!

That's why I'm talking to you, now. I want to come back. Isn't there anything you can do about perverts who make a special point of sharing pornographic images with teenaged girls? I don't see why a sick library patron should be allowed to get people like me to look at that stuff. It's not fair! I really liked my job working with you and dealing with the public, and I don't want some pervert to have scared me into giving it up. Well, thanks for listening. Anything you can do for me would be deeply appreciated.

Break's over, darn it! I've got to get back to my new job now, preparing books for the shelves. *Borrr*-ing!

Questions for Discussion

1. Do you think it right that the young clerk was reassigned to a "safer" job?

2. What methods might a library use to prevent young or innocent (or easily offended) passers-by from seeing what patrons are viewing on their monitors?

3. Can you justify forcing a patron to leave for looking at pornographic images on the Internet? Or banning him or her from the library?

Case 19

No Place Else to Go

Josh Amdur, circulation librarian, to Ann Cameron Bowman, library director, in Ann's office

Yeah, it's true: guilty as charged: I threw a poor homeless bum out of here into the rain last night even though he wasn't molesting anybody or committing any kind of statutory offense. But there are mitigating circumstances, so before you sail into me about that, please listen to my side of the story. Let me start by saying that I consider myself a very moral and empathic person. I try to live by the golden rule. You know—Do unto others . . . .

I even do what I can to help the downtrodden, supplying food and my time at the Austin Street Homeless Shelter downtown, once a month, because I figure, there but for the grace of God, go I. Recently, I read some alarming statistics on what percentage of working Americans are just two or three paychecks away from homelessness. I figure, it could be me one day, in line for a hot meal or sleeping down by the river under a bridge. So, without wanting to sound like I'm bragging, I'd have to say that I think I'm a pretty caring guy.

Having said that, I want to explain the decision I made last evening and my reasons for making it, and I hope you will understand that I'm *not,* as some have suggested, heartless, turning a blind eye and a deaf ear to the plight of those less fortunate than myself. On the contrary, I submit that I was required by my job to make a tough choice and a hard decision. And while I'm not necessarily proud of what I did, I'm not ashamed of it, either. In similar circumstances, I suppose I'd do it again.

Now, to get down to specifics: There's this homeless guy who stumbles in here almost every day and usually stays until closing time. Let me give you a word picture, at least: He's maybe 40 years old, but could be older. I suspect that he's not really old, but just looks it because of his hard life, missing teeth, and unfortunate lifestyle. He has long, weedy-looking hair, mostly brown but shot through with gray streaks, peeking out from under a scuffed-up navy watch cap he wears all the time, even in the hot summer months. His clothes are old, stained, and threadbare, and he seems to go in for the "layered look" probably because he has to sleep under bridges or on the streets, and he figures that the more he's wearing, the warmer he'll be at night and the less he's likely to lose to thieves. Why anyone would covet those clothes is beyond my understanding.

His name? Well, I heard somebody call him "Tom" once, but I couldn't swear to that being his name, because he's your basic strong, silent type. In a typical week, this guy spends more time here in the library than I do, but he never starts a conversation, or even looks like he wants to say something. After all, you don't have to talk to anyone in order to come into a library and read books or magazines, do you?

So Tom . . . might as well use that name . . . Tom gets by without saying anything. He avoids eye contact, too. I've noticed that if I look at him, he looks away instantly, no matter what the circumstances. Other staff members have made the same comment. Not only is he not interested in conversation, but I think he's one of these guys who actually tries to be invisible.

There's nothing furtive or sneaky-looking about him though. Nothing in his demeanor or behavior that suggests he's a thief (and I consider myself a rather good student of body language), or casing the joint for a subsequent nocturnal visit. I'm guessing that Tom just wants to go unnoticed, but still, he seems to be glad to be among people. Or maybe the people are just the price he pays for a place to spend his time (when the shelters and missions are closed) that's both warm or cool, and relatively clean and safe. I don't know for sure.

So I got used to Tom being here, always among the first patrons to arrive in the morning and the last to leave at closing time. His face is always expressionless, but he doesn't lurch around like an extra from *Night of the Living Dead* or anything. No, he just has no expression: not humorous, not menacing, no emotion of any kind on his face.

Let's see . . . what else? Well, sometimes I see Tom outside these walls pushing an old rusty supermarket cart that he uses to carry his possessions around. I don't know where he got it, but it seems to be full of blankets, old towels, plastic bags full of who knows what, and various items he must've scrounged up from dumps and dumpsters. But we don't allow him to bring the cart into the library with him, even though he tries. Every day, in fact, he tries to bring that thing in with him, but the guards are under strict instructions that while Tom can enter freely, the cart has to stay outside. So he leaves it, reluctantly, outside next to the bicycle rack, and comes in without it. Who'd want to steal it, after all? Every time I see him on the street, it's with him, bulging with his earthly possessions, whatever they are. I don't really want to know, to tell the truth.

Now here's the thing: the library's code of conduct defines behaviors specifically banned from the library, and, by and large, the code works all right. Anyway, it mentions by name things you're not allowed to do in the building, like fighting, loud talking, smoking, bringing boom blasters or animals in, not wearing shoes or shirts; the usual stuff. But something's missing from the list, and that's where I ran afoul of Tom, or maybe it's more fair to say that he ran afoul of me. There's nothing about smelling bad.

Nothing on that subject, at all.

I know it must be hard to maintain an acceptable standard of personal hygiene when you're living out there on the mean streets. I'm just grateful that I've never had to find out. Tom, living as he does, with no visible means of support, can't be expected to come in here every day with a freshly starched shirt, clean pants, shoes without holes in the soles, as well as being clean, well-scrubbed, and fragrant, can he? So for the homeless ones, men and women alike, we try to look the other way. We pretend not to notice if they smell a little gamy or maybe have dirt or greasy stains on their clothes. Different rules apply, and we don't really mind cutting them some slack. But yesterday evening was one of those times when it became impossible to ignore Tom. As "officer of the deck," I acted. I was in charge, and I did what I thought the situation called for.

So, last evening, we had the usual crowd of people in here to study or find good reading or just to get out of the rain. I saw school kids of all ages, adult patrons, and a few family groups. Nothing out of the ordinary. Tom, of course, was here, too. He almost always is, especially on rainy nights. Now, normally, when Tom passes by, you may notice a funky aroma coming off him, but it's not that strong and you figure, hey, it's only Tom, and you forgive him and continue with what you were doing. The least we can do on a cold, rainy evening is to let a guy like that stay in the library until closing time, especially since there's no record of Tom giving anyone any trouble. So he smells, so what? Other people smell, too.

There was this lady with a beehive hairdo, and when she walked in the building she trailed a cloud of mixed hairspray and perfume like that French skunk in the cartoons. You know, the one who thinks he's Maurice Chevalier or somebody, trying to make time with a female cat who accidentally got a white stripe painted down her back? Yeah, that one.

So anyway, Tom is sitting in one of his favorite places in the library, at one of the index tables in the Reference room, specifically the one where we keep the *Readers' Guide* and other indexes that we still take in print format (despite so much information available via the Internet terminals). He'd been out in the rain and was dripping; if he smelled bad dry, he was even *worse* wet! He was just sitting there, reading a magazine, I think, and tuning out everything else. I've seen him over there so much, I consider him part of the furniture. And so do the security guards, Matt and Mike, because they never hassle Tom anymore about his slovenly appearance and filthy clothes. Live and let live, that's not a bad motto, as long as nobody's being hurt.

But then this middle-aged woman came walking up to me at the circulation desk, where I'm on duty, and said, "Excuse me, young man."

"Yes? May I help you?" I inquired, smiling.

"Well, there's this man over there," she began, haltingly. I'm thinking, oh, no, not another flasher or stalker. Please! We were having such a nice, quiet evening, here. I just want to finish my work, get on home, and watch Monday night football with a few beers and a bag of microwave popcorn, that's all.

"What's he doing, this man?" I asked, not *really* wanting to know.

"Well, that's just it," she said as she wrung her hands. "He's not doing anything specific, but . . . well . . ."

"Give me a hint," I said. "What is he doing, *exactly*?"

"Well, he . . . sort of . . . smells."

"Smells?"

"Bad. You know, like B.O.? Smells!"

"Ohhh!" I said, knowing it was Tom we were talking about now. I peered around for a guard, but whoever was on last night wasn't accessible at that time. "Well, I'm sorry, ma'am, but what would you like me to do about that?"

"Do?" All of a sudden, she was no longer shy but was beginning to get a little angry with me for being slow on the uptake. "*Duh!* I want you to throw him out of the building, and tell him not to come back in here until he doesn't give off that horrible odor anymore."

I really hate to hassle ol' Tom, who's probably just a good man, down on his luck. Besides, it was really coming down hard out there. So I tried to reason with the woman. "Just a suggestion, ma'am," I said, "but have you tried just not sitting in his vicinity? I mean this library has lots of tables and plenty of other places to sit."

"That's the problem," she explained, coming down off her outrage, a bit. "He's sitting right in front of the index I need to use, so I can't just avoid him. And I'm not talking about a minor problem with perspiration. I mean, this man really has a terrible and offensive odor."

I sighed and told her that I'd see what I could do, then asked her to wait. I walked into the Reference room and over to Tom, who was drowsing over a magazine. Sure enough, he was giving off a rather strong smell of wet, dirty clothes, unwashed body, and, probably, greasy matted hair. He was rank, all right! I looked around for a guard again, but no sign of the big man in blue. I had to do something about it. I couldn't just turn and walk back to the waiting woman without getting something accomplished. So I cleared my throat and said to the man hunched over his magazine, "Uh, Tom?"

Nothing. No sign whatsoever that he'd heard me. It occurred to me that he could be a deaf mute. After all, I had never really spoken to him, nor had I ever heard him say anything. So experimentally, I called his name again, only louder. I considered underscoring my words with a discreet poke on his shoulder but decided not to do that, for two reasons. In the first place, it's good practice never to touch a patron unless permission is given, and in the second place, I didn't particularly want to bring my finger into contact with the stained and discolored fabric of his jacket. As a third consideration, you never really know what might happen when you poke someone. Tom could have a concealed bayonet or something under his jacket, and I wouldn't know it until I got the point, in a manner of speaking.

But this time, Tom heard me. His shaggy head rose from its position over the magazine, and he looked up at me with red eyes and a look of mild curiosity, nothing more. Now that I had his attention, I pressed onward. "Tom?" I said, "I'm wondering if you could be persuaded to take your magazine and move to a table over there in the corner?" He regarded me steadily, thinking it over. Then, for the first time in all the months I'd noticed Tom coming in here on an almost daily basis, I heard his voice.

"Why?" he growled in a tone halfway between metallic grinding and an outboard motor starved for lack of fuel. I guess it'd been a long time since he'd spoken.

"Because other people want to get to the index tables and use them, that's why. So how about it? Be a good guy and move away from here."

"Well, let 'em come, then," he croaked. "I ain't stoppin' nobody."

This was awkward already, and I could see that Tom wasn't going to make things any easier. "Well, see, some people won't come over here because of the way you smell, so we thought maybe if you'd just go sit over there in the corner, everybody wins. That way, other people can get to the indexes, you can still sit and read, and the problem is solved. So what do you say?"

Tom appeared to mull my suggestion over, and then raised one arm and waved it in dismissal. "Tell you what you do, buddy," he said, "You just go back to your desk and leave me alone." While his suggestion was, of course, unhelpful to solving this problem, his waving that arm so furiously gave me the full effect of his odor, but even that wasn't the worst part. I'd have to say that the smell was mild compared to the burning of my eyes.

Tom had had enough of our discussion, and he returned to his magazine. That left me with several unhappy options: I could insist more strenuously that he leave his seat, with unknowable consequences; I could walk into the back to the staff room and get Matt, our chief of security, on his case (Matt's six foot six at least, as you know, and good at intimidating people when he needs to, even though he's gentle among friends); or, finally, I could walk back to the woman and report that I'd struck out in my attempts to get the homeless man to see sweet reason, and then apologize for her inconvenience and admit defeat.

As I was pondering these depressing options, an idea struck me; but, first, before making any decision, I walked to my desk and consulted my copy of the library's code of rules and regulations to see if there was anything in the rules about smelling bad. Not surprisingly, there was nothing about offensive odors in the rules. Returning to the front desk, I asked the impatient woman to grant me a brief interval before I took any more action. Reluctantly, she agreed to the delay.

Then I rushed into the staff room where big Matt was sprawled on a couch, sipping a mug of hot coffee and looking at a copy of *Sports Illustrated*. I put the problem to him, asking him to do something, because as the security guard on duty, the ultimate decision was his. Matt looked thoughtfully down at his hands for a moment, and said, "I'll tell you what, Josh. I've had a lot of smelly people come in here on my watch, and I've worked out a sort of rule of thumb that I use at times like this. Wanna hear it?" I nodded affirmatively.

"Well, if I can smell a person's body odor—we're not talking about cologne or hairspray here—from more than six feet away, then out he goes. If I have to get closer than six feet to detect such an odor, then there's room for negotiation. Then, I'd probably give him a choice: either he moves it elsewhere or out he goes.

"I don't know . . .," I mused. "Why six feet? Isn't that, well . . . arbitrary?"

"Could be," agreed Matt, "But it works for me. You got a better idea?"

I didn't. So Matt and I went back out to the Reference room, where Tom's foul stench could be detected from at least *twelve* feet away, and Matt must have decided that the time for talking was over. He loomed over the shabby man and, glowering down, told Tom in a flat tone of voice that he was going to have to leave for the good of everyone else in the building.

As expected, Tom objected. He said that he was a citizen like everyone else. He said that he had a right to visit a public library, and demanded to know of some law that said that he had to smell a certain way. He added that it wasn't by choice that he lived on the streets or in shelters and that if he wanted to while away some hours in the library on a rotten night, he should be left alone to do so. Finally, he shouted about lawyers who would sue the library for depriving him of his rights.

With that, Matt poked Tom gently exactly the way I was going to, 15 minutes earlier, and quietly said, "All right, buddy. No fuss, now. Just get up and leave quietly."

"Suppose I don't?" challenged the furious Tom, refusing even to stand.

Matt drew himself up to his full, imposing height and gave him a baleful look. "You don't want that," he observed conversationally, but his meaning was clear. Obviously, it was clear to Tom, too, because without further delay, he got up, scuttled to the front door, and as he was about to rush through it, turned around and shouted (startling at least half the other people within earshot), "Hey, they turn us out of the shelter after breakfast and tell us we can't come back until dinnertime. I need a warm and safe place to hang out, and, I'm sorry, but I don't got no private shower stall or designer soap!"

Matt took a single giant step toward him, and Tom was gone—out into the wet, windy night, where I watched him retrieve his shopping cart and trundle it down the front walk. It took at least 20 minutes after that—maybe more—before the air exchange in the library's air-conditioning plant could make Tom's awful stench go away, and at least 10 more before that poor woman ventured over to the index table and sat down and started to take notes.

Maybe that's the end of the incident. I hope so. But you never know what's going to happen. So here's my question: Did Matt and I do the wrong thing, and could we get sued for doing it? What were we supposed to do? After all, when you balance the right of one miserable homeless guy against those of maybe another 99 people in the building, I say, it's a no-brainer. Majority rules, in a case like that, doesn't it?

Questions for Discussion

1. Do you think that Matt's arbitrary "six foot" rule is a reasonable guideline, or is it arbitrary, capricious, and unfair?

2. How should a library handle a patron whose personal odor is so foul that no one else wants to go near him?

3. If you needed to add a provision on offensive odors as an addition to the library's code of conduct, how would it be worded?

Case 20

Best Rates in Town

Al Schumacher, owner of Crazy Al's Motors, to the Honorable Michael Willis, Pecan Grove city court judge, in chambers

Yeah, Your Honor we plead guilty to all the charges the cop just read out, and yeah, those fines you've slapped us with are just and fair. But I think there's blame to spread around, in various ways, and so, if you're not too busy, let me have a few moments to explain what we were doing and why we were doing it. Is that possible? Thanks, I really appreciate that, Your Honor.

First off, I want to make it clear that the lady in question stays out of it. Do what you want to me, but her name has *got* to stay out of this. Agreed? Good. I knew you'd understand. As to the charge, please understand that in no way am I trying to skate out from under the fine I gotta pay. I mean, I know that what we were doing in the library yesterday was wrong or at least against the rules, but I just want to offer my side of the story. You've already heard what that security guard had to say, and looking at it one way, he was telling the truth, but . . . well, let me give you my version, and maybe you'll see why the blame should be shared by several parties.

What? The parties, you mean? All right, there's me, there's the woman I was arrested with, there's that overgrown security guard who was maybe too zealous when he caught us, and, finally, there's the library itself, for negligently leaving doors unlocked, like the one we took advantage of to find us some privacy. Seems to me, a public building should make sure that doors to places where they don't want people to enter are locked at all times, wouldn't you agree?

Move it along? Right. I know you haven't got all day, so here's my story.

Well, to begin with, as you've probably guessed, this woman and I are married but not to each other. Your Honor, you and I are both men of the world, am I right? You know that people who aren't married to each other get

126

together sometimes for things like what we were doing, all the time. It's not right, maybe, but there it is. In the abstract, I deplore adultery and infidelity, myself. Does that make me a hypocrite? Maybe, but if so, I have a lot of company. No! I wasn't accusing *you* of anything, Your Honor! I'm just saying that there's a lot of that sort of thing around, that's all.

I won't go into all the sordid details of this woman and me, but I hope you'll believe that we're truly in love—desperately, totally, madly in love. It's just . . . well, we both have kids who are growing up, and neither one of us would have an easy time of seeking or getting a divorce. So we . . . yeah, all right, we cheat. That's not the word I was going to use to describe . . . Well, I *know* what it looks like!

We're not proud of it but we do it. Sleazy, you say? I can't think of it that way. But see, here's the thing: we started seeing each other first just as friends who happen to go to the same bar. But one night, she and I started talking, and we discovered that we had a lot in common and we really liked each other, and we were both stuck in unhappy marriages. So, we . . . started consoling each other, and it just sort of went on from there, know what I mean? Sure you do. Again, I'm not proud of having a secret affair, but we do hope to be together and married to each other some day, when our school-aged kids are older and more able to accept what's happening.

She and I get together as often as possible, without our spouses knowing what's going on. No, my wife doesn't know about this, and I hope that I can count on your keeping my secret. I mean, that unfortunate incident in the library yesterday shouldn't bust up two marriages, should it? Please let me continue. Maybe you'll agree.

So we've been going to motels out by the airport once or twice a week to spend time together in private, without worrying about prying eyes. Modestly priced, clean motels where they don't ask any questions, and I always pay cash only—no credit card receipts—for five or six hours of privacy. But when I go home, I swear I try hard to be a good husband to my wife, and I guess my ladyfriend tries to be a good wife to her husband—who, from what I've heard, doesn't really deserve it. But that's another story.

Guilty? Yeah, I feel guilty, but not as guilty as I'd feel if we were just, you know, horsing around out of boredom or revenge or curiosity or whatever other reasons adulterous people give to justify what they're doing. No, we're really in love, and one day—we've sworn it—we'll do the right thing; divorce our partners, and get married to each other, and I know this sounds corny, but live happily ever after.

Anyway, about yesterday. Here's the play-by-play. See, we try to get together and go a motel about twice a week—that's what keeps us from going crazy while apart. Like Tuesday evenings, when "I have to work late" and her husband goes bowling. That usually works. We have a standing arrangement on Fridays, when she drops her kids off at school and is free until about five or five thirty. As the owner of my own used car lot, I can pretty much arrange my own hours on the job and spring free whenever I want. All right. Let's cut to the chase.

Last week was utter chaos. First, my daughter got sick, and I had to stay home with her on Tuesday evening, so that killed any chance of a get together. Then, Friday, which is normally "our" day, my ladyfriend called it off because she was sick, herself. That meant that yesterday was going to be the first time we could be together in a long time, and then, even *that* fell through. Her jerk of a husband came up with something she had to do for him in the morning, which meant we couldn't spend the whole day together. The best case scenario was that all we could manage was two hours. Two lousy hours to spend together!

Please don't look at me that way. Don't judge me until you've heard me out. That's all I'm asking. So anyway, by yesterday, we were both going out of our minds with longing. But with so little time, I couldn't see the point of spending $50 plus tax for two hours of motel time, so even that was out. Just to be together for a while, we decided to meet downtown for a snack and take a walk, and that was going to have to be it until next week. Of course, it was broad daylight and we had nowhere but one of our cars to be alone. People like us can't just go make out in some lover's lane somewhere in broad daylight. How'd that look if the police cruised by and busted us? Besides, we're both married. Not supposed to be together at all, let alone all wrapped up in each other. Get the picture? I hope so, because here's where it starts getting . . . weird.

All right. We met downtown, and we'd already accepted the idea that it was just going to be a brief encounter, so we went to a fast-food place for lunch, figuring that if anybody we know saw us there, we could explain easily that we just happened to walk into the same place and when we recognized each other, we decided to share lunch. That'd look innocent enough, we figured. After that, we took a walk, being careful not to walk too close together or to touch. We walked to the library next door, because she wanted to check to see whether some novel she'd put on reserve had come in yet, and I went along because . . . well, because it was our day together, and I just didn't want us to go our separate ways yet until we really had to. Like I said, we're in love. We're not just, you know, messing around, we're genuinely in love—doesn't that count for something, I hope?

So we were in the library, and while my ladyfriend was standing in line at the circulation desk, waiting to check out the book that'd been held for her, I walked idly around the big reading room, looking at books, atlases, and other stuff they have there, when I found myself standing in front of a wooden door with a handle. The door was closed, of course. And . . . I don't know why . . . curiosity, I guess, I just reached out and jiggled the door's handle and . . . it opened! So, I took a look inside, you know? No plan, yet. Just curious. Nobody was in that little room, but it had a green felt couch, a coffee table, and a floor lamp. That couch looked really soft and inviting, too. What was it for? I don't know. It was a really small room—maybe some of the staff go in there and take naps or something. It certainly wasn't big enough to be a break room. Just a tiny room, but clean and tidy, and there was that green couch with a couple of bolster pillows or cushions sitting on top of it.

So I'm looking at that couch and thinking about that door I came through—a door that looked locked and probably was supposed to be locked, but wasn't. And that's when I get this big idea, one of those ideas where you know it's crazy and you should forget about it, but . . . well, once it gets hold of you, it won't let you go. Anyway, I reach a decision: I leave the little room, careful to see that the door doesn't latch or lock behind me, and I look around casually to make sure that nobody is paying attention to me or that door I just came out of.

Then I walk over to my ladyfriend, who's waiting for me by the front door, and I lead her over into a far corner and whisper my idea to her. At first, she's, like, totally negative about the idea. Tells me to forget about it. But our little "thing" is pretty intense, and I can see she's hesitating, thinking it over. I whisper in her ear that since we have maybe 45 minutes, tops, before we have to say goodbye and head off for home in separate cars, and since it's been a long time, we should take advantage of this opportunity that fate has brought us.

Well, when I assured her that I'd found us a private little love nest where we could be alone together for half an hour, she gives me this nervous smile and tells me to head on back into the little room, and, if nobody else seems to be watching, she'll join me there in five minutes. The idea is so exciting that my pulse is pounding, and I just give her a look and turn and walk around the big room again, trying to look as nonchalant as possible. When the coast is clear, I open the door again, enter the little room, and close it behind me. Five minutes later, my ladyfriend slips in, locks the door behind her and jumps into my arms. Well, we're on the couch in seconds, you know how it is.

To tell the truth, I don't remember much about the next 20 minutes, except it's even better than our usual times together, because of the excitement about finding, by accident, a place to be together when our usual plans fell through. But then . . . at a particularly compromising moment, we suddenly hear a key in the lock and this big, security guard walks in with a magazine in his hand. I guess it was his break time and he was planning to spend it sitting on that couch, where he could read and relax.

Frankly, I didn't have any idea who was more shocked, him or us. I guess the woman gets the prize for being the most shocked, of course, because her clothes are everywhere, but the big guard gasps and looks like he's about to have a heart attack or something. Before we can do much more than cover ourselves, this big guy is shouting questions at us, like how the hell we got in there, and what we thought we were doing. I thought that it should have been plainly obvious as to what were were doing.

Your Honor, one thing he said is something I want to clear up. Remember, we were both stunned and shocked when this big guy burst into that room, and so when he asked, why did we pick the public library to carry on our affair, I'm afraid I ventured into a bit of what you might call inappropriate humor, which was bad judgment, I admit, because there was nothing humorous about the situation. But when that guard asked why we'd chosen the library to do what we were doing, I didn't think about it, I just said, "Why here in the library? Well, for openers, it's a lot cheaper than the Holiday Inn." I regret the flip tone of my retort, and wish I'd never said it. Heat of the moment, is the only excuse I can come up with for that remark, and I wish I could take it back.

I admit that we were caught doing something we weren't supposed to be doing in a place where we weren't supposed to be. After the shock and confusion, the guard gets his composure back and rumbles that he's going to leave for ten minutes during which we are to get ourselves "presentable" and then he'll be back to take our statements. Our statements? Give me a break! Why did we need to make statements? Wasn't it clear enough what'd been going on? But he walks out and closes the door, leaving us time to get back together.

A million thoughts are whirling through my head during those few minutes. I admit I actually considered bushwhacking the guard when he came back and taking the woman's hand and making a break for it, but I could see that my ladyfriend was in no emotional condition to run anywhere, and besides, I'm not a violent man. The guard's just doing his job, after all. But then, he comes back inside the little room and starts calling us names.

Now, I don't care what he called me. Sticks and stones, and all that. But what he called the woman I love? I really wanted to bust his jaw for using those words about her. I still do. Then he said he needs to see identification, and seeing no choice (he's a really big guy, after all), we got out our wallets. He looked at our driver's licenses and took down our names and addresses. And that was that: we left without any more discussion and agreed to present ourselves voluntarily here in your office today.

If we showed up here, he said he wouldn't go to the cops or say anything to anyone else. But if we didn't come here today, he said he'd take what actions he thought would be necessary. So here I am. Yeah, I came alone. I hope you aren't angry that the woman isn't here. She's too embarrassed to talk about this with anyone and terrified of her husband finding out. Please don't punish her, Your Honor: We're both throwing ourselves on the mercy of the court.

So, do what you have to do to me (even if it kills my marriage and alienates my kids), but please—*Please!*—leave her out of this! I'm begging you. Fine us for indecent exposure or immoral activity or misusing a public place, I'll cop to that and pay the fine immediately, as long as it doesn't get onto any police blotters or any place permanent. But just *me*, all right?

I just want to say one thing more: That library guard might have been shocked to find us doing what we were doing in his broom closet, or whatever it was, but he had no right to verbally abuse the woman I love. Words like those he called her have no place in a civilized discussion over who did what, and where. Still, given the circumstances, we'll be willing to drop any slander charges, if the guard is willing to look the other way concerning what we did and accept our solemn promise that we'll never to do anything like it again in the library.

Finally, I hope you'll agree that the library is at least partly at fault for leaving that door unlocked, where members of the public can gain access to unauthorized and off-limits rooms. I mean, what if we'd been dope pushers or users, looking for a place to shoot up? See what I mean? Proper library security would have required that a door like that be kept locked at all times, right? That's why I'm saying that the library is just as remiss as we are in this whole mess.

Well, that's all I've got to say. Thank you, Your Honor. I know you'll do the right thing. I think I've committed no crime. Yeah, all right, a misdemeanor, maybe. And I *am* complying with the guard's proposal for resolving this matter speedily and without anyone getting hurt, in any sense. Finally, please bear in mind that the big guard subjected me and my ladyfriend to the kind of verbal abuse that should bring immediate dismissal from his job, but in light of everything, I'm willing to overlook what he said in exchange for no further mention of this matter and no paperwork going into the legal system.

Will you please think about this delicate matter carefully? Here's my card. That's my work number—please don't call me at home, for obvious reasons. I'll await your verdict, which I'm sure will be both just and fair. And by the way, if you're ever in the market for a quality used car, I promise to make you a sweetheart deal. A bribe? No, not a bribe—just a show of appreciation, that's all. See you, Your Honor! Have a nice day!

Questions for Discussion

1. To what extent do you think the library was negligent for leaving a door unlocked?

2. As the library director, hearing about this event, what would you say to your security guard about his conduct in this matter?

3. What security implications for the future can you extract from this case?

Case 21

Stealing Is Stealing

Pat Sanchez, city manager, to the Pecan Grove City Council, at its monthly meeting

Thank you. Please enter that into the minutes and let's move on. Next item: It was recently brought to my attention by Ann Cameron Bowman, who, for those who can't place the name, serves this city as director of the Pecan Grove Public Library, that for calendar year 2001, an estimated total of 15,283 books are missing—or at least not located. I took the liberty of doing the math, and that number represents 13.2 percent of the total. Think of it: 13.2 percent! Approximately one eighth of the total collection, to put it another way. An appalling statistic, I grant you, but I don't tell you this for shock value alone. The real question is: What do we do about it?

The problem of theft, pilferage, shrinkage, or loss, take your pick, has, in my opinion, reached epidemic proportions. Let me make an analogy between the public library and the bookstores in our area to make my point: while bookstores, not impervious to theft and shoplifting, generally have reasonably strong defenses against such problems, libraries have considerably less, and sometimes, virtually no defenses. In other words, I maintain that public libraries could profitably borrow security ideas from bookstores, and here are my reasons: both libraries and bookstores deal principally in books and other media; patrons (customers, clients, or whatever you want to call them) visit in search of reading matter or printed publications; materials are arranged in order in aisles, rows, stacks, and ranges; browsing is encouraged; and, finally, admission is free. Though I keep hearing people say that bookstores and libraries are different, I disagree.

You may be thinking that comparing the library to a commercial bookstore is a case of apples and oranges. They're different concerns, and because of their differences, they cannot—or at least should not—be compared as though they were similar. So is it fair, then, to measure our civic library against a typical large bookstore and assume that the same rules apply? Let me open the discussion by stating, in typical politician's fashion, that I can see both strong similarities and equally striking differences be-tween a public library and a commercial bookstore, and I'd like to enumerate them before this council reaches any decisions on what to do about bolster-ing security in the library.

Perhaps some of you are thinking, they're only library books, it's not like they're personal property. So while you may care, you just don't care that much. Other civic problems probably concern you far more. What's the big deal if a few library books go missing every year?

Let's examine this argument: First, a library is different from a book-store in that it purchases its materials with tax-derived funding and its use is free to the public, making it possible for citizens to avoid buying the books for themselves. In this sense, the library serves as a useful community col-lective, returning intangible educational, social, and recreational benefits to all taxpayers, whether they actually use the library or not. Most of them don't, by the way. Ann Bowman informs me that her best guess is that no more than one quarter of the city's populace could reasonably be identified as "library users," however you may wish to define that term.

Unlike our library, a big bookstore is a for-profit corporation, and most of this city's commercial bookstores are branches of large chains, with head-quarters located elsewhere. Profits are paramount in the decision-making process as to what to buy and make available in a general bookstore—and little attention is paid to such conceits as social justice, equality, conflict resolution, and the like. Putting it simply, what's available is what's likely to sell. Less popular items are either not available or must be special ordered for those who request them.

The demand principle governs bookstores' decisions as to what to pur-chase and what to stock on their shelves, whereas a public library—while it certainly cannot ignore the demand principle and sees to it that people get what they want—still feels some responsibility to culture and society. Therefore, a library stocks the classics, important literature and social thought through the ages, and whatever else society deems to be both wor-thy and relevant.

However, it is safe to say that bookstores and libraries—while they may have different motivations and principles—are enough alike in substance to warrant a simple conclusion, which I shall now state (you might want to write this down). Ready? Here it is:

Stealing is stealing. I'll repeat that. Stealing is stealing. Or so I believe, although the matter is open to discussion.

By this assertion, I mean that when materials get stolen from either a library or a bookstore there are always serious economic consequences, and I firmly believe that appropriate security measures to reduce theft are equally necessary and desirable in both institutions.

Now let's consider how bookstores deter, or at least deal with, theft. I've had several chats recently with bookstore representatives, and I believe I am by now well enough versed on the subject to be able to list the following equipment and measures that bookstores commonly employ to avoid theft, or failing that, to make theft more difficult:

- Anti-theft gates at the doors, designed to lock and sound an alarm whenever any person attempts to leave the store with something that has not been purchased and run through a magnetic scanner that neutralizes the magnetic charge.

- Surveillance cameras, usually placed high up on walls just beneath the ceiling at various places around the store, capable of keeping an electronic "eye" on customers. By the way, it is frequently not necessary to have either film in the cameras or trained security staff watching their monitors (as, for example, they do at gambling casinos and other establishments where games of chance are played for money). The mere presence of such cameras, blinking, turning and swiveling as they scan a room, has been demonstrated to be a deterrent to crimes like shoplifting and book mutilation in bookstores.

- A uniformed security guard situated in the front vestibule of a bookstore serves to "remind" people to go through the check-out lines and pay for their purchases rather than just leaving with books on their persons.

- Store employees, wearing blazers or other apparel imprinted with store logos, who are trained to double as helpers ("May I help you find something?") and guards ("Excuse me, but did I just now see you accidentally place a book under your jacket?").

- Unobtrusive store detectives, frequently hired on a seasonal basis, such as during the busy six-week period leading up to the Christmas holiday, who are dressed to look like ordinary shoppers and pass themselves off as such. While they appear to be browsing, they are actually taking careful note of others in their area, and are ready, when necessary, to call ahead to the front door guard with a description of anyone suspected of having "boosted" books or other merchandise and trying to leave with it without going through the process of paying.

Other methods of book retention have been considered or even used by commercial bookstores, such as magnetized labels that trigger alarms if they are removed from the building without being discharged; subliminal tapes mixed in with the "muzak"; exploding cartridges secreted in purloined books; sensitive sound devices that can reveal unnaturally high stress levels in the voices of book shoppers (based on computer analysis of eye movements); colored goggles that reveal high stress levels; or even robots programmed to identify theft and deal quickly yet safely with perpetrators.

Among the problems with all of these technology methods I just listed is that they are usually just prototypes, are often very expensive (and thus far beyond the library's means), and potentially fraught with ethical problems, which could lead to bad publicity. No bookstore can afford that.

Libraries, of course, have considered many of the bookstores' methods, but the most significant difference lies in the fact that most libraries cannot afford them. As public facilities, run on a not-for-profit basis, libraries simply cannot afford to buy or lease such state-of-the-art security systems; and besides, the library—unlike the bookstore—belongs to all of us, and thus runs on the general philosophy that the fewer barriers placed in the way of those seeking knowledge, understanding, entertainment, or even a few hours' quiet respite from the rat-race world outside, the better.

Once again, the principal difference between a public library and a big bookstore is the profit motive, which drives decisions as to what bookstores buy and sell. So the question becomes: If an individual steals a book (allow me the use of this generic term, although the stolen item may be a sound recording or video) from a library, is it the same thing—and should it be treated in the same way—as theft from a bookstore, where shoplifters are routinely detained and turned over to the police? In simple terms, do we prosecute? Is it worth the trouble to try to get people sentenced and compelled to do jail time or community service for ripping off a book or two from the library? I submit that whether we're talking about a six-buck paperback novel or an exquisite gift-boxed set of coffee table books for Christmas, the *principle* is exactly the same.

Should the fact that the theft is not from an individual or corporation but rather from a public facility make any difference in the handling of those who are caught trying to steal books? I think not. Consider the economic parallel: eventually, when a bookstore experiences enough loss or shrinkage in the book stock due to theft, they must either declare bankruptcy and go out business or be forced to raise prices (or slash discounts). Should the library act similarly? And if so, how would that work?

We must ask ourselves which forms of interdiction practiced by bookstores are equally appropriate for libraries and which forms are not? Now, I admit that the average citizen in Pecan Grove, if asked, would not become unduly alarmed about the rate of loss at either the bookstore or the public library. Most folks think of our public library as worthy but dull. Maybe that's the real problem: apathy. A prevailing public attitude of "Oh, well, big deal!"

Clearly, loss from libraries is not generally regarded as terribly important, because it's nobody's personal book that's stolen (even though, in a real sense, it's *everybody's* book; folks just don't realize it). Would that help account for the fact that libraries are notorious for lackluster interdiction of petty thieves and shoplifters? I say it again: whether public library or bookstore, stealing is stealing, and the same rules should apply.

Well, I've said what I had to say on this subject. Thank you for your attention. Any questions or comments?

Questions for Discussion

1. What characteristics differentiate public libraries from commercial bookstores?

2. If we operate on the principle that "stealing is stealing," how does that change our stance on security?

3. Can you see any downside to getting tough on book thieves and prosecuting those who are caught?

Case 22

Everybody Out!

Matt DeWaelsche, head of security, to Roger Dimick, chief of detectives for the Pecan Grove Police Department

Blame it on the weather, might as well! To begin with, it was one of those nights. The weather was unbelievably rotten last night, as you no doubt recall. It was like evening all afternoon, so I never really noticed darkness falling. It rained hard and steadily for hours and when the fire alarm went off just after dark, my first thought was, "Why me?" My next thought was, "Why didn't I buy that condo in Florida (when it was still affordable) and retire before it came to this?"

At our library, we take the rules seriously. We operate by the book, most of the time. One of the rules is that we hold monthly fire drills, just to keep in practice in case a real fire or other emergency takes place. We have a staff member—have you met Sam?—who's been appointed as chief security officer, but he leaves at five thirty every day. For some reason, bad things tend to happen after five thirty, usually when it's dark outside. That means that I have to be the one—in my capacity as, ahem, Head of Library Security, to take charge when a problem hits.

Management always picks some nice day for those drills—and it's always in the daytime—when I'm told to ring the fire alarm and evacuate the building. Piece of cake. When it's, like 60, 70 degrees outside and sunny—or even on a crisp clear winter's day—I find that people may grumble, but they don't protest or balk too much when they're told that it's only a drill, but that they're going to have to leave, and to be sure to take all their belongings and gear with them.

Usually, they're back inside the building, doing what they were doing before within 20 minutes, 25 at the outside, and it doesn't present too much of a hardship. I decide when to pull the switch, but, of course, I don't follow any recognizable pattern. Predictable fire alarms would defeat the purpose, you see. I make sure that we do those monthly drills when management says, but at random times of day.

Then there are times when someone sets off the fire alarm as a prank. Teenagers, usually, bored and in need of a little excitement. It doesn't happen often, but when it does, I do everything I can to identify the little . . . darling . . . who pulled the red lever, and on two occasions, I actually got 'em arrested for it. It's a violation of the city code, after all, to report a fire when there isn't one. These punks ought to be prosecuted and placed on a year's probation, at the very minimum, with community service, if you ask me.

Now, last night, as I'm sure you recall, was the coldest night of the year. I'm sure I don't have to tell you that. You probably had to leave the pipes running in your home like I did, because the temperature in the low teens and a wind-chill factor of minus faggedaboudit combined to make it a terrible night to be outside. And when the snow—changing to sleet, then changing back to snow—began, I thought, "Perfect! Just what we need. A cold wave." That's why when the alarm got pulled, I had the dismal thoughts I just told you about. On the coldest night of the year, I knew I was in for one hell of a time getting people to leave the library, unless of course, flames started licking at their heels.

Since it wasn't a drill, my first job was to investigate. Turns out, it wasn't some punk kid pulling the alarm switch just to liven up a dull evening of homework, this time—this time—it was an actual electrical fire. No, not some kind of "towering inferno" sort of thing, but it was a sure enough electrical fire in the transformer room. Some thin but acrid smoke came rolling through the building and frightened everybody. Normally, when people smell smoke, they don't have to be told what they need to do. They head for the exits on their own because everyone understands fire and nobody wants to get burned up in one. But because of the terrible weather last night, even when the fire alarm went off—and kept on blasting—almost nobody ran, or even *walked*, outside.

Well, I followed standard procedure anyway, meaning I had to evacuate everybody—and that means everybody—from the building in anticipation of the fire trucks rolling up and sorting out the problem. First, when that smoke began coming from the back of the building, I ran back there and investigated and saw that it was a small electrical fire. I quickly shut off the generator and was gratified that that seemed to quench the source of the smoke, even if the whole building was suddenly on emergency lighting. Outside, there was a nasty mix of snow, sleet, hail, and frigid wind, so I thought it best to rush out to the public area to reassure the folks out there that there was no real emergency, no blaze, and that everything was under control, but that they would have to leave the building, in compliance with the city fire code.

The PA system had been disabled with the rest of the power, so I raised my voice (I have a really loud voice when I want to project it), and I announced, "May I have your attention, please? Folks, there is a minor malfunction in the generator room, causing a temporary power outage. There's no cause for alarm and the smoke you smell is just residual. To repeat, there's no reason to be alarmed. There is no fire.

However, in compliance with the city's fire code, every person in the building must evacuate the building at once in an orderly and calm manner and remain outside until the Fire Marshal arrives on the scene, inspects the generator room, and pronounces this structure to be safe once again for occupancy. Everyone please leave by the front exit immediately. Anyone needing help or special assistance, please make yourself known to me and I'll do my best to help you. Please gather all your belongings, now, and proceed to the exit. Thank you for your cooperation."

Even though there weren't all that many, most of the patrons in the library immediately headed for the doors. When it's that kind of weather, sometimes you could throw a live grenade into the reading rooms and nobody would get killed. I figured most of the usual crowd were probably at home, shoes off, blankets draped across their laps, watching something good on TV.

But there's always one, isn't there? Somebody always has to be an individualist. This little old man trudges up to me and puts a veined and spotted hand on my sleeve and peers up into my face. When he spoke, I detected a foreign accent, but I'm not too good at that sort of thing. I don't know, Russian, maybe? Polish? Maybe Czech. He was from some Slavic country, anyway. "Podden me," the old guy said, smiling with a mouthful of gaps in his remaining teeth. "I dun't mean to make no trouble or nothink, but didn't you chust say that dere is no ectual fire?"

I scowled down at him, annoyed at the distraction from all the things I had to do. "Yeah, that's what I said, buddy, there no longer seems to be a fire. I nipped it in the bud, and it won't become one. But the fire code still states that all persons . . ."

"I'm chust esking, is all," he said. "And my next qvestion is, If dere's no fire and no danger, then vy must ve be leavink the building on a night like dis?" He gestured toward the windows where little sharp sounds—sleet or small hailstones—were doing a tap dance routine on the glass. A few bystanders nodded their agreement. Why, indeed, I could almost hear them thinking.

A lot of nervous glances went toward the window, where swirling snow with a bite in it from the wind was starting to drift. Down on the next corner, suspended stop lights could be seen through the windows, doing a crazy dance on their own wires over the street. No doubt about it: mean night! But I had duties to carry out, and besides, what I was doing was not only orders, but in the best interest of this complainer and all the rest, couldn't they see that?

"Look, sir, I don't have time to argue with you," I said, trying to control my mounting irritation. "Let me do my job, all right? My job is to see to it that everybody leaves and that's what I'm going to do, with or without your consent, so if you'll just head on out the door and let me do my job."

"Oy!" He exclaimed, and turned to a knot of people who had stopped in their march to the front doors and now stood around us listening intently. "Another pogrom! Next, he's going to be sayink that he's chust following orders, I betcha." He glared up at me, now. "I hoid dat line before, sonny boy, beck in the camps, you know what I'm talking about? And efter the war, at Nuremberg, I hoid it again. 'Chust following orders,' said all dose Nazi butchers in defense of their ections in the camps."

Enough of this, I thought. What does my doing my job have to do with SS guards at Auschwitz or some place. I mean, gimme a break! I addressed the old man again, taking a sterner tone "Look, this isn't a debate. I don't have time for this. I'm not playing with you, old man. So get out of this building—*now*—or I'm going to have to help you leave."

"Vat're you, t'reatenink me?" He turned to the onlookers. "You pipple are all vitnesses to dis! Look at me! A helpless old man, and a Holocaust victim, yet, and you're t'reatenink me? Look!" he shouted, rolling up the sleeve of his overcoat and displaying some faint blue numbers tattooed into the flesh of his forearm. "Know how I got dese?"

No one remaining in the building seemed to be thinking about leaving by now. They were watching our standoff. I suppose this was better than TV to them. But for me, this was turning into a nightmare. One little old man was somehow persuading dozens of other people to resist a perfectly logical order, sanctioned by the city. The idea that there was any similarity between my doing my job and some SS goons back in the camps was ludicrous. I would have laughed out loud if it hadn't been such a potentially serious matter.

Well, eventually, everything got sorted out, and no one was hurt, despite a lot of destroyed umbrellas when they got outside into that crosswind, but next time, it may not lead to such a happy outcome. So, any ideas for dealing with crowd control that I haven't thought of yet? I'd really like to know. One thing I worked out on my own is three good rules to cover emergency evacuations in the future: Rehearse, rehearse, and rehearse.

Questions for Discussion

1.   Are there times when normal rules about evacuation of a public building should be disregarded?

2.   How could Matt have persuaded the elderly man to leave the building without resorting to shouting, tugging, or threatening?

3.   Given that there seems to be no immediate danger, could you justify letting people who don't want to leave stay inside where they're warm and safe from the storm?

Case 23 _____

Here's Lookin' at You, Kid!

Andrea Meeden, Webmaster (Pecan Grove Public Library), to David Rubin, head of Internet services, City of Pecan Grove

Dave, I must tell you about a serious problem; one that's only likely to proliferate, because of the widespread use of computers in this community. Is it a crime? Well, I thought so, but let me tell you about it, and you decide for yourself. My take on it is that it *is* a crime, all right, but I am not sure that it's been classified as such by the penal code of this state or Pecan Grove. And besides, as they say, the devil's in the details. One day, though, there should be something about it in the criminal code, because we just can't let this sort of thing go on. Something's got to be done. Anyway, let me tell it from the top.

It happened last year, before we installed that expensive firewall on our information system, which, despite the cost, seems to have paid for itself already in the light of what it has prevented. Not for lack of trying, though. Seems like unauthorized people are always trying to break into our files, for whatever reasons. In fact, that's why we installed the firewall in the first place, because we became aware of the vulnerability of our information to what we're now calling information bandits. That's one of the most interesting aspects of library security, if you ask me. Information theft: a new type of theft.

Think about it: If someone comes in and steals something tangible, you lose it, and you either set about trying to get it back or to replace it, or you write it off as part of doing business. If someone does something antisocial in our building, we can summon the police, provide eye witness testimony, and possibly get the perpetrator put away or at least off the streets. But information theft is a whole new type of crime, and one where the authorities and library leaders are still making up the rules as they go along.

Some interesting things have happened to me in connection with my job of being Webmaster for an increasingly technical library system, but I guess this one stands out. It started a year or so ago, just as summer was giving way to fall, when I discovered that some anonymous hacker had made a few rather clever and unobtrusive incursions and unauthorized entries into our files, and then "lifted" some of the library's proprietary information. A sign of the times, I guess.

In the old days, if anyone took library property, like books, computers, or even boxes of sticky notes, there was a reasonable chance that the thief might leave some evidence of some kind, like maybe fingerprints. But electronic fingerprints are another matter, entirely. Some electronic sneak-thief was somehow finding his way past the defenses we had in place at the time (password access to all files and different levels of access to sensitive materials), and once inside, was rummaging around.

That's something we don't want to encourage, as you can appreciate. For a parallel situation, imagine that someone waited until you weren't home, broke into your house without shattering a window or breaking down a door, and got inside. Now imagine that once the intruder was inside, he walked around, checked the drawers in your bedroom dresser (but didn't take anything), inspected the contents of your medicine chest, used the bathroom, used one of your towels, then went to the refrigerator, found a can of beer and some cold cuts and bread, located a bag of chips in the pantry, organized a snack, and sat down to watch television in your living room. After an hour or so, let's say he put the dishes in your sink, yawned, stretched, went out the same way he came in, and then went home to sleep. The question is: Was a crime committed?

That's what these intrusions were like, except the way this guy operated, he didn't exactly "take" anything from the library and nothing is missing, so calling his actions *theft* might be a bit of a reach. But he *did* enter without our authorization or our knowledge, made himself at home, and exited, possibly leaving a trap door of some kind that would make return visits easier. How would you feel about that? Violated, maybe? That's what a lot of victims of break-ins say when they discover that their home has been used as a temporary shelter or snack bar. So would you call what happened to us being violated? Right. So do I.

You see the parallel. Someone found his or her way past our defenses and into our computer files, rummaged around, possibly downloaded some of our information for purposes unknown, and then left—all without ever physically coming into this place. For all we know, this guy is in Alaska or someplace. And the worst part of it is that we were completely numb to it while it was happening. Didn't find out about it for weeks. No way we could tell—at least at the time—that he'd even been here! Frightening, I'll tell you. Violated by the slickest of thieves, with no evidence of the theft.

But I caught him, eventually. Yeah, I figured out who he was and actually tracked him down. Yeah, that's my proudest accomplishment. Or it could have been, anyway. Figured they ought to pin a medal or hero button on me . . . except for one thing, which I'll get to in a minute. But let's stick with the good news, first: I actually caught this guy, like Sherlock Holmes knew who to look for from a single dropped sweet wrapper or some of those recent forensic detectives can tell who had been at the scene of the crime from DNA or hair and fiber.

Here's how I did it: About once a month, I run a routine audit, and display on my screen at the master console a record of all access to the library's proprietary files. It's standard practice, and while it's expected of every city agency, not everyone actually does it because it can be really boring. But I do it conscientiously because it's part of my job.

Last September, I was spending my usual hours scanning endless lists of identical looking entries on the master log of people who had been into our budget files. At first, it was just the usual events, but then I found something that didn't match up. We're not total doofuses when it comes to protecting ourselves at this library. Only five members of the staff (including myself) can gain access to the budget file, and we all know the importance of protecting our information from prying or malicious eyes. I mean, yes, this is a public institution—our budget is not a state secret or anything—but think about the mischief someone could get into if they got into our budget and maliciously transposed numbers, deleted items, or replaced figures. Of course, it wouldn't have to be malicious. It could be done out of another motive: a prank, revenge, or just to see if he could do it.

So, I started scrutinizing the files even more carefully after that. I remember distinctly that muggy day, when I was going down an endless list of entries into our budget file and trying to keep from yawning, when suddenly one of those entries jumped out at me. Why that one? Because it was made at 03:04:28 on 09.15.02! Get it? That means that someone on Saturday, September 15, at 3:04 in the morning, was messing with the budget file. Three in the morning! Who does *that?*

It was highly irregular, because the five people who can access that file: Ann, the director; Mike, the associate director; Karen, Ann's administrative assistant; Donna, Mike's secretary; and me, had never before (to my knowledge) got up at (or stayed up until) three in the morning, and thought, you know, "I can't sleep. Guess I'll just go over to my computer, bring up the library's budget file and do some shifting of numbers." Especially on a Saturday morning, five or six hours before most people are up and stirring and thinking about breakfast. See why that alarm bell went off in my head?

I was puzzled, but I assumed that all I had to do was to look at the user I.D. of the person who had been so industrious or insomniac as to have done that, and then I'd know who it was. It's my job to recognize the passwords of those with high-level authorization, but I'd never seen the little grouping of letters that was printed alongside the time/date group for that three A.M. entry. It read: SPRWZRD@AOL.com. Hmmm, SPRWZRD. I thought to myself: Superwizard? Sounded like just the kind of self-promoting name that some kid-genius hacker might use, but perhaps I was jumping to conclusions or stereotyping. When I double-checked, I realized that SPRWZRD corresponded to none of the passwords in my file, or those stored in my brain, for that matter.

Now, I was alarmed. Quickly, I typed in my own access number and got into the budget file. To my considerable relief, it looked fine. I went over it carefully, but couldn't find anything amiss. All of the columns added up, and every debit and credit was carefully accounted for. What a relief! For one hot moment, when I'd found that suspected intrusion, I'd been terrified that someone had either deleted, scrambled, or siphoned off the funds in the various categories, but everything seemed normal enough.

Next, I turned my attention to our intruder, hoping to find out who SPRWZRD was. That part was surprisingly easy. It just so happens that at home, I'm one of AOL's 30-or-so-million subscribers, and there's a column on the tool bar on the screen called "AOL Members." Not really expecting to find what I was looking for, I entered SPRWZRD as a user ID, and, lo and behold, there was a profile identifying him as a single guy, a computer fanatic living in Middleburg, no more than 30 minutes away from here by interstate highway. It even provided his name, Lyle, although I knew that could be a bogus name. A lot of people on a system like AOL don't give their real names, for fear of stalkers, irritating spammers, and other unwanted messages.

So I thought about Lyle in Middleburg and his possible motivations. It didn't look like he'd done much of anything sinister to our files. I consulted the most recent printout and compared, and he hadn't done a thing that I could detect. Then I thought, if Lyle is smart enough to get into proprietary (and well-defended) information, why would he be so silly or thoughtless or just plain dumb as to leave his "footprints" on his intrusion, so that someone like me could follow it directly to him? I couldn't figure it out. The easiest way to get that mystery to unravel, I decided, was to alert the authorities, and so I did.

I called the local police and told them what I knew—or at least sus-pected—and they agreed that this Lyle character was someone they'd want to have come in for questioning (even if the specific charges hadn't been de-cided, yet) and asked the Middleburg police to pick him up. It was easy enough to get his address and full name, Lyle Metcalf, from directory infor-mation. That same afternoon, a detective in Middleburg said that a Mr. Metcalf, age 22, was in custody, and being cooperative and even chatty, al-though he hadn't yet implicated himself or confessed to anything, as yet. If I wanted in on the interview, I was welcome.

I really wanted to get to the bottom of this mystery, so I drove to Middleburg, arriving on the scene at police headquarters within an hour. When I arrived, I joined a group of detectives at a table across from a small, slight, and pale young man, sitting facing them. He might have been ner-vous, surrounded by all that heat, but he sure didn't show it, except for the observable fact that he blinked more often than most people do, which could mean something or nothing, I don't know.

When I was seated at the table, the chief of detectives, who introduced himself as Dick Russell, said to me, "Ms. Meeden, you were invited here be-cause it appears that if this suspect is guilty of anything it's got to do with your library and its information. So before we turn to Mr. Metcalf, here—who, by the way, has said that he will make full disclosure of his ac-tivities when you're here to hear it—let me get a few things down on tape for the record, all right?' I nodded my agreement and he pushed a button on a small tape recorder.

"All right, here we go: your name is Andrea Meeden and you serve in what capacity for the Pecan Grove Public Library?"

"My title is Webmaster," I replied, "But if it's more convenient, you might call me chief of computer security, at least in a case like this.

"Okay, I will. Now, Ms. Meeden, how long have you served the Pecan Grove Public Library in this capacity?"

"I just celebrated my fourth anniversary as a library employee, but the official title of Webmaster has only been mine for the past 18 months."

The Chief made a notation on a yellow pad. "Now, for the record, will you please state the duties you perform as Webmaster for the Pecan Grove Library?"

"Certainly," I said, and I gave a brief resume of what I do for my employer.

"Thank you," said Chief Russell, "And now, I think we're ready for you to confront Mr. Metcalf, who has been read his Miranda rights, but has waived them, saying that he's willing to talk openly about his activities. That right, Mr. Metcalf?" he said, turning to the man in custody.

"Please, call me Lyle," said the young man, with a big, toothy grin. "And sure," he said. "Ask away. I don't mind questions a bit." I was about to speak directly to the guy when Chief Russell held up one huge paw in warning, and then pointed sternly at Lyle.

"You realize, I hope, that anything you say may be used against you in a court of law?"

Lyle waved a dismissive hand. "Sure, sure. I was given my rights. Ask me anything. I've got nothing to hide." He looked directly at me with a friendly, encouraging look, as if urging me to direct my inquiries at him. This was sort of unnerving, because most of the bad guys you see on *Law and Order* or *NYPD-Blue* are either hostile, sullen, or nervous looking. Not our boy Lyle, though. He looked as though he was competing on one of those game shows where the correct answers could make him a millionaire, and he's already been briefed on the correct answers. So since everybody was looking at me, I cleared my throat and stepped up to the plate.

"Mr. Metcalf," I began.

"Lyle," he reproved, gently.

"All right, Lyle. Have you ever had occasion to access the Pecan Grove Public Library's proprietary files?" He grinned.

"Frequently," he said. "And to save you some time, most recently, in the wee, small hours of a particular Saturday morning, last month." What? I just blinked at him. He was making this so easy, I couldn't believe it. What'd they do, those Middleburg cops, dope him up with truth serum or torture him, or maybe offer him a deal if he'd confess? But hey, if he was really that eager to be forthcoming, I was willing to meet him halfway. More than halfway. I really wanted to get to the bottom of this. But before I could ask my next question, he spoke first.

"And by the way, Ms. Meeden—I hope you'll permit me call you Andrea—I congratulate you for using your sleuthing powers to track me down so quickly. Some of the places I hit never catch me, you know, and others take weeks, or even months."

"Thanks," I acknowledged the compliment, despite my anger at him, because I was proud of myself for the logical train of thought that had brought me to him. "Fine, call me Andrea, if you prefer. Now, Lyle," I said, "tell us how you did it, how you managed to break into our files without identity theft or securing any of the existing high-level passwords."

"Perhaps not," he said, sounding playful.

"Please?" I said, not understanding.

"Trade secret," he said. "I'll freely confess what I did and even why I did it, but the "how" of it? I don't want to tell you, because I might want to come pay y'all a visit again, some day."

I decided to pounce on what he said he *was* willing to tell us. "All right, why, then? Why did you hack your way into our budget file late at night, look around, presumably, and then just leave again, without taking anything?"

"What makes you think I didn't take anything?" he said, grinning.

"Well, because nothing's gone," I explained, knowing even as I said it that it wasn't the most helpful thing I could say in serving my cause.

Lyle feigned surprise. "Oh, but if nothing's gone, exactly what crime do you suggest I'm guilty of? I'd really like to know!"

"Information theft!" I said, wishing I were more sure of my facts and definitions.

"Excuse me?" said Lyle. "Wouldn't the word 'theft' imply that something had been removed, taken, or illegally plundered? Since you, yourself, say that there's no evidence of anything missing, I submit that I am guilty of no crime, no infraction of the laws, and I demand to be released from custody with a full apology and a ride home." I could see that most of the large men around me didn't care for this guy's playful, boastful tone, but, of course, no one had any cause or reason to take action against the harmless looking little man seated in our midst.

"But you admit that you gained illegal access to our information, and you did God-knows-what with it when you got into it!" I blurted, forgetting to be calm, as I'd promised myself. But Lyle just sat there, clearly enjoying himself, then he gave me that pleasant smile again.

"Prove it," he said, softly.

"Well," I said, "will you promise, at least, to stop breaking into our files and accessing our proprietary information? If you will, I suppose I'd be willing not to press charges."

"Charges?" said Lyle, all exaggerated innocence. "What kind of charges? You don't got no steenking charges." I knew he was doing a bit from *The Treasure of the Sierra Madre,* one of my favorite old movies, but I refused to smile or acknowledge the reference.

"But you stole our information! You can't do that!"

He just grinned and said, "So, you're saying I stole your information? Fine. How come you still have it, then?" That stopped me cold. It was a good question. A very good question, in fact, one requiring an answer, too. Got to work on that. And that's how we left it. He was right, you see. The rules of evidence are pretty clear. No theft, no harm, no crime.

The Middleburg cops released him and even drove him home, which must have been galling for them. There was nothing left for me to do but drive home, disconsolately, where I violated my own rule and had two large, strong drinks with dinner, instead of my customary can of Diet Coke. But if there was any silver lining in all these black clouds of vulnerability and frustration, it's this: This sad little chapter in our lives has resulted in the purchase of our present good, reliable firewall, which isn't necessarily going to keep people like Lyle out of our files, but it ought to make the task a lot more difficult.

Well, that's about it, I guess. The whole story. Anything else, I'll give you a call. Wait a minute . . . I just remembered something . . . something really disturbing. As I was leaving the Middleburg police station and trudging sadly to my car for the trip back to Pecan Grove, I heard a friendly voice behind me calling my name.

"Yo, Andrea!" said the voice. I turned around, knowing even as I did whose voice it was. But what do you do when somebody behind you calls you by name? You don't think about it; you just turn around. There was Lyle Metcalf, smiling his sunny smile, standing next to a huge beat patrolman who looked about ready to murder him.

"Here's lookin' at you, kid!" Lyle called softly, tipping an imaginary hat in my direction. Again, with the Bogart. Gimme a break! For one hot minute, I felt like charging over to him and kicking him very hard where I figured it would really hurt. But of course, I didn't. I just got into my car, backed out of my parking space, and drove on home. And that's how we left it.

Nothing of the kind has happened to our library since that date, but every time I check the logs, I hold my breath, waiting for something that I figure is only a matter of time. One day, Lyle will be calling on us again. I'm almost sure of it. Maybe the new firewall will keep him out, but I wouldn't bet on it. Hackers are out there 24/7, thinking up new ways to get around our defenses, and no firewall can be expected to intercept all attempts at intrusion. No, it's only a matter of time. I can definitely say that we're better off with that firewall than without it, but that doesn't help me sleep better at night. Not really.

Questions for Discussion

1. How can information theft be considered a true crime, when it doesn't result in anything being lost?

2. As Andrea, what might you try to do to deter the Lyles of the world from successfully breaching a library's security?

3. How can a firewall be configured to admit only authorized passwords, while trapping and thwarting the rest?

Case 24

Death Threat

Caesar Jaramillo, field agent for the Federal Bureau of Investigation, Pecan Grove office, to the FBI director, Washington, D.C., by e-mail, via an encrypted secure channel

To: Director, Bureau Headquarters, Washington D.C.

Status: Secret/Priority Handling/Encryption Protocols Observed

From: Caesar Jaramillo, Field Agent, Federal Bureau of Investigation, Pecan Grove Office

Subject: Death Threat against POTUS

Date: 22 September 2002

Pursuant to standard order PR-482 that we in the bureau take all death threats against high public officials very seriously, especially in light of the past year's events, I am informing you, sir, of one I consider to be quite serious. I realize that since the World Trade Center and Pentagon strikes, there have been many such threats—most of which have turned out to be bogus—but in this particular case, I suggest we take a recent threat against the president of the United States (POTUS) as very credible, and act accordingly and immediately. Briefly, here are the details:

I was summoned to the main building of the Pecan Grove Public Library last week on 11 September (the anniversary of the World Trade Center disaster of a year ago) to investigate what a reference librarian (calling in an agitated state) described as a death threat to the president, found in a message displayed on one of the library's public Internet terminals. I immediately drove over to the library, interviewed the librarian who had called, and am now reporting my findings to the bureau for advice on a course of action.

I am aware, of course, that death threats of this kind often turn out to be false alarms, hoaxes, or misinterpreted remarks, and that several such threats are received each week across the nation; but it is my judgment, based on 14 years in the field and a wealth of experience, that this one is either genuine or worrisome enough to warrant a full-scale investigation. One of the library's 16 interactive Internet terminals had been used—by a person or persons unknown—to send a message to the president of the United States in the White House that contained a specific and clear threat to his life.

Among thousands of e-mail messages sent in various directions by persons using free access offered by the library, this message was different from the idle and non-specific threats that most famous people receive, at one time or another. This one said: "Mr. President, enjoy your Christmas holidays, because you definitely won't be around to welcome in the New Year."

That message has since been analyzed by a local trained professional psychiatrist assigned to the bureau. Her recommendation was unequivocal: we should go all out to catch whoever sent that note, because this one doesn't strike her as an idle threat from a merely angry or disappointed voter letting off steam. She thinks this one is "the real deal," and cautions that the perpetrator intends to follow through on that threat if he or she gets the opportunity.

Lending urgency to my recommendation is the fact that the president is scheduled to visit Pecan Grove next month for a speaking engagement and has been invited to appear subsequently at a party fundraiser, after which he is slated to address the local Chamber of Commerce. Needless to say, these appearances could present opportunities for our potential assailant to carry out his or her threat.

Should anything untoward befall the president or anyone else in his entourage during his visit, not only would the nation be thrown once again into utter turmoil, but the consequences for my city's prestige and reputation would be incalculable. This makes tracking down and eliminating this threat of paramount importance. A psychological profile of the writer of that message reveals a troubled, but highly intelligent, and strongly motivated individual.

The librarian who reported this message to me—Ms. Mary Rhoades— the head of reference services at the local public library, says that she first became aware of the message this morning when she was summoned to one of her department's computer stations by a frightened young female patron who told her that there was something she needed to see displayed on the screen of a terminal that had been used previously by someone no longer present. I personally interviewed both the librarian and the young female and am convinced that they are both telling the truth.

Specifically, here is the text of the message, scanned in its original appearance into this communication. For the files, I have recovered and hereby copy text of this morning's death threat message:

> Mr. President:
>
> You may be riding high in the public opinion polls, and, despite the controversy surrounding your election, you may think you have a mandate from the people to push your wrongheaded agenda, make war on other nations, and appoint judges who share your political views on important issues. However, because you have already done serious damage to this nation and promise to do even more damage to it in the rest of your term of office, we—the enlightened few, the true American patriots—have decided that it is necessary to end that term, and your life, abruptly.
>
> We are coming for you, Mr. President, maybe not today or tomorrow, but we are definitely on our way. We will not rest until you are dead, and thus no longer capable of following your benighted and dangerous public policy agenda.
>
> Enjoy your Christmas holidays, Mr. President, because you definitely won't be around to welcome in the New Year!

There was no signature or sender identification. Of course, I am aware of the standard federal penalty for making death threats against high officials. Anyone sending a communication to the White House that contains a threat of bodily harm to the chief executive of the United States is committing a serious and punishable federal crime. The prescribed penalty for making such a threat under provisions of the U. S. criminal code ranges from 25 years to life imprisonment in federal prison, depending upon circumstances. The operative question is whether our perpetrator is aware of this, or even cares. The consulting psychiatrist is of the opinion that whoever left that message on the library's computer screen is beyond caring.

Ms. Rhoades theorizes (correctly, in my estimation) that, having issued his or her dire warning, the perpetrator, his or her task accomplished, promptly left the building, perhaps intentionally omitting the proper sign-off procedures that normally reset the Internet welcome screen program for the next user. Our suspicion is that the culprit wanted the death threat to be discovered, although it is possible that the perpetrator assumed that sending a communication from a public library would create a protective cloak of anonymity. I have interviewed Ms. Rhoades and the young patron (a teenaged girl) in depth and am satisfied that neither of them had anything to do with the death threat against POTUS, just as I am equally convinced that this threat was not a prank.

Promptly learning the identity of the perpetrator is our first priority. Ms. Rhoades reports that, upon examining her sign-up sheet used at peak times (e.g., evenings and weekends) when traffic is high, revealed that a person who signed in as J. W. Booth was listed as the previous user of that terminal. We are proceeding under the assumption that such a name is not a coincidence, and that the choice of an infamous assassin's name is another clue as to the intentions (if not the identity) of the perpetrator.

I have had my operatives perform the standard fingerprinting procedures on the computer in question, but the librarian reports that in a typical day, as many as two dozen people might touch the keyboard, screen, or mouse connected to a given terminal, so apprehending a suspect as a result of print analysis is a remote possibility. We are also aware that the perpetrator may well have worn rubber gloves in sending the death threat, meaning that no incriminating prints would be found.

Bureau files reveal that death threats against public officials nationwide are almost routine. However, my fellow agents and I are experienced and well trained in a variety of techniques of sorting out real threats from spurious or idle ones, as well as pranks. Additionally, we will not hesitate to call in the bureau's operatives if the job becomes too sophisticated for local analysis.

I therefore recommend that the Secret Service be warned to be extra vigilant in watching over POTUS as our investigation proceeds. Locally, immediate action will be taken to investigate, arrest, or detain the perpetrator of this threat, and to conduct a skilled interrogation to discover how serious the threat was, and whether the perpetrator acted alone or whether there are others involved in a conspiracy. This may involve "rounding up the usual suspects," as well as more extraordinary actions to ensure public safety, at least for the present, but as you, yourself, have said, "Unusual times require unusual measures."

I have run into a minor snag in my countermeasures, however, and would like advice as to how to proceed. As a first step, I immediately attempted to enlist the library's cooperation in helping us find the perpetrator of this clear threat by calling us as soon as he or she shows up again to use the Internet computers. Disturbingly, I encountered resistance against this goal, however. The library disclaims responsibility for the content of messages sent or received on their Internet terminals, and, furthermore, Ms. Rhoades reported that her staff will not spy on citizens. She added that she and her hard-working reference staff haven't the time to monitor every

Internet user and every transaction, in addition to being worried about the various privacy and civil rights issues involved in such surveillance.

At my request, she allowed me to hold a brief special all-staff meeting anyway, which was held this morning at the downtown library. After introducing myself, I formally requested that all reference librarians and clerks cooperate in all ways possible with our investigation, including making regular rounds behind Internet terminals, then ascertaining, to the extent possible, what people are reading or looking at, and—should any suspicious activity be observed—calling the FBI's local hotline immediately.

In furtherance of my requests, I passed out business cards to everyone present and urged them to report anything suspicious, no matter how trivial or unimportant it might seem. In parting, I thanked them in advance for their cooperation and said that the bureau has every confidence that the library staff will be active partners in tracking down any persons in the community who intend or threaten to use violence to make political statements.

I hope that I have not overstepped my authority here, but, in view of the clear and present danger presented by the threatening message, I have ordered Ms. Rhoades and her staff to "keep an eye" on all Internet users for us. I was tactful; rather than threatening anyone who did not comply with charges of obstruction of justice, I attempted to appeal instead to their desire to prevent violent acts, as well as their sense of patriotism and civic pride.

Despite my attempt at persuasiveness, there was more resistance on the part of the library staff. Several said that what I was asking them to do amounted to spying on their patrons, and they were not comfortable with that. They cited librarians' principles of intellectual freedom and privacy for their patrons, and one or two even refused to comply with my directive. Finally, growing impatient, I cited the tragedy that took place in Dallas, not far away, 40 years ago, and asked them how they would feel if such a tragedy occurred here in Pecan Grove, especially if they might have helped prevent it but declined because of abstract principles of intellectual freedom and civil rights. Thinking about that seemed to sway some of them, but, I fear, not all of them.

We have thus ordered full cooperation from all library personnel in helping us to apprehend the criminal who sent the threatening message to the White House yesterday. Any staff who flout our order and are caught doing so may be punished for obstruction of justice. I pray that it won't come to that, but you never know.

Given the nature of the threat, I took the action I did because I judge this problem to be gravely serious. I shall keep the bureau continually informed on any developments, and my staff and I pledge to be all over this matter until the perpetrator of the threatening message is caught and off the streets. I shall personally supply the bureau with daily progress reports, and I predict confidently that we will find this deranged individual and put him or her out of business before any tragedy or loss of human life can ensue. In the unlikely event that we are unsuccessful in closing this case by next month, however, you will doubtless advise the White House that the bureau cannot recommend that the president's trip to Pecan Grove go forward as planned.

Questions for Discussion

1. What are the implications for personal privacy when a library requires Internet users to provide and leave a photo ID or other proof of identity?

2. Would you, as head of reference, assist the FBI in tracking down and apprehending the perpetrator of death threats, even if it means "spying" on patrons?

3. If you refuse to cooperate because of privacy and freedom issues, how would you justify such a refusal to the FBI?

Case 25 _____

Just Paperweights

Andrea Meeden, Webmaster, to Paul Holser, head of technical services by telephone

Paul, the repair guy from the computer company was just here, while you were in your meeting, and to put it bluntly, the news isn't good. Forgive me if I'm belaboring the obvious, but once a virus gets into one computer in a network, it spreads—like a human virus—to all the rest, unless immediate remedial steps are taken to contain the damage.

Well, unfortunately, such steps were not taken in time this weekend. It's nobody's fault, at least nobody on the library's staff, but we still have a problem of major proportions that we need to discuss. In my view, it's mainly because the city refused to heed my repeated warnings and vetoed my proposal that we purchase and install a new firewall system.

Who's sorry now?

Here's what I think happened, although I can't be absolutely certain. Every morning, one of our Reference clerks comes in early, turns on each Internet-equipped terminal, runs its diagnostic programs, and waits until the operating system reaches the "Welcome to the Pecan Grove Public Library!" screen, indicating that the terminal is ready for use. This procedure has worked well enough for a long time, day in and day out, and it worked on Friday morning as well, at least for most of the machines. But when terminal number 14 switched over from the welcome screen, the clerk told me that the usual symbols and wallpaper were nowhere to be found. Instead, the computer's screen consisted of a depthless, blue-sky background.

When I got there and verified the problem, I guess I said something stupid like, "What the . . ?" Then I started troubleshooting, checking the usual problems. The machine was clearly turned on, the power light was glowing, and I could hear the fan in the back whirring away. I tried restarting, but the same screen appeared. So I took the machine back to my desk for a check. I rebooted and even shut the power off and on again maybe half a dozen times, but I only saw that blue sky and nothing else that would suggest that lurking somewhere in the guts of the computer was the usual organized hierarchy of folders, files, and gateways to more information. Frustrating!

I tried again and again, until finally, reluctantly, I had to admit defeat. For whatever reason, terminal number 14, while the others continued to work perfectly, failed to boot up its operating system. Suddenly, unaccountably, there was nobody home. *Tabula rasa*. Blank screen, no matter what I tried. Now you know me: I may get frustrated, but I love a good challenge, so before I made a call to our service provider, I went out front to see if any of the other terminals were affected.

At random, I sat down at terminal number 6 and established to my satisfaction that it was running normally. I clicked on a few icons at random and got into one of the Internet search engines, just to satisfy myself that everything was normal. Still curious, I tried three others, also at random, and had no difficulty getting them to go through their paces either. That convinced me that the difficulty—while puzzling—was at least confined to only one machine. Didn't seem like any kind of spreading virus, at that point. At least the problem was contained. All in all, I figured, it could have been a whole hell of a lot worse.

When I got back to my desk, I still wasn't ready to concede defeat. So I tried everything I could think of to make number 14 behave, but nothing helped. Among other hopeful remedies, I tried turning off the machine and then on again, unplugging it and then plugging it back in; unplugging the keyboard cable, and the mouse connector, not because I really thought it would do any good, but because I was desperate and figured it couldn't hurt. And it *didn't* . . . hurt, I mean. I even tried talking to the machine, first in a cajoling voice and then threatening to send it to the city dump. But whatever I did, the screen adamantly, infuriatingly continued to show pure blue. No files. No applications. No Internet icon. Nada. Just blue.

Still, at this point, I didn't see it as all that much of a problem. I went back out front, placed an "in the shop for scheduled maintenance" sign on the dust-ringed spot where the computer had sat, then, once back at the afflicted machine, I shut if off. Finally defeated, I made a service call to the computer company that installs and services our computers under our annual contract. I still wasn't alarmed. I figured that when you have all those terminals, and one goes down, it's no biggie. After all, 15 out of 16 ain't bad, right? It's a decent percentage, wouldn't you say? Even though we've become a busy public Internet access center, the difference between being able to have 16 users online and 15 is only about a six percent reduction in service capacity, and besides, whatever was wrong seemed like a minor and temporary glitch in an otherwise routine day.

Let me tell you what I think: I've been using computers on a routine basis for the past 25 years, and I still think the remarkable thing is not that one of them breaks down from time to time but rather that so many of them continue to work perfectly. It's like a story I know about a dog who reputedly was taught to play chess. When observers criticized the dog for losing a few games, his owner turned to the critics and said, "You miss the point: What's remarkable is not whether my dog wins or loses at chess, it's that he can do it *at all* that counts." And that is my point: When 15 out of 16 computers are running hot and normal all day, and just one is "sick," I'd rather point with pride to the healthy ones than lambaste the manufacturers or programmers because one of them crashed.

So, like I said, Friday, I called the contract service and asked them to put a priority rush on a site visit. Unfortunately, the woman I talked to said something mysterious about how "a lot of this stuff was going around," like we were discussing the flu or something. I guess in a way, we were, actually. She said a technician couldn't come out until Monday, so there was nothing to do but wait.

But today, Monday, I got another nasty surprise, much worse than the one that hit me Friday. Saturday, the same clerk went up one aisle and down another before opening time, turning on all the terminals in the Internet bay, but this time, to her growing alarm, all of the remaining ones that had worked fine on Friday had gone the way of their sibling. Each and every one of them revealed only blue, yawning space where icons had been only a few days before. How's that for a way to start off the weekend?

This morning, when I drove into the parking lot, I didn't even get a chance to get out of my car with my cup of fancy coffee. The Reference clerk came rushing out to meet me—and from the way she was running, I could tell that either someone had died or that there was a computer problem even worse than the previous one. I knew something was up, because in the two years she'd been working here, she'd never done anything like that before. One look at her face told me that we had big-time trouble. She confirmed my intuition in a few breathless sentences.

"Andrea? Remember the trouble with terminal number 14 on Friday?"

"Sure do. Why, what's up?" I asked, fighting down my alarm.

"Well, I hope I'm wrong about this, but it looks as though *all* the Internet terminals have come down with the same virus or whatever that number 14 had. Now there's a double row of blank screens, and I'm guessing whatever the first one had is catching and has spread throughout them all."

"Calm down!" I said. "Let me have a look." We walked inside together.

Once inside, I hastily removed my coat, bolted the last of my cooling coffee, pitched the empty paper cup into the wastebasket 20 feet away— nothing but net—and walked quickly around to Reference and the banks of terminals only to discover that what I'd heard was true. To tell you the truth, I didn't need visual confirmation; I'd known already from the look on that kid's face and the shake in her voice. Big-time trouble.

As of this morning, we have on our hands a crisis of major proportion. That's no exaggeration. After all, it's one thing to have a down terminal, or even two or three. But *all* of them displaying blank screens? Crisis. They've all been wiped clean, somehow, by something—a virus, a computer glitch, an act of God, who knows? As you can appreciate, not having Internet access for the public nowadays is just not an option for a library. What it means is that, as a community information center offering our patrons free Internet service, we are *toast!* Put simply, as an Internet facility, we're—temporarily at least—out of business. For now, all of our Internet machines have become little more than paperweights.

Hell of a way to start off a week, isn't it? I hate to be the bringer of bad news, but here's my report: Every public access terminal in the place is now *kaput.* There is one bit of better news, though: this morning, I walked into the administrative office to report the problem and was relieved to see Karen, the secretary, word processing away. It seems that her computer—and the rest in the administration suite—are completely unaffected by whatever horrible thing has descended on our public Internet terminals.

What accounts for the difference? My guess is that the difference is that the public computers are all linked together on the same LAN or network, while the office computers are standalone, and so escaped the fate of the public machines. Thank the Lord for that anyway! But the problem remains that we have no Internet access computers to offer our demanding public, and worse yet, no real explanation for what's happened to them. "Some sinister force" as an explanation, probably isn't going to get the job done.

Well, when I realized how bad things were this morning, I sort of dithered around in a highly agitated state for a while. But before the library opened and patrons began to come in, I posted signs at the entrance to the computer bay, informing the public that—temporarily—no Internet service would be available.

Some of them grumbled, as you might expect. There was one kid who said he had taken the bus all the way downtown to use a library computer instead of going to school today. Too bad. He's not a happy camper, to say the least. One irate woman promised to send a strongly worded letter to the mayor concerning taxing citizens for services and then not delivering those services. As the "techie" in charge, I seem to be blamable, so people blame me. I defended myself—and my balky machines—as best I could until the repairman could arrive.

Finally, at 10:45, today, Fred, the uniformed technician from XYZ Solutions strolled into the library, expecting to have to jump start just one machine. He seemed genuinely surprised to find out that it was all of them he'd be dealing with. I led him to the computer bay and showed him the problem, and after he opened his enormous tool box, revealing a very impressive array of utensils, ranging from replacement disks and diagnostic readouts to screwdrivers and socket wrenches, he told me he'd appreciate it if I didn't hang around and kibitz but would busy myself elsewhere and let him do his job. So I came here to report. I can take a hint; besides, I have plenty to do in the back.

Twenty minutes later, Fred found me, and with a shrug and a grin, he said, "Listen, lady, I'm telling you what you got here is the kind of virus that chicken soup isn't going to fix." He elaborated, of course, adding that once one of those hellish things gets into one terminal on a network, it starts replicating itself at a dizzying pace, and it'll spread its virus throughout all the other members in a nanosceond. Worse yet, he said, by the time you notice it, unless you're really lucky, it's usually too late to do anything about it, except cry, and promise to do a better job of guarding against such things the next time.

Half an hour later, he left, saying he'd consult "headquarters" and get back to me later today. So here I am, waiting. At this juncture, by accident or on purpose, someone or something has taken down our entire public computer system. Who? Why? Your guess is as good as mine. But that's almost beside the point, isn't it? The end result is that this library is now the proud possessor of two rows of gleaming paperweights, until further notice.

And if the efforts of Fred, the XYZ technician, don't manage to restore what we've lost, well, then we could have a riot on our hands with zero Internet access for our patrons. But it's XYZ's problem, now. All we can do is wait and hope. My question isn't really so much how did this happen, but rather, how could this have been prevented? Also, when we get our system restored, how can we keep such a thing from happening again?

Questions for Discussion

1. How can a library protect against people opening programs, inserting viruses, and going away, leaving the computer "sick" and unable to function?

2. How can a virus in one computer be prevented from spreading from one machine to another until all are affected?

3. How can public access Internet terminals be fitted with safeguards to prevent future incidences of this type?

Case 26

She Said/He Said

Steve Glass, reference librarian, to Apollo Joven, head of circulation, in the break room.

Wait 'til I tell you what happened today. It'll knock your socks off. You know, working in a library is not like being a beat cop or anything, but my job has its occasional share of drama, let me tell you. I mean, a public library, by definition, is a public place, meaning that all sorts of people can come in and use our services. And they do, *oh Lordy,* they do! You know this as well as I do.

We get students looking for a quiet place to do homework, and homemakers who need a good read when the kids are down for their afternoon nap, and of course, the business community. We get priests and ministers and rabbis and even mullahs in here. Doctoral students and high school dropouts. And our share of strange ones, too: you've seen the sort of people who walk, stride, crawl, stumble, or slither through our doors. Bums. Vagrants. The homeless. Criminals, sometimes, looking to find an open purse or a wallet unguarded.

But this morning, we had the kind of patron I really hate: a flasher. Your basic exhibitionist. At least this lady who came out of the stacks in hysterics, screaming like crazy, *said* he flashed her.

He denied it, of course.

Who was he? Well, Matt the guard calls him Walter. There's nothing particularly unusual about him. He's maybe 5 foot 6 and wears thick glasses, with duct tape holding the frames together. Wears different things, different times of the year, but certainly never the kind of raincoat or trench coat I always imagine a flasher to have on. Today, maybe because it's summertime and hot out, he had on some kind of Hawaiian shirt. You know: loud colors, big patterns. Pants, of course, but I didn't really notice what kind he had on. Gotta work on being more observant, I guess.

So anyway, just after opening time, when I unlocked the front doors and turned on the electronic foot treadle gizmo for the "in" door, he was the first one to walk in. Sometimes there are a lot of people waiting outside for us to let 'em in, and when I'm late opening up, I get complaints. Especially when the weather isn't nice, like on cold days, or rainy mornings. But this morning was warm and muggy and I made sure that I unlocked the doors for the four or five people milling around outside the front door at 9:00 A.M. on the dot. Technically, that shouldn't be one of my duties, at all. I mean, I'm a professional—with a master's degree from an accredited program of library and information studies. But hey, somebody's gotta do it, so I'm elected.

Where was I? Oh, yeah, this morning. Walter in the Hawaiian shirt. At 9:00 sharp, I unlocked the doors, stepped back, and maybe half a dozen people strolled in. First among them was Walter. Today, like always, he was wearing a baseball cap, that loud Hawaiian shirt (I hate those things, but they must be popular, you see them everywhere), and non-descript slacks and shoes. Certainly, he had none of the fevered look we tend to associate with flashers. You know: sweaty face, nervous, darting eyes, averted gaze. Actually, when I stepped back from the door, he smiled—a kind of friendly smile—and said, "Morning!" as he walked past me, turned right, and wandered out into the stacks. Just planning to while away the hours reading, I guess. Or so I thought. Turns out, he was interested in something else, from what this lady says, but before today, who knew?

One thing I learned from the police report was that if he actually did what she said, he was not a previous offender. Unless he had just moved to town, this guy had never been booked or run through the system for flashing, peeping, aggravated sexual assault, pedophilia, or anything like that. And what he's accused of doing, by the way, isn't consistent with the standard flasher incident you read about in the papers. I mean, the typical flasher waits for a victim, usually female, often young, then chooses his moment, does something like clear his throat to draw attention to himself, and then, uh, well, exposes himself. Fear is what he wants. Fear and loathing, I guess. For some perverted guys, that sort of thing must be a turn-on.

But not this Walter. I don't think what he's supposed to have done—while clearly illegal and beyond the limits of acceptable behavior—was premeditated. In a weird way, it's even possible that the woman precipitated the whole thing. But she was extremely insistent. One thing this job has taught me is that there are people—some of 'em normal looking—who walk among us with, I don't know, bad chemicals in their heads or faulty wiring, maybe. And when something upsets or compels them, they just act out. So that's what Walter did, according to the distraught lady. He acted out. The operative word is *out*.

Here's what our complainant said: About quarter past nine, she came into the library, looking for some books on gardening. She came to my desk first—I remember her—pleasant looking, fortyish, blonde hair with streaks or highlights. She asked me to point her toward books on gardening. I gave her the Dewey numbers for such titles, and directed her to the back stack area where we keep them. After she disappeared into the stacks, she also disappeared from my mind, because I took a call from somebody wanting some information on building permits, and I got seriously busy. Had to really concentrate.

Fifteen minutes later, when she came out crying, she said that in the stacks, she became aware that a man in the next aisle was humming off-key, very loudly. But not any kind of tune she recognized. Just humming, loudly. She decided to ignore it, as she browsed through the range of books on gardening, but when the humming got even louder, she decided to walk over and ask the hummer—as politely as she could—to hold it down, so that she could think. So she did. Politely, she said.

But apparently her request enraged Walter who began shouting at her that it was a free country and a free library, and if he wanted to hum, he'd hum all he wanted. The lady says she quickly decided that starting a confrontation in the dim stacks far from the front of the building with a rude man was probably not a good idea. But she couldn't resist passing one more remark. As she walked back around the stack to the adjacent aisle (looking at a book she held in her hand and not at Walter), she admits that she said one more word: "Jerk!" I mean, I'm not a part of this, and I wasn't there, but it seems like she was entitled to say such a thing. When a person is being a jerk, it's not forbidden to say so, is it?

She told me that after she said that, Walter started humming even louder. So she decided to just grab some books and bring them out to the front where she'd be away from him. But she had to choose which ones to bring out, and as she was engrossed in a description of organic flower growing, she was suddenly horrified to discover that Walter had followed her around the stack aisle, unzipped his fly, and waved himself, right in her face, saying, with a grin, "Yo, lady! Jerk *this!*" I know . . . it isn't funny, really, but it's just so . . . well, you know . . .

Needless to say, the poor woman didn't stick around. No, she came flying out of the stacks, sobbing and breathless, rushed over and told me what happened. For a while, I couldn't understand what she was trying to say, but when I got the idea, I told her to wait, and eased into the stacks in the hopes of catching this guy in the act of . . . well, whatever it was he was doing. But when I got there, there was Walter as she'd described him, reading a book, and humming quietly to himself.

When I walked over to him he looked genuinely startled. I asked what he was doing and he said, "As you can see, I'm reading a book. What makes you ask? Is there a problem, here?" I took a moment and noticed that he was all zipped up, whatever that's good for. I stood there for a while longer, trying to decide how to describe the problem as related to me by that visibly upset and shaken woman. Finally, I opted for the truth. In my experience, artful dissembling might work for other people, but the truth works for me almost every time.

"Lady out there says you exposed yourself to her, just now, buddy. Any truth in that?" I watched him carefully, and saw surprise, shock, and slowly building outrage flash over his face. He took off his glasses and wiped them carefully on a red patterned handkerchief that he took out of his back pocket.

"Unbelievable!" he said. "Why on earth would I do a thing like that? She's crazy, man! Crazy or a liar, one. I was just scratching myself, is all. Ain't that allowed?" I stared at him.

"I'm just telling you what she said. Now let me ask you something else: why would she make up a story like that? Right now, she's out there, trembling and acting really shaken. I can't figure out why she'd invent such a story, can you?"

"Beats me. I don't know what she's talking about," said the little guy. "I shouldn't dignify such accusations with a response, but I have nothing to hide. If somebody did do that to her, you got the wrong guy. No way I'd do that sort of thing in a library, or anywhere else. What would I get out of it?"

"So you deny it, then?" I asked, just for confirmation.

"Deny it? Certainly, I deny it! Categorically, I deny it. Tell me, did that lady say I, you know, molested her in any way? She talking attempted rape? Taking liberties?"

"Not exactly," I said. "She just says you exposed yourself and scared the bejabbers out of her. That's why I haven't called the cops . . . yet. I wanted to hear your side of the story before I decided what to do next." Walter grinned at me.

"Well, do me a favor and tell that lady out there that she ought to quit smoking those funny little brown cigarettes before breakfast. Hallucinating, that's what she's doing. She's made the whole thing up, I tell you. But tell her I don't need an apology, just tell her to leave me alone. That way, we can all get on with our day."

I was getting exasperated, because I knew the woman wasn't going to be happy if I told her to forget about it. "Look, are you sure you didn't, oh, I don't know, accidentally forget to zip up after using the men's room, and she misinterpreted your intentions, or something?" To my surprise, I found that I was trying to invent plausible explanations for his alleged behavior. At that point, I just wanted the whole sordid business to go away.

"Tell you what," said the little guy in the shirt printed with hula girls and palm trees. "Bring her out here. Or I'll come there, whatever you want. Let her repeat what she told you to my face in front of witnesses. Then I can sue her for slander. Yeah, I'll get a high-priced lawyer working for me on contingency, and I should be able to pick up enough money from winning my case to spend next winter in Hawaii or Jamaica or someplace." I shook my head.

"I don't think she wants to be anywhere near you, so that's not going to work." We were at an impasse, so finally, I went back out to the Reference room where I found the woman seated as far from the stack entrance as she could get, and called the police, just to make an official report about the situation. Here's the gist of the conversation I had with the desk sergeant on duty yesterday. I'm not condemning him, or accusing the police of indifference, but, well, you decide.

"Pecan Grove Police, Central Precinct. Sergeant Reilly speaking. How can I help you?" he answered.

"Good morning, Sergeant. This is Steve Glass over at the Main Library. I need to report a suspected flasher back in our stacks. Can you send an officer over to investigate?"

"Let me get some information, first, all right? You say you have a flasher? So what's he doing, your flasher, at this moment?"

"Well, that's the problem. A female patron came running out of the stacks screaming that the man had exposed himself to her, but when I went to investigate, the guy was just sitting there, all buttoned up, and reading books."

"A-ha! I see. Reading books, is he? Sounds pretty dangerous. What kind of weirdo goes to a library and reads books, I wonder?" I could have done without the sarcasm, but I remained silent. "And what, specifically, did the woman say he did to her?" asked the amused sergeant.

"She says that, in the course of an argument, he unzipped his pants and flashed her."

"Go on. What else? Did he touch her? Assault her? Grab her purse? Try to get up close and personal with her? Give me all the salacious details."

"No, she didn't say that, but she insists that he did what I just told you, and she wants something done about it. Come on, Sergeant, isn't that a crime?"

The cop sighed deeply. "Well, there are crimes and there are crimes, know what I mean? Look, pal, you have any idea how many homicides get committed in this city every year? Care to hazard a guess?"

"No," I muttered. "Couldn't tell you. Too many, though."

"You got that right. And don't forget rapes, robberies, burglaries, drive-bys, drug busts, bar fights, race riots, and other forms of assault. You following me, so far?"

"Yes, but . . ." He went on like he was explaining something to a young, slow child.

"So with all the serious crime we got to fight in this city, together with the fact that the taxpayers voted down an increase in the police budget last year, I'm sure you can see that we have to assign higher priority to serious crimes like the ones I just mentioned, and a much lower priority to stuff, like, oh, say, shoplifting, jaywalking, watering your lawn during drought conditions, and . . . can you guess?"

"Exhibitionists?" I supplied on cue.

The sergeant laughed. "Now you're getting it. You're a bright boy. I like that. Why do you work in a library? Have you ever considered a career in law enforcement?" I was getting exasperated.

"So, bottom line, you're not going to do anything about this guy?"

"Did I say that?"

"Not in so many words, but . . ."

"From the way you describe the situation, this guy allegedly exposed himself to a lady, but now everything is all safely tucked away and he's just reading and humming to himself. Do I have it right?" My turn to sigh now.

"I guess so, but what do I tell the woman? That you're not going to take any action on her complaint?"

"Tell her that we'll investigate," the sergeant said. "Look, we're having a pretty busy morning fighting crime, here. A stabbing, already, an ongoing investigation of a murder, and an apparent suicide. But, tell you what. I'll send an officer around after lunch to take the lady's statement if she's still there, and the suspect's, if *he's* still there, and of course, yours. That's about all I can do for you at this point. Unless there's an emergency, of course. That gets to the head of the priority list. So, are you reporting an emergency?"

I asked him to hold the phone a moment while I scurried back out to the stacks. Walter was sitting quietly at his reading table, several books in front of him, making no moves toward anyone else. I watched for a moment or two, but the only physical thing he did was moisten a finger and turn a page. He was humming, but it didn't seem to be too loud, and anyway, humming isn't mentioned in our list of unacceptable conduct. Objectionable language, yes! Humming, no. We might want to talk that over at the next staff meeting. So I left and trotted back to the telephone.

"No, sergeant. No emergency."

"Look, son," the sergeant's voice took on a kindly, fatherly tone, "you're probably new at this. After a couple of years, you'll develop a sixth sense for who's a real threat and who's just being a nuisance. This guy sounds like a nuisance, even if he did choose a rather dramatic—and illegal—means of making his point. But you can expect an officer to come over there in about an hour, give or take, and he'll take statements from everyone who's a party to this incident. Sorry, that's the best I can do."

Sighing, I thanked him and hung up the phone. Then I went over to the woman and explained the situation. She agreed to wait around, but I noticed that she was keeping one eye on the stack entrance. Then, I occupied myself with other matters, as best I could. A full *three* hours later, a large street cop walked into the library and asked for me, but I had nothing to tell him. By then, the lady and Walter, the possible perpetrator, were both long gone, and it was just a normal, quiet afternoon in a public library. Ho-hum.

The way I see it, the problem of someone accusing someone else of flashing is one of evidence. Got to catch criminals in the act, or it doesn't work. A hidden camera or something—that'd do the trick. Besides, I don't think Walter is really a criminal. Poor impulse control, perhaps, but he doesn't seem like a sexual predator or anything. He's never touched anyone inappropriately, to my knowledge. Just seems to act out when he's feeling hassled, or maybe he just likes that sort of attention. Sick? Possibly. But criminal? I don't know. What a world. But I'll keep an eye on Walter from now on—I've got his face memorized. Next time, he's in here, I'll point him out to you, too. I suppose the sergeant was right: working in an urban public library comes with its own set of problems. What're you gonna do?

Questions for Discussion

1. How can a library try to discourage exhibitionists from displaying themselves to others?

2. When it's a case of she said/he said, how much responsibility is there on a library employee to figure out who's telling the truth?

3. How can the library best cultivate good relations with local police so that officers will take incident report calls seriously and act speedily?

Case 27

Sieg Heil! or Whatever

Steve Glass, reference librarian/electronic services, to Carole Miller, vice mayor, City of Pecan Grove, via telephone

I have never been very keen on the idea of filters imposed on Internet computers. Too much Big Brother government intrusion into people's freedoms, if you ask me. Besides, as a librarian, I stand opposed to any form of de facto censorship. And I know that you feel the same way. Great minds, and all that. We share the belief that in order to have the freedoms Americans hold dear and to comply with the simple provisions of the First Amendment to the Constitution, it's necessary to leave our patrons pretty much alone when they go searching for information on the Web, wherever it takes them. Restrictions on Web searching should come from parents, not civil authorities.

That said, I need to add that I do recognize the need for certain limits on freedom, and our recent "Nazi" incident definitely demonstrates that need.

A contradiction? Maybe, but I still believe that censorship of the Internet is a matter between kids and their parents and not a role that we librarians should be asked to play. Yeah, it's true; there are abuses. Every once in a while, somebody uses one of our terminals to go on the Web to access pornography (no, don't ask me to define that term, but like that judge said, I know it when I see it). But there's no earthly way that we could—even if we wanted to—monitor the activities of every user sitting at every terminal to make sure that their Web searching meets some arbitrary standard of decency, or whatever you want to call it.

Still, I'm willing to admit that I was shocked to have discovered today that some hate-filled member of the community (or maybe a whole cell of them, who knows?) has been coming in here to run a Web site that advocates and promotes nazism, anti-Semitism, racism, genocide, and hate. We need to find out who it is and put those sick puppies (assuming it's more than one misguided wretch) out of business, at least as far as library use is concerned.

Yeah, I know: cracking down on these bigots violates the First Amendment—the one I just cited in defense of leaving people alone to pursue avenues of investigation freely without government interference. So I contradict myself. Sue me.

I agree that nobody wants to have this community equating our free library, and its policies and actions, with those of the Ministry of Truth in Orwell's *1984*. Remember that book? But should the First Amendment be interpreted as offering protected access to porn sites, hate sites, and even kiddie porn? I don't think so. Freedom is a double-edged sword, wouldn't you agree?

Here's what we know: Someone (and again, it may be more than one person) has been using our library's Internet terminals to enter hate speech chat rooms; contact like-minded, maladjusted people elsewhere; and, most significantly, to operate a Nazi propaganda Web site out of this building under our very noses without us knowing anything about it . . . until now.

I first learned of what was going on last week, when a patron happened to look over at his neighbor's monitor and saw what was there. He said that the bright red and black swastika filled the screen, so it was hard to miss. Once I was alerted to the problem, I did some unobtrusive surveillance and found several other people doing the same thing—at least looking at sites where the swastika was prominent, anyway. So I waited until one patron left, did a recovery routine on his terminal, and found a page of Nazi propaganda so vicious that it sent chills up and down my spine. Not just political stuff—this site actually advocated killing certain groups of Americans and seizing power.

Maybe now you see why I say that, without our knowledge, our library has become de facto state Nazi Party headquarters. The return address for the site is our own building, a clickable link entitled, "How to contact us." Our library! You should come over here and see the artwork, if that's what you would call it: swastikas everywhere; photographs of Hitler on almost every page, arm raised to salute screaming crowds; and cartoons that first appeared in a newspaper in Germany back in the 1930s, showing caricatures of Jews with big, hooked noses trying to degrade and debase Aryan children. Disgusting. Some are more recent, American images: a big Nazi banner in a parade carried by a pair of brown-shirted thugs that says in English, but in Germanic lettering, "Hitler was Right!"

Remember: these images are mounted on a Web site that uses our library as a mail drop. There are hundreds of others: disgusting caricatures of Jews, Poles, gypsies, and others targeted for concentration camps and eventual extinction by the Nazis before and during World War II, and the list goes on and on in sickening detail. These twisted people don't spare African-Americans, Hispanics, Arabs, or gays from their jeering depictions, either.

It's clear that the American Nazis hate everybody who isn't like them! The worst part is that every post that gets sent by our anonymous bargain-basement fuehrer ends with a call for new members, financial support, and enlistment in the cause: the use of any means necessary to purify *AmeriKa* (they spell it with a *K)* of mongrel races and to preserve the purity of white people, which they call the only superior strain of humanity. Amazing what filth flows from such disordered and hate-filled minds, isn't it?

Just blowing off steam? Idle talk? Possibly, but I don't think so. Think back . . . in the past few years, several local synagogues have been desecrated and churches of various denominations have been spray painted with swastikas. Some other groups' religious services have even been disrupted by gangs of thugs and rowdies, bent on destruction and intimidation. So it isn't just speech we have to worry about. You know that old saying, Actions speak louder than words? These guys believe that, too, evidently. What frightens me is that other vandals and destructive delinquents out there might get inspired by Web sites like the one I've discovered right in our own public library. So should we allow it to continue? You tell me, but I think not.

Well, there's a lot more to tell, but I only had 10 minutes to talk to you, so I hit you with the headlines first. Solutions? Here's what I think should be done, but we'll need the city's approval before we can move forward with any plan, which is why I called you about it. First, we need to do what we can to shut down the Nazi Web site immediately, then we need to ban the perpetrators of this dangerous hate speech and other filth from our library. Extreme? Well, I don't know about that. Think about the "clear and present danger" provision of the Supreme Court's decisions on censorship.

I say letting Nazis and other hate mongers spread their calls to violence and solicitations for new members constitutes clear and present danger to a lot of people. Sure, maybe we ought to do something about pornography sites, as well, but it works better to tackle one problem at a time, and these Nazi punks are priority one. At least they are for me. My family's Jewish, as you know, so I'd be affected immediately and personally, if these bozos ever came to power.

The problem is that when we find out who's been doing this, they'll probably turn out to be American citizens, who, of course, enjoy and can claim rights and freedoms under the Constitution. We're going to have to tread very carefully in seeking to deprive them of their privileges. There are several pertinent legal issues, in fact, and we're going to seek legal advice from the city attorney before we take any action. But I have prepared a rough agenda of first steps for your approval. Let me run these ideas by you.

First, we need to identify the person or persons running the Nazi Web site out of our library. I have several suspects, but no names and no absolute proof yet. This investigation may entail a good bit of surveillance, even if the thought of walking around behind our Internet users and, well, spying on them is sort of distasteful, and possibly even risky— you can never tell. These guys could be armed, so it'd be nice if some plainclothes police were detailed to help in this, just temporarily, as back-up. Might be trouble when we roust these guys, who knows?

Next, when the authorities deal with members of this group, it might look like we are taking a selective approach to the confidentiality and privacy of our patrons. We will need to handle the public relations fallout carefully. That's going to be troublesome, and we're going to need your help. But I hope you agree that there's a need to put this Web site out of business or at least to get its point of origin out of our library. Now, I may be overstating my case, but I see clamping down on the Nazis in our midst in the same way as rooting out the confederates of the terrorists who blew up the World Trade Center. The right to strike pre-emptively at terrorists trumps issues of privacy.

Finally, we need to establish some specific guidelines for appropriateness of Internet use on library terminals without appearing to be pro-censorship. This could be the hardest thing of all to accomplish.

Please understand, I'm not advocating filters on all of our public Internet computers. That would be going too far. I've read about people who couldn't access information about breast cancer because the word *breast* was filtered, and one guy who complained that he couldn't access information about Super Bowl XXX because of all those exes (which pornographers often use to advertise sexually oriented materials on the Web). But with or without filters, something needs to be done to prevent this problem from recurring before it's too late!

I realize that some of the things I'm recommending might present headaches and even lawsuits for the city; not just the library. That's why I called you before taking any action. But to my mind, we can't just permit these maladjusted hate spewers to use our library to promulgate their views and agenda. So if you don't specifically forbid us to go forward with our plans, we're going to spring into action starting today. If we let everyone with a cause or a grievance use our Internet terminals to recruit for membership in their hate groups, we are, in a very real sense, I think, sanctioning terrorism by our inaction. And I say that just can't be allowed. What's your take on this?

Questions for Discussion

1. What are the differences between a patron accessing a Web site from one of the library's Internet terminals dealing in such things as bears, orchids, bundt cakes, and "Elvis Lives" fan clubs, and one that promotes Nazi propaganda?

2. Does a person who comes to the library to access or disseminate hate speech and calls for genocide have the same rights as one who merely comes in to use the Internet to look for information?

3. If the perpetrator of the Nazi site is caught in the act, what should the library administration do?

Case 28

Who Watches the Watchers?

Ann Cameron Bowman, library director, to Pat Sanchez, city manager, at city hall

Pat, I know city government is concerned about security in our library, and I'm grateful that you have taken such a personal interest in our problems and have called me in to discuss them. Let me give you a status report on our security upgrades, to bring you up to speed on both the improvements that we've made recently and the challenges and problems still facing us.

I think you'll be pleased that we've upgraded our security without having to spend inordinate amounts of additional money, which is the neatest trick of the week. I mean, with a hefty budget increase, or a grant, or some earmarked funds for security purposes, sure, it'd be a piece of cake. But without any additional funds, well, I'm proud of what we have accomplished, even if big challenges still lie before us.

To begin with, we've installed new technologies that make breaches of security much more time-consuming and harder for the bad guys out there who might want to do disruptive things to the library, for whatever reason. There are new surveillance cameras (although just between us, except at the front desk, we don't always have film in the cameras, or personnel to watch the film).

Also, we've equipped all doors to the outside with alarms, and most of the building's windows are alarmed. Motion detectors, operating automatically at night, alert the police station two blocks away whenever there is an unauthorized entry. Finally, we have competent security guards on duty from noon to closing every day. It'd be nice to say that we're covered *whenever* the library is open for business, but we're grateful for what security there is. (Some libraries, we know—even three of our own branches—make do without any security guards, whatsoever.)

Our next year's budget requests a fairly large increase in funding for library security, which we hope the city council will take to heart and consider with an open mind. I don't have to tell you about the well-publicized incidents that have taken place in our buildings over the years, and we're well aware of what could happen if people with evil intent decide to use the library to do their violent deeds. Speaking of violent deeds, I would like to remind you gently of the incidents that have occurred in our library in the past year, incidents that take place almost always in public areas, where innocent people can be suddenly thrust into harm's way. There were

- No murders, at least this year (so much for the good news).

- One stabbing with a knife (thankfully, just a wound in the arm).

- One attempted choking of one patron by another, ending with the arrest of the aggressor.

- Numerous occasions of suspected or witnessed drug sale or abuse, including an apparent drug overdose in the ladies room of the downtown library.

- Six fist fights or assaults with fists.

- One patron slapped by another (nothing hurt but some dignity).

- Two counts of attempted arson (neither coming to much).

- One apparent suicide by a deranged man with a history of severe mental problems, who swallowed a whole bottle of tranquilizer pills at one go and then went quietly off to sleep.

- Two muggings; one inside the main building, the other outside on the library grounds. Three other muggings in or near the Lakewood branch.

- Numerous stolen items of apparel or personal belongings, including a fur coat and a gym bag containing cross-trainer athletic shoes.

- Many wallets or purses reported stolen.

- Three reports of men exposing themselves to women or girls in the stacks or reading rooms.

- One attempted sexual assault (the inappropriate laying on of hands).

- A reported stalker (who kept staring at a young female employee).

- Countless cases of verbal abuse of other patrons or of library staff.

- Obscene or threatening telephone calls (causing fear and anxiety in female staff members).

I guess that's the lot, at least of incidents that were reported. Such a list of crimes and other offenses probably pales in comparison with a similar list of incidents down at any corner bar, but remember: we need people to think of the public library as a safe haven from life's cares. Reasonably safe, at any rate. In today's world, none of us is completely safe anywhere, as we both recognize. But *reasonably* safe—that's essential to our library's mission of serving the community. After all, if folks worry that the library is *not* a safe place to visit, attendance will fall way off. Without patrons, I shudder to think of what would happen to our budget or our staffing level.

Still, when you think about how many people walk through our doors in a calendar year, it's remarkable how few of them turn out to be up to no good, or how few just lose it and act out their aggressions in our building. While such things do indeed happen, we like to think that we're doing a good job of keeping library incidents in which patrons are endangered down to an acceptable minimum. I mean, we can't prevent such things from happening entirely, but when it comes to deterring the public from doing what they please in our public areas, well, we like to think that we're on top of it. Really, it's remarkable, given the fact that we don't have either the money or the human resources to watch everybody, and it might not be universally appreciated if we did. Surveillance, after all, just doesn't seem American somehow, am I right?

What else? Since you ask, there is something else, and I guess now's as good a time as any. Put it this way: it would be nice if we could always assume that the only risks to security for people, library property, and everything else came only from the *outside*. Outside? I mean from our patrons—outside in the sense of them versus us. See what I mean? People who come in here are our guests, clients, audience, patrons, whatever. A lot of librarians sometimes think that our building would be a great place to work if we just didn't have to open our doors each morning and let the thundering herd of beasts enter and roam wherever they like. That's when our troubles begin.

Well, yeah, of course that's the whole point. We need customers. Without visitors, there wouldn't be any point in having a library—at least a building with books in it—would there? That "thundering herd" is, after all, composed of people who support us, pay our salaries, and give us a reason to open those doors. We accept that. We also like that the public is welcome to come to the library. It helps justify our existence. But we maintain a security posture to protect people in the building from each other. Call it the human condition. People can be violent or at least unpredictable.

But there's another problem we don't like to admit to but we sometimes have to deal with. Protecting people not from the actions of deranged members of the public but protecting them against staff. That's right, *staff*! Surprised? You shouldn't be. Staff members are people like everybody else, and they suffer from the same stresses and problems with finances, relationships, and depression as the general population. Of course, none of us on staff is *supposed* to go crazy or anything; presumably, we are all screened for histories of violent behavior. But you never know. Today's gentle soul could conceivably become tomorrow's ax murderer, and even the meekest library staffer could, under certain stimuli, be driven into an insane, murderous rage. I don't enjoy telling you this. Frightening to contemplate, I know, but true, all the same.

I work a public desk, and there are times when I wish I could wear a bulletproof vest, a hardened plastic helmet, and have various new technologies that can alert me as to which people are potentially dangerous. There's been talk of giving staff members—especially the evening shift—extra pay for working in a combat zone, like downtown or at the Lakewood branch on the west side. But almost all our security measures are designed to protect us against *them*. Suppose . . . just suppose that the bad guy is *not* some enraged library patron. What if it's a library employee instead? Don't kid yourself that it couldn't happen. It has, it can, and it will again . . . somewhere. No matter how we try to screen our staff, any one of them could erupt.

But assuming that we don't have any violent criminals on staff, let's just talk about thieves. We're getting pretty good at catching book thieves before they make off with our property, but what about inside jobs? I read in an article not long ago that inside jobs, in fact, are the hardest crimes for corporations or retail establishments to detect and combat. Think about it: if you're the boss or owner, you gotta trust somebody, right? But what if that somebody on the inside—trusted and apparently normal—is really a kleptomaniac, just waiting for an opportunity to steal something. I don't have any figures on what percentage of our annual book loss comes from members of the staff, but I'd bet my next paycheck that it's more than a little bit. Temptation, after all, could happen to anybody. The enemy could be inside the walls.

Pat, you have a master's in business administration and—if I remember right—you minored in criminology, which is one reason why I'm here to ask for your assistance. We at the library think we have a handle on most of the problems that might arise from the public end of things. But what if the person doing the misdeed turns out to be one of us? What if the person who pilfers books or supplies, or runs amok with a weapon, is a card-carrying member of the library staff?

I know that new hires are screened routinely by the city's personnel office and that such tests are supposed to detect and eliminate people who aren't "normal" before they start to work for us. But what about the ones who passed those tests with flying colors several years ago or who never took them because they were hired before employee testing began? Now they're "grandfathered" into the system.

I don't want to give up any names, but we have a few employees who may well be under rather unusual levels of stress in their personal lives just now. So what should we do? What *can* we do? Are we permitted to require them to submit to psychological evaluation and counseling? I can see a lot of problems with that idea. Might be better for now just to keep watching them—maybe that's the safest course.

Or we could reassign the ones exhibiting stress symptoms to jobs where they don't interact with the public. Think that's a good idea? Difficult, but doable, I suppose. What I need is ideas. We want to do the right thing. But what *is* the right thing? Can you help us out, here? We accept that incidents occur in the library, but we don't want to find out that the one causing the next one is one of us.

Questions for Discussion

1. Do you think that people, by nature, are dishonest or potentially violent, requiring that even members of a library staff require watching?

2. Are mandatory pre-employment psychological tests a good idea to reduce the worry of inside jobs?

3. What forms of surveillance, if any, are appropriate to staff members as they work?

Case 29

Un Nouveau Espèce
de Voyeur

Carl Davis, reference librarian, to Mary Rhoades, head of reference

Yo, Mary! Mind if I pick your brain a minute? Something happened yesterday, and I'm wondering if you can shed any light on the subject. Even if you can't (because this is a seriously tricky problem), I think it's something that needs to be talked about at our next Reference meeting, so that everybody understands the problem, even if they can't necessarily do anything about it.

Yesterday, we had a lot of people in here using the online Internet terminals, as usual. So many, in fact, that we were using the sign-up sheets and half-hour appointments to make sure that everybody got a fair turn. Well, at about half past three, I passed along the rows of terminal stations, just to—you know—eyeball what was going on, and I saw this weird little guy standing a few steps behind one of the Internet users. What caught my attention was how intently he was looking at her fingers—not at the screen but at her fingers—as she went online to surf the Net, check her e-mail, or whatever.

Sometimes—I don't know how to explain it—I get a tipoff that tells me that something's wrong. I call it a "tell," an expression I got from a book I read on poker, back when I thought maybe I could supplement my income by becoming a card sharp—not by cheating but just by knowing more than the other players did, which would give me an edge.

In poker, a "tell" is like, maybe somebody looks at his two down cards in a hand of seven card stud and they're good ones—say, a pair of aces or some other high pair—then he does something he doesn't ordinarily do, unconsciously. Like what? Well, one guy, whenever he had a good hand shaping up, cleared his throat several times, while another guy would take a small stack of chips and place them protectively on top of his down cards. That meant he thinks he's sitting on a powerhouse. Time for an observant player to fold. If you watch closely over time, you pick up on other players' patterns—certain behaviors when they're bluffing. If they have a bust hand, they might display a facial expression of disgust, however brief. That's a tell.

In all the years I've been a Reference librarian, I think of myself as having become a better than fair student of human behavior. There are always tells, if you know how to look, and they'll give you clues as to what people are doing or going to do. No, not always. Sometimes, I've been dead wrong. Some bluffers never give themselves away. But in general, I think I'm pretty good at picking up on it when somebody's scamming somebody else. Of course, some people are good actors; the better the actor, the better he can fool you.

But I digress. Back to the problem at hand. Yesterday, this sweet-looking, middle-aged woman waited her turn, and when it was finally time for her half hour she seated herself on down for some surfing. She started typing away merrily on the keyboard, and as I walked by, I noticed that the woman was accessing her AOL account, and had just typed in her user number. Next, the system asked for her password, which she typed in, but for security reasons, instead of seeing those characters on the screen, all the observer can see is a series of little black dots. Good system: prevents onlookers from glancing at her screen, reading the password, and either remembering it or writing it down, for later use. That sort of theft is easy to bring off, trust me.

But that little guy lurking around behind her: he had a definite tell—staring intently at peoples' hands He was standing behind her about five feet, and when she got to the first screen of AOL, he leaned forward and peered intently. But he wasn't watching the screen. No, he appeared to be watching her *fingers* and whispering to himself, as though trying to memorize the password she typed in to activate her account and begin her AOL session.

If somebody's got good distance vision, he's in. Or soon will be. The poor, unsuspecting woman didn't know it or even suspect, but she was extending to this enterprising crook the right to access her AOL account as long as he likes—to download pornography, join hate group chat discussions, or (like someone did here not long ago) send a death threat to the president. And as far as the people receiving those messages can tell, they came from *her*.

I saw this guy doing it, but I couldn't do a thing about it! Too risky. Can't bust a guy for staring, right? Even the police couldn't do that. No probable cause, like they say on the cop shows. But the next time that clever identity thief (unless the woman changes her password, of course) accesses AOL, he can surf to his heart's content without her knowledge or consent, entirely free.

Huh? A crime? Hell, *yes,* it's a crime! When a guy like that gets caught, the judge ought to throw the book at him. Internet identity theft should be punished in the same way as other identify theft, such as using a stolen credit card to charge up a set of new radial tires, or something. But in order to bust somebody for doing a thing like that, you've got to catch 'em at it, and that isn't easy, as you can imagine.

That guy I eyeballed stealing that lady's password, he could go home and use his new identity from his own computer. How am I going to catch him doing that? He was just watching, that's all. Whatever I felt like doing, I couldn't stop him and accuse him of anything. I just watched helplessly while he strolled out the front door.

That's why so many guilty people get off. Seeing a crime is one thing; proving it, that's another. For this guy, it was probably like finding money in the street. In fact, since that lady turned out to have one of those unlimited use accounts, she might never have known that this parasite ripped her off, and would have spent many happy hours living large off her account, if I hadn't brought it to her attention. Probably the only clue she'd get is that once in a while her password would be listed as "in use" or "busy," and she'd just figure it's a computer error or something.

So yesterday when I saw this dude—with thick glasses (probably magnifying lenses, it occurred to me later) and some kind of greasy looking baseball jacket—just lurking around by the terminals, standing behind this lady, and watching her access her AOL account, I moved in his direction. When he saw me coming, he just turned and streaked for the front doors, before I could even stop him for questions. There's another tell. The guilty ones leave as soon as they know they've been spotted. I knew what I couldn't do, but at that moment, I confess I had a sudden impulse to chase him down outside and plant my big fist in his nasty little face, but, of course, I'm too under control for anything like that.

Then later I thought it over: How could I prove anything even if I did detain him? Watching somebody else sitting at a computer is no real offense, is it? If I accused him of anything he'd probably have said, "Hey, all I'm doing is using my powers of observation; how is it *my* fault if other people are careless?" You've got to admit, it's a reasonable question. Once he was in the wind, however, I knew I had to do something. So I walked over, tapped the woman on her shoulder and informed her of what I believed had just taken place. Told her she'd best change her password immediately, and, just to be on the safe side, to change it regularly, like, say, once a week. Case closed, this time, anyway. At least I hope so.

I'm seeing you about this because I figure we need to be more aggressive in pursuing a policy of getting library users to be more careful when they enter their passwords. We installed privacy shields around the monitors of our computers to help protect against having children suddenly encounter pornographic images, but I think we neglected to consider other things that someone could do to misuse our public Internet workstations.

I've got to get back to my desk now, but one last thing: Funny—I always thought I knew what the word *voyeur* meant. Just a fancy French word for the kind of dirty old man who comes in here and sneaks peeks up the dresses of young girls, I thought. But yesterday, I learned somebody can be a voyeur just by standing around and watching fingers dance over keyboards. *Un nouveau espèce de voyeur* is a new type of information thief and a new problem patron to watch for. So about what I did yesterday, tell me: the next time I see some creep standing around staring hard at a computer user's fingers, what should I do about it?

Questions for Discussion

1. Would Carl have been justified in detaining the man he suspected of identity theft and questioning him?

2. Was Carl correct in figuring that since he had no justification for accusing the man of anything specific, he needed to talk to the woman involved immediately?

3. What might make the library-using public more aware of identity thieves, so that they can help the library protect privacy?

Case 30

The Customer Is Always Right

Harold Pennigan, reference librarian, to Ann Cameron Bowman, library director, in Bowman's office

About last night? One thing I've learned since I started working here is that you can't really tell much about people just from the way they present themselves. To look at this guy last night, he seemed like just the kind of person we'd welcome in here: impeccably dressed, mannerly, and using our business materials. You know the type: three-piece suit, razor-cut hair, expensive-smelling aftershave, and handsome, in a squeaky clean, professional way.

So when he walked over to *Thomas's Register*—you know, those enormous green books that provide classified business information, such as who makes widgets, or fire extinguishers, or helicopters—and started taking notes, I put him out of my mind. After all, he seemed to know exactly what he was doing, and since he didn't seem to require any help, I figured, it's not as though I didn't have lots of other stuff to do this morning. So I just gave him a smile and a nod when he looked over at the reference desk and then forgot about him.

Maybe about half an hour later my phone rang. Somebody wanting me to consult *Moody's Industrials* for some company data. With a little effort, he could have found it for himself on the Internet, but I guess if everybody did that, I'd be out of a job and the library might close, so I'm grateful that some of our patrons are still too lazy, technology-challenged, or busy to look up stuff like that themselves. Anyway, I got the information I needed from the caller, and got up to walk over to the index table where we keep *Moody's, Thomas's,* and a few more of the standard business and corporate reference titles that people consult frequently.

I remember I was wearing my new shoes yesterday. I had worn the heels and parts of the soles off my usual, comfortable, work shoes, and decided that I was overdue for a new pair of shoes. So I splurged a little and invested in a good pair of those rubber-soled, posture shoes that are supposed to be like a vacation for your feet, and I was eager to try them out with a typical day of chasing around the Reference area.

As you know, comfortable shoes are a must in our line of work. Sometimes I actually walk upwards of five miles, and on Saturdays, even more, moving from the reference desk to the shelves, out into the stacks, over to the computer terminals, and then to the index tables. How do I know? Years ago I bought a little gizmo called a pedometer, and every once in a while I'd wear it to work. It's an unobtrusive little thing that attaches to my belt buckle and is worn over on one side. Every time the leg on that side takes a step, it moves the needle of the pedometer a bit, and it adds up, you know? At the end of the day, I can see how many miles I actually covered, although it doesn't differentiate between work-related and lunchtime walking, but close enough.

That's how I know that my legs carry me anywhere between five and seven miles on a typical day. I'd say that five miles a day is a rather impressive amount of walking, given that my doctor defines my job as "sedentary," suggesting that I just sit in one place and don't move around much.

Yeah, right, about my new shoes. The old ones had developed squeaky soles, and, when I wasn't walking on carpeting, they made a sound when I walked, but my new ones allow me to walk almost silently, which I guess is what made it possible for me to sneak up on the guy in the Armani suit and catch him red-handed, even though I wasn't really trying to sneak up on anybody, but that's what happened.

To get to *Moody's Industrials* meant passing the place where we keep all those big books of *Thomas's*, and I must have been pretty quiet getting over there. Then I heard a tearing sound and I noticed, to my shock, that the businessman in the expensive looking suit had just torn a full page out of one of the *Thomas's* volumes. Funny thing: the ripping sound made more noise than the sound of my shoes on the carpeted floor.

I was so shocked by what I had just witnessed that I didn't think about what I was saying; I just said it: "What are you doing?" I came out with, probably too loudly, because everybody within earshot looked startled and turned our way. You know—when people just stop whatever they're doing and cock their ears? Like that. I didn't mean to embarrass the man or call undue attention to his actions; but I guess I did, because his face turned crimson, and he got the look of a kid caught with his hand deep in the cookie jar.

We just stared at each other for a long minute, both probably trying to think of something to say. Then he got a sheepish look on his face, quickly followed by a look of irritation, which soon changed to one of fury.

It was pretty clear to me what he'd been doing. No other explanation fits the facts, as they say on those law shows on TV. He had been tearing pages out of *Thomas's*, not bothering to take notes or carry it over to one of the copy machines. And instead of having the good grace to look embarrassed, or contrite, or ashamed, he decided to cop an attitude with me. That's right, instead of a lame explanation or apology or anything that a person might say when caught stealing—if what he was doing can be called stealing—he got angry with me for calling him out on it! It only took him about 30 seconds to go on the offensive, and I use the word offensive advisedly, let me tell you.

He glared at me, and finally said, "What are you looking at?"

"You," was all I said, feeling a little bit angry, myself. "I am looking at you." He gave me a defiant look.

"Well, whatever you think you just saw, you're mistaken, and I resent the implication, so I'm going to take your name, and then I need to speak to your superior immediately! My guess is that you'll be out of work, this time, tomorrow. What's your guess?" I just stood there, gaping at him, wondering how he had managed to put me on the defensive, when I'd caught him so clearly vandalizing library property.

"My name's Harold Pennigan, sir," I said, "and if you wish, I'll personally conduct you to the director's office immediately, if I can get someone to take over my desk while we're gone." So I called Steve Glass, who was in the back, to come out for a few minutes and spell me while I came up here with our . . . guest. The man repeated, as we walked to the stairs, his intention of getting me fired, and for a moment, angry words tried to make their way out of my mouth. Then I recovered myself and modulated my voice. "Yes sir, I think we both need to see the director, so please follow me, if you will," I said.

Before we reached your office, I realized that what I had witnessed was only the tip of the iceberg. Sticking out of his poorly closed briefcase was a whole sheaf of long, onion-skin pages torn from various volumes of *Thomas's*, and before he quickly stuffed them farther down into his bag, I could see maybe a dozen full pages and a whole bunch of smaller torn-off paper scraps. I don't know how many, because he was doing his best to conceal everything.

I was astonished at his—oh, what is that word Steve uses to mean brass, effrontery, cheek, gall, stuff like that? It's Yiddish, and he uses it to mean having a lot of nerve. I hate it when a word gets away from me, don't you? Wait. It's coming. Give me a minute. Ahhh, yes! *Chutzpah!* That's the word, although I can't say it like Steve does. Gotta work on that. Anyway, chutzpah is what this guy was showing me. He was dead-bang guilty, no question, and he even had what looked like a whole briefcase full of evidence, but by counterattacking, he was trying to put me on the defensive, as though *I* had done something wrong. Now, that's chutzpah!

But I wasn't about to back down, not when our copy of *Thomas's* was missing who knows how many pages. That's an expensive set, know what I mean? Missing pages makes it much less useful. Also, a library that loses enough pages from a much-used reference work has to decide whether to attempt to locate, copy, and tip-in the missing pages to make the book whole again, even if not pretty, or to bite the bullet and break down and buy a new set. And because we're having a lean year, this guy's actions were not without consequences. Not if I could help it. No walk for him. I'd caught him red-handed! He was going down!

So up the stairs we went: this guy in a power suit, with a confident swagger, an attitude of command, and a way about him that suggested that he is sublimely comfortable inside his skin, and then little ol' me—one year out of library school, dressed modestly in my usual go-to-work clothing and feeling rather small and insignificant standing next to him.

But I had the moral high ground, and besides, I couldn't just give him a pass, could I? After all, I'd caught him in the commission of a crime. Or is it just a misdemeanor? Anyway, this guy wasn't just stealing from the library, he was—if you look at it a certain way—stealing from the whole community, because all the other people who might consult *Thomas's* after this wouldn't have the whole set to look at because of this guy's selfish acts. So I was just as angry as he was when we arrived—side by side—at Karen's desk and asked whether you had time to see us.

"What's it about?" asked Karen, looking from me to the irritated man and clearly bursting with curiosity. Karen's nice, but she's one of those people who always has to know who's doing what, and why. Not a bad sort, Karen, but a major gossip. Karen never seems to accept that I might need to talk to you privately—no, she's just *got* to know the nature of my request and would probably love to have a concealed microphone inside this office just to hear what gets said. In fact, I wouldn't be surprised to learn that she does—and maybe one of those little hidden cameras, too.

So anyway, Karen said that you were out of the library but you were expected back any minute, and if the gentleman and I would please be seated, we would get a chance to talk to her soon. We sat down, but not next to each other. No way were we going to sit next to each other. The next 10 minutes had to be among the most uncomfortable 10 minutes of my past year. I sat in one chair, and the businessman took the other, but we didn't say a word to each other. In fact, we didn't even look at each other, although he kept making those exasperated sighs and expressing a kind of ticked-off aura that was for me almost like sitting too close to a pizza oven.

At one point, he reached into his briefcase—the one I'd seen him put the pages from *Thomas's* into—and extracted a cell phone. He called someone—probably his own secretary—and irritably announced that he was unavoidably delayed but would be back in his office in about an hour, and would she please juggle the rest of his schedule so he didn't have to cancel any appointments. I realized that he was an important guy, but I had dealt myself into this hand, and I was going to play it to whatever showdown awaited me.

Besides, I was in the right, wasn't I? I mean, he was a thief or at least a vandal, and I was reporting his activities, so why should I back down? Just because a crook doesn't act guilty and hangdog doesn't change the fact that he's a crook, does it? So I really had no choice: I had to go through with this, or I'd be looking the other way to assaults against library materials. But I was dreading the next scene in this little drama of ours, I'll tell you that.

Fifteen or so more minutes passed. Karen offered the man and me coffee, but I didn't need anything that would make me any more nervous, and the man simply said, "No, thanks!" and kept staring intently at the paintings on the walls. Finally, you came into the office, greeted me and looked questioningly at the man with me.

"Harold and this gentleman are here to see you," Karen said, "if you have a little time. Here are your messages." She handed over a few pink slips and returned to her correspondence, or at least she pretended to return her attention to her word processor. But I could tell that her ears were pricked up like a hunting dog's.

At your invitation, we all walked into your office and found new seats. You closed the door for privacy and went back to your desk where you raised an interrogative eyebrow.

"Harold?" you said, after studying the face of the silent but fuming man next to me, "Let's start with you. What's this all about?" Before I could speak, though, the man spoke up first, to my relief, because I really didn't have a clue as to what sort of opening statement might come out of my mouth, or what the consequences of what I said might be.

"Ms. Bowman," said the man in a steady but aggrieved voice, holding out his hand to you. "We've met before. I'm Jason Ludlow, CEO of Ludlow Industries."

"Oh, yes, Mr. Ludlow," you said, after a brief blank look, and I guessed that you didn't have any recollection of either Mr. Ludlow or his company. Ludlow might have been fooled by your quick recovery, but I've known you long enough to know when you're faking it. "Welcome! Now, how can I serve you?"

Ludlow told his version of what had happened, only he got most of it wrong. Bass-ackwards, as they say. The way he told it, he was just innocently sitting in the business index section of the reference area, collecting information, when I accosted him (I didn't really care for the word—it makes it sound like I went after him physically or something) with wild accusations of vandalism and embarrassed him greatly by shouting (I didn't shout, although, I admit, I might have been a bit more subdued in my tone, but people who are shocked or surprised can't always watch the volume of their voices, right?).

He said I accused him (which I didn't) of something he didn't do and added that he was considering bringing legal action against both me and the library for "pain and suffering." He said he wanted me to be dismissed immediately, but he didn't really wish to be harsh or punitive, so he had decided to bring the matter before you, as a first step.

You're always thoughtful in dealing with the public, Ann, and I admired the calm way you asked him what he wanted, what would satisfy him. "Well, for openers," he began, "I demand an apology for the way I've been treated by this librarian."

At this, I opened my mouth and croaked a furious, "An *apology?*" but a sharp look from you shocked me into silence.

"I think disciplinary action against this rude young man is in order, as well," Ludlow continued. "I'm not trying to tell you your business, of course, but if someone in my outfit behaved toward a visitor the way Mr. Pennigan did toward me, I would fire him or her on the spot. At the very least, I'd place a formal reprimand in his personnel folder and throw in a good talking-to about public relations and common courtesy to clients."

Once again, I made as though to speak, remember? But you gave me another one of those looks, and I didn't say a word. "Exactly what was it that my staff member accused you of, sir?" you asked, peering intently at the man.

"Well, he seemed to think that I had taken pages out of some library books. What's worse is that he called his suspicions to the attention of everybody else in the room, causing me to become the subject of unwanted scrutiny. Let me tell you something, and you, too, buddy," he said, acknowledging me for the first time since we had entered the administrative suite of offices, "my company employs over 50 people, and bills half a million dollars a year. As founder and chief executive officer of the company, I earn well into six figures each year. I own a house, a yacht, and a vacation home up in the mountains. Now does that strike either of you as the sort of person who would steal a few trivial items—or parts of items—from a library? I don't think so. If I wanted to, I could buy all the reference books I like. Or I could send my assistant or any of my other staff out to buy those books and not even worry about how much they cost. So the idea that I might steal whatever this misguided, delusional employee of yours says I did is ludicrous, wouldn't you agree?" When he had finished, you nodded thoughtfully, and turned to me.

"Well, Harold? What about it? Let's hear your side of this story."

Dozens of things I might say tumbled through my mind, but at that point the only lame thing I could manage to say was, "Oh, Lord!" Thirty seconds passed, while I pondered how to begin. Finally, I had it. "If the gentleman will permit, I think a quick look in his briefcase will reveal a few dozen torn and ripped-out pages of our *Thomas's Register* and will prove which one of us is telling the truth."

You thought about this and finally said, "Mr. Ludlow, it would certainly expedite matters and resolve the issue if you would allow us to look inside your briefcase," you said, gently. He looked angry again.

"Forget it! No way should I have to submit to such an indignity. What's in this briefcase," he cradled it to his chest," is nobody's business." I remember how you looked pained at this.

"Well, sir, I can't compel you to show us, but I must conclude from your disinclination to do so that . . . how shall I put this . . . you have something to hide. Therefore . . ."

"All right! All right!" Ludlow growled, scowling at the floor. "So I removed a few lousy pages from some of those huge books. Big deal! So what? Each one of those books has thousands of pages, so I don't see the tragedy if a few of them aren't there. I mean, who has time to write all that stuff down? Besides, I didn't have a pen with me." After that, Ludlow seemed to run out of bluster and threats and confined himself to mumbled responses to your questions.

Finally, realizing that he was free to go, he got up, took the briefcase full of stolen pages, skulked out, and vanished down the stairs. I opened my mouth to speak but you looked at me a long moment and placed your finger across your lips signaling that I should be quiet. I tried again to say something, but you silenced me, remember?

"Tomorrow," was all you said.

"But . . . but . . ." I stammered. "Tomorrow," you repeated. There was nothing left to say, so I got up, walked out the door, and followed that crook down the stairs. But today is the tomorrow you promised me yesterday, so I'm here to ask you how the customer can always be right, when this guy was so darned wrong!

Questions for Discussion

1. What are some effective ways of preventing library patrons from incidental acts of vandalism or theft?

2. Is the customer *always* right, no matter the circumstances, in disputes with staff members?

3. How can security in public buildings be enforced in such a way that the public is not made to feel that they are entering a mental police state, where everyone is under surveillance or suspicion?

Case 31 _____

One Hail of a Night

Roger Dimick, chief of detectives, Pecan Grove Police Department, to the chief of police, by telephone

Good morning, Chief! Huh? Oh, almost nine o'clock. Sorry to bother you on your day off, but we have a situation on our hands, and I need to talk to you about it. What's it about? Last night. Were you awake sometime after midnight, after all that heat lightning and then it began to rain? You were? Then I don't have to tell you about how we got a cloudburst after a bunch of thunderclaps, and even, in some places, golf-ball-sized hail.

No, I didn't call you with a weather report. So here's the problem: Somebody broke into the downtown library last night, and the results aren't pretty to say the least. It was some of those kids who mess around in the park next door to the library—you've seen them—hanging out until all hours. They got themselves caught in the downpour and were getting pelted with hailstones and no place to hide from the storm, so they decided it would be a good idea to wait out the storm inside the library building.

Only thing though, they didn't seem to notice or care that the library was closed. So finding the building locked, the perps tossed several large rocks through one of the library's back windows. That's how they got in; those rocks were still on the floor this morning. They didn't trip the burglar alarm, of course, because the chief librarian told me that the city's budget had turned down the installation of security sensors on most of the building's windows for the duration of the current budget crisis.

I know times are tough all over, but only the front and back doors and the large plate-glass windows in front were wired to the alarm system, so when the rocks sailed through the back window, no alarm went off. Once the window was busted in, it was a simple matter for the intruders to step through the jagged panes and be safely inside, out of the drenching rain and hail. It also meant that they suddenly found themselves where they could do whatever they felt like doing to the building's contents and furniture.

What? Yeah, they're all in custody, I was getting to that. Chief,

let me tell you this in my own way, all right? Anyway, there was, it would seem, a casualty. One of the intruders evidently did not enter the building as safely as his buddies did, because our investigating officers found drops of recent and still-drying blood on the floor, a table, and one of the library's telephones. Yeah, it was collected and bagged as evidence. Yeah, they all admit what they did. Whatever their reason for entering the library unlawfully—after all, it was a really terrible night to be outside—they still committed a crime and should be made to pay for it.

I believe them that their motive was not theft, but shelter, at least at first. Why? Because once inside, they didn't steal anything—they just went on a rampage, resulting in some senseless destruction of property.

Yeah, you're right: large amounts of alcohol were probably involved, because the uniforms found an empty jug of wine, but that excuses nothing. Crime is still crime. In any case, there was one hell of a huge mess on the floor this morning when the library custodian reported to work at 7:00 A.M. He quickly phoned the director first and then my dispatcher, to report it. I interviewed the custodian, Chris Cree, who told me that it looked like one mean mother of a tornado had blown through the west side of the building's ground floor, leaving a path of devastation in its wake. He's right about that, no doubt about it.

Damage report? Got that right here, Chief. Got a preliminary list of what's broken or smashed, and there might be more later, after the staff has more of a chance to take inventory. Maybe 200 books were strewn on the floor of the Reference department. No books seem to be missing, and a quick check reassured the library staff that nothing was removed. I saw for myself that a large Webster's dictionary that the library has owned since anyone could remember was ripped out of its loose binding, shredded, and crumpled into unrecoverable pages. Ever seen that book? So big, it sits on its own stand. Anyway, it's a total writeoff. That baby's gone.

The interior doors between the reference and circulation areas and the rest of the building had been closed and locked at closing time last evening, meaning that the devastation was confined to those rooms only. Thankfully, no damage or sign of forced entry occurred in the children's room or upstairs in the library's administrative offices. None of the Reference department computers seemed to have been touched, either out of reverence for the technology (which I personally find unlikely) or a simple act of omission on the part of those drunken punks.

A globe of the world on a free-standing spindle was at first thought to be missing, but a check of the library grounds revealed that the stand was lying in the mud just outside the shattered window. The globe had evidently been used as a soccer ball in a pick-up game after the storm. Want to hear the ironic part? The petty cash drawer in the circulation desk was still closed and locked; apparently not even tampered with. Contents amounted to maybe 15 or 20 bucks, but that would bear out the theory that money wasn't the motive for the break-in.

So let me get to the bottom line. The city's claims adjuster estimates $5,000 in damage in glass replacement and general cleanup costs. Insurance ought to cover it, and it could have been a lot worse.

How is it that they are in custody already? Another victory for the adroit application of accepted police procedure and maybe a little bit of luck. Of course, it didn't hurt a bit that one of the guys was found sleeping it off behind the circulation counter, either. One thing led to another, and this morning, a couple of uniforms made arrests of the other two perps after the sleeper gave up his two friends in exchange for vague promises of clemency in exchange for his cooperation. To summarize, all three of them are now downstairs in the lockup, where they belong. But not for much longer.

Turns out they're first offenders, with nothing more serious than drunk and disorderly charges on any of their rap sheets. You know Judge Willis, Chief? Yeah, that's the one: Hizzoner Bleeding Heart Willis, who thinks that there's no such thing as a bad boy. Well, guess who caught the case? I know. It's starting to look a lot like Willis and I are going to have a difference of opinion as to how senseless and stupid crimes committed by bored and hammered kids ought to be punished. Yeah, they're all going to make bail soon, and they'll be sent home in the custody of their parents. Off? Well, they didn't exactly get off, no. But it's pretty certain that none of them is going to be serving any time, and that really bugs the hell out of me.

It happens I actually know one of the young guys involved. He was a high school friend of my son, Jimmy, but they're not friendly anymore now that Jimmy is away at college in the East and this kid is unemployed and getting stupid drunk almost every night. Anyway, an hour ago, I walked into his cell and asked this kid, "Why did you and your pals do such a stupid thing?" I thought it was a fair question; I was trying to understand. And can you believe it? This punk tried to excuse what happened.

He said, 'It was late, we were drinking, we were sitting out the rain, and then it started to hail like mad!' " Like that excuses what he and his buddies did. Go figure. Want my take on it, Chief? I say, nothing justifies breaking and entering a public building, whether there's theft or not, and if I were the judge in this case, I'd see to it that none of these punks would be outside and walking around for at least the next two years. The more we coddle these louts, the bolder they become, I say. But then again, I'm not the judge. Willis is.

Yeah, they lucked out this morning. Because they were all young and had no previous criminal records, Willis gave them a sweetheart deal I still can't believe. They all pleaded guilty to various minor charges, got fined for damages to the library building and property, and were sentenced to community service and a year's probation. Community service and probation!

Now, they're all going home and their mommies will probably be serving them hot chocolate! Gimme a break! I've been in law enforcement for 30 years, as you know, and I honestly don't know what the world's coming to! But that was what they got, and we're all going to have to deal with it.

So anyway, the judge got real cute at the sentencing hearing. Willis said he thought it would be appropriate if these young guys did their hours of community service in the same library that they vandalized. Needless to say, the library director, Ms. Bowman, wasn't too thrilled about that, but what could she do? Well, sure I protested, but I'm a cop and he's a judge. Not my decision. Willis called it poetic justice, or some such.

But when I called the director to tell her that the same volunteers who would assist with the cleanup and recovery of the library were going to be the same vandals who trashed their building in the first place, she got pretty upset. Her actual words were, "No, way, José!" Privately, I think she has an excellent point. But the judge insists that this is going to happen, and the library director was compelled to soften her stance on accepting these . . . young men for community service. Otherwise, she would be in contempt of court.

Me, I think it stinks. But he's the judge. So I'm headed over there now to the library to try to set up a trial period of community service for these three perps for the good of everybody concerned. No discussion. The judge isn't kidding around. He really means it. He says it's a done deal, and the library just needs to find some useful work for these guys for the next several months. Unreasonable? Well, certainly I think the judge is being unreasonable, and I'm betting you do, too; but I can't talk the judge out of his decision, and the director just needs to accept it.

Well, that's my story, Chief. Sorry to start your day off with such a problem, but you're the police chief around here and I figured I'd better put you in the picture. That's why they pay you the big bucks, right? Everybody wants to do what's right, but what can we do when a bleeding heart judge issues a ruling? About the best we can do is impress on those boys how close they came to doing some actual time in the city jail, and what'll happen if they get up to mischief during their time of working in the library.

I'm really sorry to have to hit you with this problem on your day off. Yeah, all right. Got it. Tomorrow. See you then. For now, I'm planning to be there bright and early in the morning when those punks report for work at the library, just to make sure they understand what's expected of them. I'm halfway hoping that some or them—or even all three—fail to show up. Then I can issue arrest warrants, and even Judge Willis wouldn't be able to stop us from running them through the system.

Enjoy the rest of your day off, Chief. See you tomorrow. And thanks!

Questions for Discussion

1. How could the library's "hailstones" incident been averted?

2. How should the library ensure that the judge's ruling is complied with, yet no further mischief can be acted out by the delinquents?

3. As a librarian, what duties would you give the perpetrators of library vandalism as community service workers to minimize the possibility of any further damage?

Case 32

Stark Staring Mad

Michael Chitwood, associate director, to his wife, at the dinner table at home

Something weird happened today about half an hour after I got back from lunch. I was at my desk in my office. Donna buzzed me and said she was sorry to bother me, but there was a woman outside with a rather unusual problem, and since Ann was on vacation, she was going to turn it over to me. You know how Donna loves a practical joke, and from the tone of her voice, I knew this was going to be something ridiculous. "And what is the nature of her problem," I asked in a bantering tone. "Give me a hint, at least."

"It's . . ." Donna hesitated, "well, tell you what. If you don't mind, I think it's something she needs to tell you, herself."

"Then send her in," I said. I didn't have anything special on my calendar for the next 30 minutes or so, and it was as good a time as any. In a few seconds, Donna stepped in, trailed by a small, mousy, and extremely ill-at-ease woman of perhaps 40 years (although I could be wrong about that; I'd starve as a carnival age guesser), dressed in a plain drab blouse and skirt.

"Hello!" I said. "Michael Chitwood, assistant director, but make it 'Mike.' " I smiled encouragingly, but the woman, her mouth working, couldn't seem to find a way to start speaking. So I shifted my gaze to Donna, who is normally never at a loss for words. "Donna?" I said to her, "Who is our mystery guest, and what is her quest?" I was then introduced to Ms. Teresa Flores, who looked startled at hearing her name but bobbed her head in acknowledgment, then just stood there silently, shifting from foot to foot.

"Ms. Flores," I said in the warmest tone I could muster. "Welcome to my office. Please sit down." Wordlessly, she sidled into one of the guest chairs. "Would you like some coffee?"

"No, thank you," said the woman, "but if you have a cold soft drink, I could certainly use one. Or if not, a glass of cold water. What's happened to me just now has made my throat so dry that I can hardly swallow."

"Donna?" I said, "Please get Ms. Flores . . ."

"It's *Miss*, but you can call me Teresa, Mr. Chitwood," said the woman, smiling slightly for the first time, "and if there's anything diet, that'd be great."

"Diet Coke?" asked Donna, smiling. "I always keep cold ones on hand."

"Lovely," said Teresa as Donna departed to visit the little fridge we keep in the back room. I smiled at my visitor again.

"Why don't you call me Mike, while we're at it? That way, we're all friends, while I figure out what I can do for you." In half a minute, Donna was back at her regular duties, and my guest was taking long, greedy pulls on a frosty can of cola. I still didn't know what it was about, so, after a decent interval, I leaned forward and gently inquired, "Now, please. In your own words, tell me, Teresa, how may I serve thee?" She put the drink down on the table next to her chair.

"There's this man . . . ," she began, "down there." She pointed downward in the direction of the main rooms of the library. Now we're getting someplace, I thought.

"Right," I said, gently. "A man . . ." This was designed to be a furthering response, intended for her to get on with her story. Please! I thought to myself. Not another pervert or flasher! I harkened back to that recent incident I told you about, remember? The time when a distraught woman accused a man of exposing himself to her in the stacks, but for lack of any evidence or corroboration, there was nothing we could do. Now this! If some sickie was turning this poor trembling woman into a basket case, well, that shouldn't be permitted in a library, or anywhere else.

Teresa's mouth worked soundlessly. Time passed. So I tried again, "And this man . . . what, exactly, was he doing?" Finally, she regained her power of speech.

"Well, that's just it. He wasn't actually *doing* anything that was . . . you know . . ." I didn't know, but I could take a guess.

"Why don't you just tell me what he *was* doing, then?" I said. "Whatever it was, it's upset you enough for you to come up here to talk about it. So, . . ." once again, I gave her my comforting smile, "just tell me what he did, and we'll see what can be done about it." She cleared her throat nervously, and took another slug of her drink before speaking.

"He . . . he stares at me." I sat back in my chair slowly.

"I see," I said, not seeing, really, much of anything. "So this man stares at you. Go on." Time passed. I was aware of traffic sounds outside and the hum of the air-conditioning, but the woman didn't have anything to add.

"That's it," she said, finally. "He just wouldn't stop staring at me."

I decided to try to get some more information out of her, if I could. "Can you put the look he was giving you into words? I mean, was it a leer, would you say? Or a wink? A menacing sneer? Or a lascivious grin, perhaps? In your own words, tell me what kind of expression he wore on his face when he stared at you."

"Expression?" Teresa looked puzzled. "I don't know. Maybe that's what frightened me so much. He didn't have any kind of expression on his face. Just a flat, constant, stare. Right at me!"

"No gestures?"

"Gestures? Oh, you mean like . . ." Her right arm made a vague flutter in midair and then returned to her side. "Well, no. Like I said, just a flat stare."

"And how far apart were you and this man when he was staring at you?"

"Oh, maybe 25 or 30 feet. I'm not good at estimating distances. But I mean, it's not as if he looked like he might or even could reach out and try to touch me or anything. I'm not accusing him of . . . assault. But he stared and stared at me until I . . . well, I burst into tears and jumped up and ran into the ladies room. But then when I was in there, I thought that he might try to . . . you know . . . come in there after me or something. So I ran out again, and I saw this sign on the wall that said "Administrative Offices, 2nd Floor," So I said to myself, 'Hey, yeah! I ought to tell someone about this guy,' so . . . here I am."

"All right," I said, trying to think of what to say that wouldn't make this poor woman any more distraught. "You're doing fine. Now, please understand. I'm not doubting your account or suggesting that you're making anything up, but let me ask you: Are you positive it was *you* he was staring at? You, and not just some specific spot in the room, or anybody else?"

"No! It was me, all right. He was staring at me. I made sure of it before I ran away."

"You made sure of it. And how did you, ah, test your theory?"

"Well, at first I just tried to ignore him. But every time I looked up, there he was, staring at me. His eyes just bored into me. I mean, he had a magazine in front of him, but he wasn't even pretending to read. He just sat there and stared at me. As far as I could see, he didn't even blink! Just kept staring. Finally, as an experiment, I got up and changed my seat to one way over by the windows, and I sat with my back turned to where the man was sitting, and for about five minutes, I didn't look around. Not once. But I felt . . . I don't know . . . a kind of heat or something on the back of my neck. Did that ever happen to you? That feeling that you're being watched?"

"Frequently," I said, and it was true. "I think we all sometimes have that kind of instinct. But please continue. What happened when you did look around?"

"Well, that's the really scary part. As I said, I didn't turn around for five minutes, but finally, well, um, I did. I guess I was hoping that he had gotten up and left, or maybe he'd focused on somebody else—anybody else! Anybody but me—but that's when I panicked."

"He was still looking straight at you?"

"Yes! Same look, same intensity. In fact, he'd actually turned halfway around in his seat so he could see me over where I'd moved to, by the windows, and even though he never made faces or leered, or licked his lips, or whispered any words, he was still staring at me."

"So, that's when you . . ."

"That's when I panicked and ran into the ladies room, not even trying to walk slowly or appear calm or anything. But when I got in there, I decided it could be just the sort of trap I didn't want to be in, so I ran out of there and came up here."

"Can you describe this man?" I asked. Yeah, I know. I asked for a description, like they do on *NYPD-Blue*. I know it was a sort of "cop" thing to do, but I also knew the police probably wouldn't respond to such a low-level problem, even if I phoned it in. Anyway, her problem sounded like something I could handle myself. So if I wanted a description of this staring man, it was up to me to get one.

"Do I have to describe him?" Teresa shuddered, and I noticed the hand on the soda can was trembling. Whatever had happened, it had certainly shaken her up, I could see that clearly.

"Try," I said in a warm and encouraging way, straight out of the administrator's manual.

"Well, he was old. Or older than I am, anyway. But not, like, a little old man, or anything. Maybe in his 50s, like you. Oh, no offense."

"None taken," I said, as she hurried on.

"And wearing a sort of beige jacket. I think it was beige. Might have been gray. I was so scared. And I'm sorry, but I can't tell you how tall he was or anything, because I never saw him standing up. Just a non-descript white man wearing a jacket, with nothing unusual about him at all, that I could see."

"Teresa?" I said, hoping to get to the point of this quickly, because after 20 minutes, I still didn't have much of a clue as to what she wanted done about the man, whether he was staring or not. "I'm not a lawyer, but I have to tell you that I haven't heard you mention anything illegal, as unpleasant and unsettling for you as this gentleman's conduct may have been. What would you like done about your complaint?"

"Done?" She gave me a look like our Bekki gives one of us when you or I utter something she finds obvious or inane. "I'd like you to go down there, find that man, and tell him to quit staring at me, or you could call the paddy wagon and have him carted away! Or throw him out and ban him for life. Punch his lights out. I don't care; have him taken out behind the building and ... Well, actually, I don't really care how you handle it. Just make him stop!"

"Well, that's clear enough," I said, "and he *should* be made to stop what he's doing, but I don't know whether it's legally possible to compel someone to quit staring at someone else in a public building. I could look it up in the rules that govern the library, but after 10 years here, I think I know them quite well, and I'm pretty sure that nothing in them explicitly prohibits staring at someone, whatever the context." Teresa now seemed to lose patience with me, and startled me by slamming her empty drink can down smartly on the table by her chair.

"So what are you telling me? You won't do anything to help?"

"It's not a question of *won't*. It's more a question of *can't*," I said, feeling suddenly tired and depressed. I took a moment and considered and rejected several strategies designed to find this staring man and get him—somehow—to agree not to stare at Teresa. But I couldn't think of anything to say that'd be useful at the moment, so I just looked sadly at Teresa, extended my arms out to my sides and raised them, palms up, in the universal gesture of helplessness or confusion. Suddenly, she burst into tears and stood up, pointing a finger at me.

"The way I see it, you've got two choices: there's caring and there's not caring," she shouted. "Which is it?"

A trick question if I ever heard one—anything I responded would make me look bad. I took my time formulating an answer. Obviously, too much time, because before I could say what I was thinking—which would have started with "Of course I care ... but what ...?"—the distraught woman rushed from the room, past Donna's desk, and out the door of the administrative suite, slamming it behind her. Her rapid footsteps could be heard pounding down the flight of stairs to the main floor.

Shaking my head sadly, I looked up to see Donna standing in my office doorway, a look of curiosity on her face. "Didn't go well, huh, Mike?" she said.

"Not really, no," I answered. Then an idea struck me, and I walked quickly out of my office and down the flight of stairs so recently descended by my agitated visitor, around a corner and into the main reading room. I don't know what I was expecting to find there, but I figured that a look-see couldn't hurt. But all appeared normal. The usual suspects for a quiet Thursday afternoon. Nobody shouting. Nobody hitting anybody. No weapons in view. Nothing out of place. I stood watching, my hands on my hips.

I could see five or six middle-aged men seated in the room, but as to whether the staring guy that had so plagued Teresa Flores was present, there were several possible candidates but no confirmation. I looked intently from face to face, but not one of them seemed to be staring at anything but downward at a book or magazine. Mournfully, I turned and trudged up the stairs again to my office. Donna met me as I walked through my door.

"See anything? Our starer still down there, is he?"

"Nada," I said, scowling. "No Miss Flores, no staring man, nothing at all."

"Phooey!" said my secretary, returning to her word processing. That pretty much summed up my feelings about the matter, as well. Phooey!

All in all, it was a minor disturbance as disturbances go. Much worse things have happened on my watch, and you know it. This time? Nobody hurt. Nobody in custody. No crimes or even misdemeanors committed, as far as I could tell. But I couldn't just forget about it and get on with my day, either. So just before I came home tonight, I reached into a file drawer, found the document I wanted, and looked carefully through the library's rules and regulations booklet. Sure enough, the offense of "staring at people" wasn't anywhere to be found. Do you think it ought to be?

Questions for Discussion

1. Under what circumstances could staring be considered a form of stalking?

2. Did Mike handle Teresa's complaint appropriately, or was there something more he might have done?

3. Assuming that you, as a library employee, wanted to get a patron to cease staring at another patron, how might you go about it?

Case 33

Honesty as a Policy

Judy Newhouse, director of human resources, City of Pecan Grove, to Kyle Bozeman, human resources, by e-mail

From: Judy Newhouse

To: Kyle Bozeman

Date: 12 March 2002

Subject: Recent Employee Termination

I received with shock and regret the news concerning the circulation librarian whom you fired on the spot yesterday for theft of library supplies. While I never had a chance to meet the employee in question, I am still saddened that a person in such a position of trust could have turned out to be dishonest, and I'm certain that you are too. Let us hope that the loss of the supplies that you list in your e-mail of yesterday turns out to be the full extent of the losses that the library sustained as a result of this former employee's actions.

I applaud your prompt action in this case in deciding to terminate this employee, and I also understand your reluctance to press charges, owing to the minimal value of what's missing. I agree that if you took her to court it would involve financial costs and many hours of release time for you to testify. So I think you did the right thing.

I also want to applaud you and your staff for performing faithfully the tiresome chore of reviewing the film in the Circulation department's security camera daily, which was the means by which you found evidence beyond reasonable doubt that the employee in question was guilty of such actions. The fact that, when questioned, she admitted her malfeasance—in exchange for your willingness to decline criminal prosecution—testifies to the effectiveness of such cameras. So briefly, before we meet to talk about this matter in person, I want to review the salient aspects of this case, and comment, where appropriate, on what has already transpired.

To begin with, because the actual monetary value of the materials allegedly pilfered amounts to less than $100, retail, what she did may be classified as petty theft, rather than grand larceny. I realize that the principle is the same, and that theft is theft, but the material loss to the library seems negligible enough to justify declining to prosecute her for her misdeeds. Frankly, it's not as though any computers went missing, or any cash from the fine drawer or petty cash fund was taken or misappropriated. Such matters would have required a stronger response.

But in view of her immediate dismissal, I submit that the woman has been punished adequately by being given the sack. For most, having crimes or sins revealed in a public forum is nearly as effective and embarrassing as having the police lead him or her away in handcuffs. More to the point, had you elected to press charges over such a piddling amount, most judges would likely have had little patience for trying a discharged employee found guilty of ripping the library off for some miscellaneous supplies from a closet or cabinet.

Now, don't get me wrong. Stealing from one's employer is never justified and is always wrong, no matter the circumstances. That said, an employee dishonestly appropriating and taking home a box of sticky notes here, a box of pencils there, and a sheaf of yellow, legal-sized pads is not really what I'd call a hanging offense. While problematic in many ways, it hardly constitutes a major financial loss for the library. Still, if we allow our employees to walk out the staff door with city property with impunity, then we, in effect, condone theft, and that is not the attitude that we wish to convey.

The problem before us is not what to do about a single thief caught red-handed on videotape; you've already seen to that. The real problem is how to choose employees who are trustworthy enough that we need not worry about employee theft or pilferage in the future. I believe that we should still operate on the assumption that, when we hire someone to a position with the city, that person is generally honest and does not have larcenous intent. But some of us yield to various temptations, as we all know.

I am also aware that some other cities in this country with populations similar to our own now routinely administer standardized "honesty" tests to all new or prospective hires, and in some cases, even to continuing employees. But I continue to resist that idea for the following reasons:

- No test can accurately measure the honesty or dishonesty of an individual by analyzing responses to specific true/false or multiple-choice questions.

- A truly dishonest person, taking such a test, would doubtless dissemble, expressing not his or her true feelings but rather what he or she thinks will be the "best" response to lead to employment.

- Conducting detailed background checks of applicants for new positions is an expensive procedure.

- As we all know, "inside jobs" cannot always be predicted or prevented.

- Attempting to "watch" employees to ensure their honesty typically breeds resentment, which is bad for morale.

Finally, I detect an undertone of guilt in your e-mail of yesterday. Kyle, there is no reason to blame yourself for having decided to hire the dismissed employee several months ago, simply because that decision turned out to be "bad." It's no one's fault, and it could have happened to anyone. In my extensive reading about the problem of employee theft, I have discovered that millions of dollars worth of cash, valued objects, supplies, and equipment go out the staff door in companies and city agencies every year. Millions! In every city and state. It's an unfortunate aspect of human nature. There seems to be a touch of larceny in every human heart. In some hearts, there's a whole bunch of it.

So what is to be done about such unfortunate incidents? We need to maintain the practice of background checks and other investigation procedures for new hires, citywide. This would include, at the minimum, checking local police records, and sending requests to law enforcement agencies concerning wants-and-warrants nationwide might not be a bad idea, either.

Of course, I accept some of the blame, myself, for what has happened. Before I gave you the green light for the library to hire the woman, I performed the standard background check, which turned out, I admit, to be inadequate. In my own defense, I remember investigating the background of your dismissed employee, and she came up smelling like a rose. No police record. Zero history of previous criminal activity. In short, no one could have suspected that she might succumb to the temptation to boost a few bundles of library supplies and take them home.

This points up the need for better security in your library building, both out front at the public exit and in back where the staff come and go. At the same time, we also need to be careful not to create an atmosphere of fear or mistrust in the library, in which staff resent being under surveillance because of the inappropriate actions of one of their number.

What is urgently needed is an overhaul of our current system of employee hiring, firing, retention, and promotion in order to attempt to identify and weed out at-risk employees who may be likely to commit theft. Could we therefore arrange to meet soon to consider some constructive suggestions for keeping employees honest?

Let's talk again later in the day and schedule a working lunch next week to discuss these matters. Monday is clear for me. As long as we're going to talk about it over lunch, why don't we check out that new French bakery, La Boulangerie, that opened recently over on Live Oak Street? If we met in front of city hall and took a brisk walk over there, it would do us both a lot of good. Besides, I hear their chicken salad croissants are to die for!

I'll be waiting for your call.

Questions for Discussion

1. How can a library best assess the honesty of its present and future employees?

2. To what extent would you place your trust in a standardized "honesty test" to weed out those with tendencies toward larceny?

3. As Kyle, would you have sought prosecution of the dismissed employee for her theft, even though the losses amounted to little in terms of monetary value?

Case 34 _____

It Takes a Thief

Ann Cameron Bowman, library director, to her husband, at home

"I couldn't believe it! This kid couldn't have been much more than 17; the kind you see hanging around malls with a skateboard and a face full of adolescent pimples, wearing his baseball cap on backward. I mean, when he walked into my office, I thought he was a teenaged relative of somebody who works here, or maybe a high school kid looking for an after-school job.

Other than identifying himself as "Billy," he stonewalled me while the door was open, saying that he wanted to talk to me, personally. He guaranteed I'd be thankful if I granted him a brief interview. He didn't look dangerous. Geeky-looking is the actual expression that seems to fit best. So I was intrigued. I figured, what the hell, I can spare 15 or 20 minutes out of my busy morning to see what this kid wanted. I allowed him to close the door and showed him to a seat.

Once Billy was sitting comfortably, he got to the point. But before you hear what he wanted, a little background first. For some weeks, now, we've noticed a frightening pattern developing as various computer files have been raided—or at least visited—by hackers, who it would seem, keep finding new, clever, and devious ways to access our files. Oh, we've done a lot of things to thwart them, and many prospective electronic attacks have been stopped cold before they could get into our system. How many? Oh, well, I really couldn't say. How can we count attacks on our computers that have been prevented? That'd be like coming up with the number of traffic accidents or airplane crashes that almost did but didn't actually happen in a particular time period, right?

Still, since we installed our new firewall to intercept and prevent unauthorized attempts to penetrate our system, I'd say that most attempts have probably met with failure. So, while I can't tell you how many of these invasions have failed, I can tell you how many have succeeded.

Five.

Five is how many (or at least how many we know about) times since the first of the year that we've been hit. Five intrusions in half a year comes to less than one a month, although I don't know whether that's good or bad. Zero would be good. Five is somewhere between annoying and alarming, I guess. But it means that five individuals, or possibly the same person five times, penetrated our firewall somehow, and, once inside, did pretty much whatever they wanted to.

Fortunately, we have ways of discovering when someone unauthorized has been shuffling through our information because the system keeps logs of users and use, time of use, files accessed, and even the identities of the individuals who got in. But that's part of the bigger problem. The system is set up to prevent unauthorized users from accessing our files, but what happens when an unauthorized person steals, borrows, or otherwise acquires the account and password of an *authorized* user?

Identity theft. Yeah, identity theft, that's what it's called. All hell breaks loose when that happens. We encourage all staff who have access to the system to change their passwords regularly, and, when possible, to make their passwords random combinations of numbers and letters that nobody else should be able to guess or figure out. But some people are awfully naive about the problem. You'd be surprised how many people, including some of our staff, choose something like their nickname, their children's names, or maybe the license tag number from their family car for a password. Dumb? Well, I think so. I mean, why not just walk around with a sandwich sign on your shoulders that says something like, "The combination to my private safe is 35L, 16R, 21L"?

Real problems arise, however, when someone unauthorized manages to glom onto the password of an authorized user, whether by going through his files, getting him to tell him what it is, or even just watching carefully when a user enters the password. The system is set up such that you can't see passwords on the screen, but all you have to do is observe from behind the user where the fingers go when the password is being entered. We have ways of protecting our information, but keeping people from watching other people's fingers? That's a hard one. Other than warning people about prying eyes, there's not that much that can be done. Warnings help some, but the problem persists.

But I digress. Back to Billy the Kid. He made me an interesting business proposition today. First, he informed me that he knew that we'd had several visitors to our files, of late. I sat there, my face as expressionless as possible, as he told me what I already knew—that certain people had been breaking into the library's files, picking through them, sometimes rearranging them, and then leaving, pretty much at will.

"But how . . .?" I blurted, intent on asking him how he knew what he knew and planning to get around to asking him who the culprits were. Billy held up a grubby little hand and smiled. He must practice that smile in the mirror, because it's, well, disarming. Hard to be angry with a kid whose face beams like that, even if he's got a bad case of acne and is nobody's idea of handsome or charismatic. Anyway, he told me that he was not there to help me identify the culprits.

"The point is, I know that your computers get hit regularly, and even though I deny all involvement, I doubt that you're interested in having these incidents continue, am I right?"

"Uhhh, riiiiight," I answered, drawing out the syllable, thoughtfully. "But if you're not our, uh, phantom visitor, and won't tell me who is, what is it exactly that you can offer that might help us with this situation?"

"Thought you'd never ask," he said, smiling innocently. Like I said, he must practice that expression in the mirror. "All right, here's the deal. What you and your library need is to hire someone who hacks into your system on purpose: a hacker, yes, but on *your* side. Someone who's technologically up-to-date on state-of-the-art hacking methods and can figure ways to fiddle even the strongest and most restrictive firewall. Someone who will identify and report on weak spots in your system and provide advice on how to fill those holes, plug those gaps, and maintain your system in such a way that it drives intruders out of their minds. You need someone . . ."

"Let me guess. Someone like you," I interrupted, somehow enjoying this verbal jousting, even though I was aware that serious matters were at stake. Billy beamed again.

"I *knew* you'd understand!" he exclaimed, adding, "I just knew when I walked in that you'd be receptive to my proposal."

"Which is . . .?" I was still intrigued, but I had several appointments in front of me, and besides, enough kidding around.

"What I propose is to become a hacker *for* the library, not against it. I'd be like a spy or picket that a general sends out to probe the enemy's defenses, look for gaps in security, and then report back. The kind of spy I'm talking about is one who looks like one of the enemy and is thus accepted by them; a spy who knows how to get them to talk freely. That's why I'm perfect for the job. Not only can I tell you about the weak spots in your defense, but look at me. I can mingle easily with other people like me—who may or may not be planning a hack—and pick up little bits of intelligence on the street about who's doing what, when, and why they're doing it. So, how does that sound?"

"Interesting," I answered honestly. "A person with your talents and abilities would be of great value to the library. But come on, Billy, level with me. Am I supposed to believe that you're offering to do this out of some sort of sincere altruism, free of charge to the library, just in the interest of helping us protect our information?" Billy's smile took on a tinge of embarrassment.

"Well, okay, you got me," he agreed. "I actually have two motives in making this proposal to you. The first one is a genuine—I swear—desire to protect your files from some nasty people of my acquaintance who might like to get into them, corrupt them, or even destroy them. And then, I guess you can figure out the other motive—I need money. I mean, what I'm offering is going to take up a large chunk of my time, right? And since I'd be working for you—in every way but officially—I don't see anything wrong with getting compensated for it. Besides, I have expenses, and my offer, well, I think you see the value of it. So I have a figure in mind."

"Finally," I said. "Here's comes the closing. All right, Billy, don't keep me in suspense. How much are you asking to work for us?"

"I'm not greedy, really," he said, spreading his hands out, palms up. "So what if you start me out at 20 bucks an hour, off the books. I'll keep a strict accounting of my time, and since I'm not on the payroll, deductions from various governments and taxing authorities won't apply. A straight twenty an hour, in cash. Then, if my services prove to be valuable, I'd like to think that you'd offer me raises."

I opened my mouth to respond, but he had one more line to deliver. "So my real question is, what'd it be worth to you if I showed you the holes in your security and how to plug 'em?"

"How many hours per week would this entail?" I asked, wondering where the funds would come from to pay someone off the books if I went for the deal. "I mean, there's the petty cash fund, and I have access to it, but an audit leading to charges of embezzlement doesn't appeal to me, and you don't want to be visiting me in jail, right?"

Obviously, my young visitor had thought about this previously. "I figure 20 per, times 10 hours a week equals $200, payable in cash, every Friday."

"Ten hours a week?" I asked in surprise, thinking that finding $200 a week was going to be a rather steep hill to climb. "Maybe . . ." Billy grinned again.

"You drive a hard bargain, you know that, Ms. Bowman?" He seemed to be enjoying this enormously.

"So do you," I admitted.

"It's money well spent, I promise you," he said. "So, do we have a deal?"

"Let me get this straight. You get $200 a week and we get full reports of your activities and discoveries, together with a description of what you did to patch the holes in our security. Is that it?" Billy nodded in agreement and made a crossing motion over his heart. He is a charming little guy, but a shakedown is a shakedown. "Perhaps," I countered, "we'll have to see. What I need is a day or two to think about this, and then, I'll have an answer for you." Billy's grubby hand shot up in warning.

"Fair enough," he said, looking ominous, "but no tricks, understand? Bring the cops into this and I can't vouch for the integrity of your files, know what I mean?" Oho! Threats and blackmail, now. Billy had, evidently, seen too many crime movies.

"No cops," I whispered.

"All righty, then," he said as he got up to leave. "I'll call you tomorrow. But remember two things: First, I have the power to bring your system down like a house of cards if you report me to the police. Second, in this business, if you snooze, you lose. The longer you wait to activate my services, the more risks of hacking from people not as sweet-natured as myself you entail." He paused at the door. He seemed so small and skinny; so young to be half petty crook and half skilled con man. "Well, I've taken up enough of your valuable time, I guess. Expect my call tomorrow, say, around 11:00 A.M.? Pleasure meeting you, Ms. Bowman. Ciao!" And out he went, grinning like mad.

Questions for Discussion

1. How can a library best attempt to render its electronic files hackproof?

2. If you were the library director in this scenario, would you accept Billy's offer?

3. Would you report Billy to the authorities for trying to shake down the library?

Case 35

See You in Court

Karen Southern, administrative assistant, to Betsy Roseman, retired homemaker, via telephone

Thursday, 9:02 A.M. Good morning! Pecan Grove Public Library. How may I direct your call?

I'm sorry, ma'am, the director isn't in now and isn't expected until Monday morning. She's at a library conference. Perhaps I can help you, though? I'm sorry, I'm not at liberty to give out that information. All I can tell you is that she's expected in on Monday morning. No, I'm sorry. We have a policy against that, unless it's a crisis or something that the director needs to know immediately. But I'm here and willing to help. So perhaps you can tell me the reason for your call, and . . .

Ma'am, there's no call for such insulting or demeaning language, and just for your information, I am not a "flunky" but rather a highly trained administrative assistant and . . . Well, yes, I understand that you're upset, and your tone of voice isn't doing wonders for my own state of mind, either. Tell you what: let's both just dial down the voltage a bit and analyze our problem, shall we? All right. Ready to be polite? So am I. Now, then, begin by telling me your name and giving me your telephone number. Perhaps if we calmly review the circumstances together, we can come to some satisfactory . . . Pleased to meet you, Mrs. Roseman. Who am I? Oh, I'm sorry, ma'am. My name is Karen Southern, and for the past six years, I have served as administrative assistant to Ms. Bowman, the library director. And frankly, when she's not available, she's come to trust me to make certain decisions in her absence, unless the associate director, Mr. Chitwood, is here, but just now . . .

No, I'm sorry, he's not here, either. So if you'll just tell me . . . Yes, I agree, it *is* unusual for both the director and the associate director to be unavailable at the same time. But something came up today for Mr. Chitwood. Well, I can understand your irritation, ma'am, but it happens that Mr.

Chitwood is taking the morning off to accompany his son to Presbyterian Hospital where, if all goes well, the boy expects to have the cast finally removed from the leg he broke playing football last fall. Oh, he'll be so glad to get out of that cast! Amazing how those young bones heal, isn't it? Why if I . . . What? Oh, yes. Sorry, Mrs. Roseman. I apologize. I do that sometimes. Just my natural inclination to be chatty and social, I guess. Makes me a good administrative assistant, I think, but the downside is a tendency toward . . . Fine, then. We'll stick to the issue at hand. Let me take some notes about your complaint, and . . .

Well, it *is* a complaint, isn't it? I see. What would you call it then? Oh, all right. I stand corrected. It's not a complaint. It's an "issue" and a request for clarification, on its way to being a problem settled. If you insist, we'll call it that, although I wish you'd . . . oh, boy! Sighing? No, I wasn't sighing. Or at least, I didn't mean to sigh. It's just . . . Anyway, please tell me what your "issue" is, and when Mr. Chitwood returns to the office, I'll have it called to his attention right away. So suppose you . . .

Uh-huh, uh-huh, uh-huh. No! Really? In that tone of voice? You don't say! He did? You were? Uh-huh. Right. I can certainly understand why you felt that way. Our Matt is indeed a very large man, with a deep voice, and while he's almost always gentle as a lamb, he can be . . . intimidating, I suppose . . . when he's standing over you and glaring downward. I fully understand.

Uh-huh. Well, here's what I can do for you Mrs. Roseman. Let me hang up now and see what I can find out about the visit that you say our guard paid you last evening, and . . . huh? Called you a *what?* Did I say that? No, it never entered my mind. Not at all. Please believe me that I didn't mean it to sound as though I was doubting your word. Of course, I believe you, Mrs. Roseman. It was just a figure of speech, that's all. I really . . . oh, boy . . . look, I have your phone number, and as soon as I learn what the guard's side of the story is, I'll get right back to you with an explanation or apology or whatever. Court? What do you mean, it's gone beyond an apology? Oh, come on, Mrs. Roseman! I think you're being a little extreme. You mean a court of *law?* With a judge and everything? Don't you think you're being . . .? Oh, now, Mrs. Roseman, I realize that you're upset, but I really see no reason for such drastic . . . oh, boy.

Yeah, okay, I hear you. I realize that you're a woman and you live alone with nothing but two angora cats for company in the house you've occupied for over 60 years. Yes, I can imagine how frightened and upset you must have been when your doorbell rang and when you opened the door our Matt loomed over you and said that, but still, going to court over it? Seems like a bit of an overreaction, at least to me.

Uh-huh, uh-huh. But it wasn't a heart attack, though, was it? I'm glad of that. Uh-huh. Oh, you poor woman! I see. All right, Mrs. Roseman, let me get off now, and I promise to get back to you within the hour with as much information as I can gather on this matter. All right? I surely will. You have my word. My name, again? It's Karen. Karen Southern, as in . . . well, belonging to the states around here. Yes, that's correct. So, give me an hour. Right. I promise. Goodbye, now.

Oh, boy.

Thursday, 1:13 P.M. Hello, Mrs. Roseman? Karen Southern from the public library. We spoke earlier? Yes, I'm calling you back with the information I promised I'd get for you this morning. Is this a good time? It is? Good. Mrs. Roseman, I wonder if you'd mind turning down the volume on the TV a bit, so I can hear you better. Ahh, that's better. One of your afternoon shows? Which one? Oh, I know. I love it, too. You know, when I get a day off, I watch it, and I've found that even when I mute the volume I can still figure out what they're talking about from the body language, know what I mean? So you're watching now? Just curious: was Monica with Jason when I called? That figures. Isn't Monica a witch? She's just so evil, the way she slinks around, don't you think? And the way she twists men around her finger . . .

Yes, forgive me, you're entirely right. I didn't call to discuss daytime TV, I called with the information you requested, that I promised to get for you. No, I'm not trying to deflect you from your anger. I just thought . . . oh, boy. Right. Let's get right to it, then. Our associate director, Mr. Chitwood, came in about 10 minutes ago to pick up something in his office, but he couldn't stay. Well, I think that's a bit harsh; normally, he works a killer week, but he has an outside life, you know, and his son's leg came out of the cast weaker than expected. So Mr. Chitwood has to take the rest of the day off, unexpectedly, to arrange for his boy to get a course of therapy for that weakened leg. I'm sure you understand that these things happen, ma'am.

Well, yes, we did chat briefly about your issue, problem, complaint, or whatever, and he confirmed that he did authorize a library book recovery program recently, whereby our security guards were sent out with lists of our most delinquent borrowers to . . . No, that's just what we call them . . . it doesn't mean . . . Well, anyway, Matt, our chief of security, was told to drive out to the homes of borrowers who had overdue books who refused or were unable to return them, despite repeated attempts on our part to recover them. What kinds of attempts? Well, everyone the guards went to see during our recent campaign was someone who had either neglected or failed to answer three attempts to recover our books.

That's right, I said three attempts. First, we send out a post card; a couple of weeks later, it's a letter; and finally, a personal telephone call from one of our staff, requesting that the overdue books be returned. When all three attempts fail to recover a book, we go to the personal visit approach. I guess your name turned up on the list of people we had to visit; and by the way, today, I checked your file on our mainframe computer and learned that you have held three of our library books over six months beyond their due dates, without any promise to return them.

You did? Are you sure? No, ma'am, I'm not saying that. Possibly you did. That's been known to happen. Sometimes it does, yes. We could check the stacks and see if they're there, but, by and large, our computer system does a pretty good job of informing us who has overdue books, and that's why your name came up on our list of . . . well, we call them delinquents.

I know how it sounds, Mrs. Roseman, but the way we use the term, it doesn't mean criminals or anything like that. Not really. Now, Mrs. Roseman, there's no need for you to . . . oh, boy.

What? No, our records don't tell us that. You're how old? Well, bless your heart! And still independent and going strong, from the sound of your voice. Congratulations! More power to you. Yes, I can see how difficult it must be for you without a car to get over to the main library, or one of the branches, and return books on time, or even at all, so that's why we instituted the program of recovery. Matt's mission was actually a public service—an offer to collect and return your books for you, that's all. What did he say to you?

He did? Well, certainly I believe you're telling the truth. It's just . . . our Matt. He is big, but it's never his intention to terrify anyone, please believe me. We just want our books back, and Matt's job is to facilitate matters by offering to collect and return your overdue books for you, saving you the trouble of having to get out, come over to the library, and return them yourself. Of course, there is still the matter of your accumulated fines for the books you held that long, which, if you're interested, comes to . . . But, uh, why don't we deal with one problem at a time, shall we?

"What? Oh, I can't believe . . . He threatened you? Matt? *Our* Matt? Oh, I doubt that. That doesn't sound like Matt at all. A little gruff, sometimes perhaps, and he may be a giant, or what passes for one to most of us normal-sized people, but he's a gentle giant in almost every case. What do I mean by almost? Well, we have occasional security problems here in the library, and every now and again a show of force is called for. I mean, when you're a security guard at an urban library, sometimes . . .

No, Mrs. Roseman, no. Please don't read into everything I say to you. I am *not* calling you a liar. I just said that I couldn't believe that Matt was capable of . . . No, they are *not* the same thing. Look, I'm just trying to . . . oh, boy. I just have a hard time believing that our longtime and trusted employee threatened you into finding those books while he waited. I hope you're not alleging that he struck you or touched you in any way, are you? Because I know that Matt would never . . .

He what? Loomed over you? And you only come up to his belt buckle, and you were terrified and actually afraid for your life? You know, Mrs. Roseman, I think that what we have here is a failure to communicate. Different perceptions of the same actions, that's all it is. Mr. Chitwood has assured me that Matt's instructions were to be gentle and polite, but insistent if necessary, in offering to return your overdue books for you. Well, yes, our Matt is well over six-and-a-half feet tall, and when he stands next to a short woman—I'm only just over five feet, myself—it can seem intimidating, but he never would have . . .

What do you mean, you'll see me in court. Oh, please, there's no need for this to . . . It's all a misunderstanding, that's all. Well, I guess I can picture how you must have felt when you opened the door and found yourself looking up into his face, but . . . Maybe he is a bit craggy, but you should see him when he's laughing. Uh-huh, uh-huh. Yes, I can understand how you must have felt.

Threatening? Yes, I'm pretty sure that threatening or menacing someone is against the law, but nobody instructed our security guards to threaten anyone into giving us back our books. Well, yes, the idea was to get tough on delin——uh, people we visit, as a direct way of recovering our missing books, but threaten anybody? Never!

Uh-huh, uh-huh. Well, I'm very sorry you feel that way, Mrs. Roseman. Listen, I don't suppose you'd accept a sincere apology from Mr. Chitwood, or even from Matt, himself, along with, let's say, complete amnesty for any fines you still owe on those overdues? If you give him a chance to meet with you under different circumstances, I think you'll find out that, despite his size, Matt's a pussycat. I mean, last year, I trusted Matt to take my children to the ball game and they all had a wonderful time. Now, do you think I would entrust my own precious children to a person such as you describe?

A psychopath? Oh, come on, Mrs. Roseman, I hardly think . . . He's just . . . well, large . . . and craggy. And maybe he was taking his mission a bit too seriously, I don't know. Oh, boy! Are you're sure that there's nothing I or any of us can say to dissuade you from taking the library to court for what you say is harassment of an elderly citizen? Well, then all I can add to what I've already said is that I'm really sorry you feel that way. No, I understand. You have to do what you have to do, and I understand how frightened you must have felt at the time, but . . . All right, Mrs. Roseman. Yes. I understand. I guess we *will* see you in court. But I hope that's not necessary, so if there's any way that we can make this right, any . . . hello? Mrs. Roseman? Hello? *Hello?*

Oh, boy!

Questions for Discussion

1. Would you authorize a book recovery program of the type described when conventional means of retrieving overdue books doesn't work?

2. How might the associate director have prepared a well-intentioned, but possibly overzealous security guard for an assignment of this kind?

3. As Chitwood, what would you now do or say to try to dissuade Mrs. Roseman from carrying this incident into court?

Case 36

The Schpritz

Joel Eatmon, sales representative for Creative Systems Solutions, to Kristina Simon, comptroller/ budget officer, city of Pecan Grove

Ms. Simon, I'm told you're the person to see about authorizing purchases for the library, so here I am, and I predict with confidence that you're going to be very glad I'm here. Why? Because I've got the solution to the public library's loss problem right here. Catch! Good one. You're holding in your hand what just may be the answer to the problem of library theft. I see a look of disbelief. Just let me explain and you'll understand.

That affordable little device you're holding, once installed on an expensive or valuable book, will, in time, cut your collection's loss rate down pretty close to zero. That thing look familiar? It should. You've probably noticed bigger versions attached to the high-end clothing you buy in stores. I'm calling it the "Schpritz" in tribute to the guy who gave me the idea. *Schpritz* is a Yiddish word for a squirt or spray. I got the name from my buddy Paul Roth. Paul is the owner of Roth's, a downtown men's clothing store that's been open for business for almost 30 years.

Now, Ms. Simon, do you mind a personal question? You married? I figured. I'll bet your husband has in his closet something he bought at Roth's. Well, Paul has a good head for business, no doubt about that, and a few months ago, I was talking with him before our weekly poker game, asking him how business was and that's when he gave me this great idea. He smiled and said, "Well, up until a few months ago, it *was* lousy. In fact, I was seriously contemplating bankruptcy and the liquidation of all my assets, but all that's changed now for the better"

When I asked him to explain, he said that he had recently turned his profit picture around. He said that he'd been drowning in a sea of red ink, partly due to competition from discount clothiers, but also partly due to an appalling rate of loss of merchandise in his store due to shoplifting and theft. He said that it had been getting harder to make a living in that neighborhood when thieves kept ripping off the items he had for sale and rushing out of the store with them before he could even shout, "Stop! Thief!" But he added that all that changed drastically when he invested in a system of cartridges like that one, filled with colored dye, that could be clamped onto expensive garments like suits, topcoats, and blazers. And he swears those little beauties brought about a complete turnaround in controlling his losses in merchandise.

Well, that was all very interesting, but what does that have to do with my line of work? After all, my company sells library supplies, right? At first, I didn't see how a library's loss problems might be connected with the problems of a commercial store trying to hang onto its cashmere blazers either. But I'm here today to pitch my idea to you. I went to the library first, of course, but they told me that you make the big financial decisions, so here I am.

Anyway, after I churned the cartridge idea around in my head for a while, I headed over to the library to see Mrs. Bowman, the director. See, I remembered that the local newspaper ran a feature story about how the library was experiencing high losses in its book collection, and I figured, why not? And that reminded me of something I'd read in a book but I couldn't remember which one, so while I was at the library, anyway, I looked it up in *Bartlett's* quotations. Turns out it was George Bernard Shaw who said something like, "You look at what is and you ask, 'Why?' But I look at things that aren't and I say, 'Why not?'" Those weren't Shaw's exact words, but you get the idea. So I said: "Why not?"

Why couldn't a library try protecting books from being stolen or walking out the door by using the same technology that Paul uses to help him make sure he doesn't lose his topcoats and slacks to shoplifters? Now you're maybe thinking that the problems of this city's library and those of a clothing store are different. But I beg to differ.

Paul said that in an effort to stop the loss of his clothing to thieves, he'd tried all sorts of things: surveillance cameras, security guards, night watchmen, theft alarms, more alert cashiers, signs (in English and Spanish) warning that shoplifters would be arrested and prosecuted, and even plain-clothes store detectives who circulated throughout the store, especially around the Christmas holidays. They looked like everyone else, but actually they were watching for shoplifters. They were empowered to detain anyone they caught—or strongly suspected—of attempting to steal items of clothing, and then they would call the police. But the losses went on.

Finally, one day, he was thumbing through a trade magazine and came upon an ad for those cartridges. So he said, "Why not?" and bought a few dozen gross of dye packets and a couple of tools for attaching them to garments, and for removing them, of course, when somebody walks out the door with something they had bought fair and square. And guess what? His rate of shoplifting has now dropped to less than half of what it was before. Must be a moral in that, somewhere, don't you think? Now you're probably thinking that dye packets and other security measures they're using in retail establishments won't work on library theft problems. The doubters say it's different circumstances. Apples and oranges, and all that. But why not?

Paul told me that just the visible presence of the cartridges helps deter theft of his merchandise, whether the things actually explode outside or not. He's also willing to bet that nobody who ever tried to steal a cartridge-equipped garment once is likely to attempt to rip him off again. Of course, he just uses these little beauties on what he calls his big-ticket items, not on $10 shirts or sale merchandise. He swears that they're amazing at preventing losses due to unauthorized removal of items of clothing from the store.

You probably know how it works: a cartridge containing a packet of colored dye is attached to a garment and it just sits there while it's inside the store, but it goes off like a tiny bomb if somebody tries to leave the store with a jacket or suit, and it marks the thief with indelible color for easy pick-up by the cops. And the cartridge is almost impossible to remove, once attached, unless the person removing it wants to destroy the garment or has a special tool that unclamps it and gently lifts it off. Only then is the item of clothing safe for removal from the store. Only then can somebody walk out of Paul's place with a purchase without risking the consequences. And here's the good part. Once people are aware of what it is and what it's for, the cartridge serves as a passive deterrent to wannabe clothing thieves. How cool is that?

But let's say somebody is so foolish, greedy, desperate or forgetful as to walk out with a big-ticket item of clothing with an ink cartridge attached. Well, that individual is in for a great big nasty surprise. Oh, yeah! That little plastic cartridge you're holding in your hand may look innocent enough, but it's a non-lethal equivalent of a miniature hand grenade. What? That sounds ominous? I hear you, but Paul said it was either that or bankruptcy, so he decided to get tough about things being stolen from his store and to take a bite out of crime. You can call him and ask him how he feels about his bold new step in security. I've got his number right here.

Anyway, like I was saying, the cartridge that's just been sitting on a lapel or sleeve of a garment explodes, schpritzing brightly colored ink in a big sort of curtain, all over the garment, the thief, and anybody else who happens to be unlucky enough to be standing nearby. *Wham!* Yeah, that's the possible downside. Innocent people standing nearby can get schpritzed, too. But the ink washes off, eventually. Just not right away. If it were too easy it would defeat the whole purpose, right?

Does it work? You kidding me? Works every time. Paul told me that he hasn't had to actually sacrifice any of his clothing to prove that the device works. The manufacturer sent him a videocassette, a 10-minute training film in which an actor pretends to be stealing a sports coat from a store. The film breaks the incident down into a slow motion sequence. An ordinary looking guy in a busy clothing store, examining a rack of blazers, looking at price tags, trying them on, and like that. Then, the guy looks carefully around for cameras and store detectives, and when he's satisfied that nobody's looking his way, he takes off the grubby jacket he's wearing and puts it on the hanger from which he's just removed a new navy blue blazer. He puts on the blazer and walks away from the rack—slowly, whistling, not a care in the world. You see the guy walking nonchalantly past the store detective, smiling at him, and then exiting the store.

Now the shot is from the perspective of a camera outside the store. The guy in the blazer takes a step outside the front doors. Nothing happens. Then, as he takes step two, it happens. From under the arm of his left sleeve, ribbons of bright yellow—like the mustard they give you on hot dogs at the ballpark—soaks the guy, the coat, and a good chunk of the sidewalk in indelible ink. And that's it.

The film freezes on the guy, looking shocked (who wouldn't?), standing there on the sidewalk dripping bright yellow, as the narrator explains that even if the guy ditches the coat now (why not? It's not as though he's ever going to be wearing it) it will be a snap for the cops to find him and arrest him because even a 30-minute shower and a whole bar of strong laundry soap won't get that ink off this guy's head and hands for maybe a week. Beautiful, isn't it?

Paul tells me that since his store installed the new technology, three unlucky people who tried to rip him off have been *schpritzed* outside his store. And once word got around, theft of his garments fell off almost to zero. I mean, people talk. Like I say, the ink—although indelible—doesn't damage people permanently (as long as they don't, like, place a cartridge in their mouth and bite down), and it's really effective as a deterrent. Now, nobody wants to risk taking the chance.

How would you feel about walking around in public with your head and hands covered in some primary color, maybe a yellow badge of shame? Embarrassed, right? And again, you'd be clearly marked for the police. Sort of like having your face splashed all over *America's Most Wanted*. Unless you holed up immediately, and stayed there until the dye faded, you'd be marked. Might as well turn yourself in—you're toast.

Downside? Well, yeah, there's a downside. Two, actually. For one thing, the company that makes these gizmos ain't exactly giving them away. The cost varies with how many you order, and the deepest discount goes to those who buy the most. But much of Paul's cost gets amortized by the money he saves in items not stolen. Then, too, there's the sidewalk outside that requires some heavy-duty cleanup after an incident. But the most serious downside would have to be that the very book your library wanted to protect with this device is ruined—absolutely totaled—when it gets schpritzed.

Hey, I didn't say it was a perfect system. Just really effective. Tradeoff, that's all. I know. That's the bad part. Reminds me of an old movie I watched on late-night TV when I couldn't sleep a couple weeks ago. There was this wanted murderer holding a gun to the head of the woman he supposedly loves and screaming to the cops outside, "If I can't have her, then nobody's going to have her." Crazy guy is willing to kill the woman he loves most, just to keep her out of anybody else's arms.

Well, that's a problem with this exploding cartridge. In protecting a rare book with one of these, the library might be ensuring that nobody's going to steal it, but if anyone does, the library loses it anyway because that book is now useless—at least the outside of it is useless.

But that's part of the deterrent factor. When people read in the paper about one of these things going blooey all over some guy or see on television what a guy looks like when he's been schpritzed with bright yellow dye, and then they see him get led away, covered in paint, to the slammer where a long stretch of time awaits him, they're going to think very hard about stealing any of the library's rare books.

So here's my offer. I called the 800 number of the company that puts out these cartridges and asked them a couple of questions about adaptability to other items . . . like expensive books and the like. My first question involved whether these things come in different sizes. Well, they do. The one you're holding is twice the size of the book model. Obviously, one that would fit down the spine of a bound book would have to be pretty small. And it won't work on paperback books, but who cares? Mass-market paperbacks are relatively cheap and easily replaced, so we don't need to protect them anyway. But one of the library cartridges can be mounted indiscreetly yet easily inside any hardbound book, and after that, things work pretty much like they do in Paul's store.

Now, you're probably interested in the cost. We wouldn't need to install these cartridges on all of your books—or even most of them. Just the big ones or valuable ones that you'd hate to lose. Naturally, you would get a discount for quantity; the more you buy, the less you pay per cartridge.

So here's my proposal. Fit these tiny packets onto all the hardcover materials in the rare book room and a few hundred selected reference materials. Then it's sort of like one of those good-news, bad-news jokes you've probably heard. The good news is that the cartridges preserve and protect the collection, pretty much ensuring that when someone wants to find a book on the shelves, it'll be there. The bad news? Well, you know. *Wham!* But if everybody understands the consequences, nobody's likely to try to rip off the library, am I right?

So I'm asking you to buy 500 of these cartridges for a start and install them in the books you value most. Then go public with what you've done and post signs warning people about consequences. Give it a three-month trial period, that's all I ask. Think about last year's library loss figures and consider this an easy and inexpensive way to turn that around. No more big reference books waltzing out the door or mysteriously disappearing. Now, if anybody is stupid enough to try to remove a rare or expensive book from the building without permission, he's schpritzed good and proper. And once somebody gets schpritzed, believe me, he's going to stay schpritzed for a long time

So what's it going to be? Green light this project, and I'll order the cartridges today and arrange for a staff training session tomorrow, meaning that you should—barring unforeseen obstacles—have the library's 500 most valuable books protected by this new technology this very weekend. Of course, I know that you'll probably need time to talk about this with the library staff and the board. Here's my card. I'll be waiting to hear from you again soon. Enjoy the rest of your day. Bye now.

Questions for Discussion

1. What's your opinion of adapting the "cartridge" security method to rare and valuable library materials?

2. As library director, if you decided to accept such a system on a trial basis (and the comptroller authorized the expense), how would you inform the public of its existence so that incidents would be kept to a minimum?

3. How would the library justify its new security measure to members of the public who—as a form of collateral damage—might accidentally get schpritzed when a cartridge went off in the hands of a thief outside the building?

Case 37

The Latest Thing in Eyewear

Jan Asuquo, grants officer, to Michael Chitwood, associate director, in Chitwood's office

Mike, as you know, my job is to write grants and submit them to various foundations, agencies, and corporations, in the hope of acquiring additional funding to supplement the library's rather austere budget. And let me add, if you will forgive a shameless bit of self promotion, that I'm exceedingly good at my job. But don't take my word for it—judge me not by what I say, but by the percentage of grant proposals I write that actually get funded.

That's a statistic in which I take a great deal of pride. A full 58 percent of the proposals I've submitted over the three years I've been working here have been rewarded with funding. Just for comparative purposes, the average success rate for grant proposals among libraries—according to an informal survey I took of my opposite numbers via e-mail—is in the low 20s, so I must be doing something right.

If I had to name one thing about the proposals I write that gives them an optimal chance of being funded, it's that I do careful research prior to writing them. By that, I mean I thoroughly investigate the funding body, trying to find out ahead of time how much money is available, what's been funded in the past, what restrictions there are to the use of the funds, and, if possible, what kinds of proposals they have rejected, and why.

Adding to the difficulties of my job is the fact that the supply of available grant money fluctuates widely with general economic conditions. For example, a few years ago, my first proposal was to a foundation for assistance with acquiring additional computers, printers, and peripherals for the growing Internet services area of the library. As you know, it was granted easily. But lately, the same foundation has shared the general economic hardships of the parent company, which has seen a downward path in its stock price. Stock devaluation means less money available for grants, leading to fewer grants.

Still, grants have never been slam dunks, as in, "Here! We have this money available. Please take some!" until now. In the past month, a particularly interesting offer has been made to us, and it is fair to say that the grant—not one of money but of expensive equipment—literally fell into our laps, and about all I had to do was to write the proposal (for their files) to suit the terms and conditions outlined by the company involved, and the grant was ours. Too good to be true? Maybe, but I'm intrigued enough to think that we ought to go for it.

What happened was that a local businessman named Maury Roberts approached me (it's usually the other way round, as you know) on behalf of his consulting firm and asked me to write a grant, which, if funded, would benefit the library greatly. That's what I said. *He* asked *me* to apply! It was that easy. Badda boom, badda bing!

He actually gave me step-by-step instructions on how to write and win a grant to get several pairs of special goggles for free. I'm nobody's fool, so I just followed the instructions like it was a cake recipe, and voilà! We win!

What kind of goggles? Here's a couple of pair. They look like the driving goggles you see in the old movies about the invention of the automobile, don't they? Not very stylish, I admit. But wait'll you see what they do. Don't ask me how they work, but they do, as you'll see in a moment. I brought along a couple of pairs and decided to arrange a little seeing-is-believing demonstration that'll convince you that I'm not making this up. They really work!

Ready to try a little experiment? Good. Here, take a pair and look them over. No, don't put them on, yet. Just examine them. Note that they're lightweight, the lenses are seated in rubber backing so that outside light can't enter, and the rubber nose piece is adjustable to fit various facial configurations including people who wear glasses. The velcro strap is adjustable. True, the sealed battery pack, which goes into the wearer's pocket or has to be carried in the hand, is cumbersome, but these batteries give several hours of use without recharging.

The developer tells me that his company is hard at work on ways to make the goggles even lighter and less obtrusive in future versions. In fact, he says, one day, a contact lens version of the same technology should be available, meaning that a person wearing them would be unobtrusive as long as the battery pack is hidden. But those refinements are still a year or two away, minimum. We're being asked to beta-test these prototype goggles, which, while sort of clunky looking, work surprisingly well, as you'll see.

All right, now that you've seen what the goggles look and feel like, let's each put on a pair. There. Now, look at me. What do you see? I'm betting you see me outlined in dark red, correct? No, that's fine. You weren't supposed to see anything out of the ordinary, actually. And that's what I see when I look at you, which, you will be happy to learn, I hope, shows only that you and I are within normal tolerances for stress and emotional upset.

All that "normal" means in this context is that you and I are seen through these special goggles as having no particular elevation in our internal stress levels. I mean, oh, yes, perhaps you're concerned about tomorrow, or even tonight, and feeling a bit uneasy about terrorism or epidemics or the stock market, but according to what I see when I look at you, your present stress level is not sufficiently elevated to trigger the goggles' telemetry circuits. What's that? Don't ask. If you don't mind, let's leave the technology to the technologists and just deal with the results of this device, shall we?

So now, let me ask you to keep your goggles on, as I will as well, and come with me downstairs to the Reference area. Be careful to hold the handrail of the staircase when we go down. One of the problems of these goggles is that everything looks red, and your eyes see most objects outlined in an even darker red. That can take a bit of getting used to. All right, here we go . . . slowly.

Now we're standing at the entrance to the Reference/Adult Services room. As you can see, there are perhaps a couple of dozen people in the room, some reading, some seated at computer terminals, and maybe a few talking or doing other things. Now let's both slowly pan—like we're television cameras—around the room, looking carefully at each person we see, whether they're close to us or far away.

Whoa! Contact!

See that man over there? Yeah, him, sitting over by the atlas stand. See it? Sort of a flaming bright red aura around his outline, like the way solar radiation appears around the sun during an eclipse. Note that while just about everybody else in the room, including you and me, has dark red or purple outlines, that guy—the one with his baseball cap turned around—looks like he's on fire. No, it's not an optical illusion. It's the lenses you're wearing reacting to high levels of emotional stress, that's all.

I've experimented like this before, putting on the goggles and walking around the library, a mall, and even once at the baseball stadium, just to see what I could see. Of course, people who see me wearing these things think

I'm a freak, or maybe a wannabe Elton John look-alike, and that's a definite drawback. Nothing unobtrusive about a middle-aged woman strolling around a public place sporting black rubber goggles with red lenses, is there? I mean, I get looks you wouldn't believe.

Yeah, you know what I'm talking about. Check out the people looking at us now. See the open-mouthed stare on that woman over there? That's typical. I tell you, I'll be glad when they start mass producing the smaller or contact lens models, or at least something less inconspicuous, anyway.

Yeah, I see you're convinced, but there's one more thing before we take these contraptions off and head back upstairs. Let's consider the man over there who's showing up with all those bright red flames or vapors around his head. According to our goggles, we are looking at a man who may not know it, but he's surrounded by an aura of high emotional tension.

What does that tell us? Well, if these things are functioning the way they're supposed to, what we know about that guy is that he is undergoing a serious amount of emotional stress at this particular moment. So the question becomes, what do we do with that information? I mean, do we tell him to chill out or give him a set to put on and show him in a mirror what he looks like to us? Should we rush over to him and ask him what's wrong? Intervene in some way? I don't think so. Besides, there could be serious legal problems for anyone who did. And who knows what else? Privacy issues, perhaps. Anything is possible.

Anyway, we all experience high levels of stress at various moments in our lives, don't we? In today's world, who's to say that stress isn't normal? A few days ago, my car was almost sideswiped by a speeder. I could have been severely injured or killed by a thoughtless turkey driving a big van with a cell phone plastered to his ear. For a few moments, I felt pure, undiluted rage. Stress? Probably off the charts. I honked my horn, but I don't think he ever noticed me as he just went on his merry way. Now imagine that you were working here and wearing these goggles and I'd just come into the library after my near-death experience. What color do you imagine I would have been at that moment? Something to think about, isn't it?

Well, let's take off our goggles now and go back upstairs and sit down to talk.

Quite an experience, wasn't it? Now that you've experienced the abilities (and shortcomings) of this new technology that we obtained for library use without any expense, I'm sure you have a few questions, so let's hear 'em.

Good question. How do we plan to use these goggles? What practical library application do they have? Well, think about it. We have security guards on duty every afternoon and all weekend. Now, what if we issued a pair of these goggles to each guard during his shift? Picture a security guard posted by the front entrance, watching people enter and leave the building. Only he's wearing a set of goggles as he surveys the multitudes streaming through the entrance. What does he see? Dozens of people outlined in a dull dark red, just the way we saw each other and most of the people downstairs a few moments ago.

But then suddenly, uh-oh! The guard sees a man coming through the front door who appears covered head-to-toe in red flames. And that's the neat part. With the unaided eye, the troubled patron probably looks like everybody else. Perhaps nothing in his facial expression or body language gives him away. But through the special lenses, our security guy gets a tipoff that this patron is seriously stressed. He'll bear watching.

Right! That's an important distinction. Normal people might glow red after encounters like the one I told you about. But only briefly. After the adrenaline stops flowing, normal stress falls off. But seriously stressed people can turn flaming red and stay red for days or weeks, and those are the ones our guards need to keep an eye on. Anyway, it's just an advisory sort of thing, a heads-up. It's not anybody's job to prevent seriously stressed people from entering the building—or to screen library staff and employees for signs of stress. But it can be a useful way of telling the wearer who, among the hundreds who traipse through our doors every day, is potentially dangerous. Or at least who should bear a bit of extra scrutiny.

Will you accept the premise that there are those among us in society who may look normal enough but are those hair-trigger guns you read about? Good. We agree then. These goggles can easily help identify those who are at risk.

So what happens if we do identify such a person? Our guards are not empowered to stop or question seriously stressed patrons. But someone wearing a pair of goggles will at least have a clue as to who might need extra surveillance, just in case somebody's high stress leads to some form of aggressive, inappropriate, or antisocial behavior.

Anyway, we're going to be famous. Thanks to the grant, we'll be the first library in the country to try out these goggles, and the results of our experience may well change the direction of library security. Who can say? One day soon, libraries might be able to do away with goggles and install some sort of electronic screening device in the doors, walls, or ceiling that alerts security staff to the presence of extremely stressed out individuals.

But I don't know if that's especially desirable. I mean, it could be another enhancement to personal safety inside our building, or another step down the slippery slope toward the erosion of personal privacy in modern so-ciety. Or both, at the same time. I've been wrestling with that problem, but I think this form of surveillance is definitely worth a try. Forewarned is fore-armed, don't you think?

Well, thanks for taking part in my little demonstration. It's almost quit-ting time now, so here's wishing both of us a stress-free drive home during the rush hour, lest our silhouettes, next time we meet, show us both to be on fire to an observer wearing a pair of these special goggles.

One final thought. The same company has, they say, in the final stages of development, another handy little device that we may be interested in beta-testing in the library. It's a gadget that you point at someone when he or she is talking that acts as a portable stress analyzer. Essentially, it does the same thing as the goggles, only it analyzes the voice, looking for ex-treme levels of stress. When it detects extreme stress, it beeps an alarm.

The company says that when that gizmo is refined, it will make it possi-ble to tell whether a speaker is under serious emotional pressure and even if he's lying. Think of the potential in that! Intriguing, isn't it? Our very own unobtrusive lie detector. Think of the applications. But it's getting late, so good night. Yeah, I agree. We live in an amazing world, don't we?

Questions for Discussion

1. What benefits can you see for security staff in using these goggles in surveillance of library building occupants?

2. What ethical or legal drawbacks can you envision if your library used such goggles?

3. Assuming that the library could secure this technology without cost, would you favor using a voice analyzer as a lie detector?

Case 38

Thou Shalt Not Steal

**Phyllis Owen, board member, to the board and
the director, at the monthly meeting**

Good morning everyone! I think everyone in this room knows how much I love to shop—that's why my husband is always joking that I shouldn't be left alone on e-Bay or allowed to watch the Home Shopping channel without adult supervision. So maybe I shouldn't have been the one to get called with this sales pitch that I'm about to tell you about, but then again, maybe that's why it was me who the salesman called, instead of Bryan, or one of you other hard-nosed business types. Anyway, I was the one he called, and I must say that I was so impressed (although I admit to be being easily impressed, sometimes) by what I heard that I promised him I'd bring the matter to the board meeting today, which is why I requested an agenda item this morning.

Put simply, I think this idea is so fascinating that we might want to consider getting it for our library. At first, when that technology vendor called me with his spiel, I really wasn't in the mood to get into conversation with a persistent salesman. I'd just come home and had maybe a dozen things clamoring for my attention and jostling for position on my "to do" list.

Then he started talking, and what he is offering our library got my attention instantly. Like the Godfather says in those movies, "He made me an offer I couldn't refuse." Or maybe it's just timing because the idea he wants to test market in our building coincides with the depressing news we've all received that the book loss rate for the main collection is at an all-time high.

So it was a combination of his company looking for a site to test its new technology and the appalling rate of our books going missing that made me say, "How soon can you get here?" when he asked to come to my home to talk. What I heard that day helped me to decide that we might very well want to consider adopting his subliminal messaging system for our library's use, especially now, before these systems get more expensive.

Subliminal? Well, you've probably heard of the concept. They tried visual subliminal images inserted during movie showings many years ago, as a way to discover whether people would behave a certain way during a movie if a single frame—so quickly on and off the screen that your conscious mind can't notice it—could induce people to go out to the lobby and buy tubs of popcorn more often than they might have otherwise.

But this concept is audio technology, which doesn't require people to look at anything in particular in order to get the subliminal message encoded on it. I think it's an intriguing idea, and, goodness knows, one worth trying, especially since the first 90 days of the contract will be a trial period, absolutely free.

So why not? Marty, the sales rep for this service, lives up in Missouri, somewhere outside of St. Louis, and I was impressed that he was willing to drive all the way down here just to pitch his system to me. But don't worry, he reassured me that we were getting a free trial period and that we are under no obligation thereafter. I have his solemn word that if our library is dissatisfied with his system, he'll just disconnect it from our sound system, and that'll be the end of it. So I figure we have nothing to lose in giving it a 90-day trial.

Now, I know you want to hear all about what it is and how it works. I've made some calls to libraries in other parts of the country, and their reviews are glowing. The creators of this system estimate that book theft, which usually runs an estimated 50 to 60 volumes a month in our system, should drop 30 percent or more after we have them install the subliminal tapes on our sound system. That's *30 percent!* And because it'll cost us nothing, that's a lot of gain and no pain for us.

What's the downside? Well, some people have been known to express alarm about what they say is involuntary hypnotism—a form of messing with their minds. And some critics complain that using subliminal technology on people without their knowledge or consent is highly unethical. So I thought about it as an ethical problem: risks versus rewards and the end justifying the means. I thought about it long and hard before I came here today to tell y'all about it.

And what's my answer to the charge that using such a system is unethical? I say, ethical, *schmethical!* If we install the new subliminal sound system, theft of materials will drop over 30 percent! How are you going to argue with that? Among other advantages, no complicated installation is required, making it a win–win situation, and, just as a clincher, it might even make our library patrons into better people—at least, in the short run.

I see some of you looking confused. Yes, I said "better people." No, nothing to do with brainwashing or thought control—at least, not the way you're thinking. This is America, and we cannot abide that sort of notion. I would never have come to you with this idea if I thought this was brainwashing.

So then let's consider what I mean by "at least, in the short run." It just means that whatever suggestion might enter your mind while you're in the building would not persist once you left it. No lingering effects.

Mercy, so many questions! Yes, I'll answer all your questions in a minute or two. But first, I guess I'd better just go ahead and explain what the system is and how it works. Then I think you'll have a better understanding of my meaning, and I might have answered some of your questions in so doing.

It's called Subliminal Synchronicity, a new product developed by SRQ, Inc., of Missouri. (If we take them up on their offer, we'd be the first library in the whole world that has adopted their technology.) Its working principle is simplicity, itself. Say you come to the library to borrow a book or two, or for any other reason at all. As you enter the building, you hear unobtrusive but beautiful and restful music, the kind that's conducive to study and not the kind they have in elevators in tall buildings. Light classics, mostly, mixed in with a concerto by Vivaldi or excepts from a Mozart symphony, or his *Eine Kleine Nachtmusik,* you know the kind of music I'm talking about?

There are various tapes available, and I listened to part of one. I think I recognized something by Chopin—he's always easy to listen to—and there was that Rachmaninoff concerto that has that pretty song in it, the one that goes, "full moon and empty arms." Anybody else here old enough to remember when that one was popular? My mother used to sing that one when I was a girl. Anyway, you can imagine the kind of music I'm talking about: easy listening, but classical. The greatest hits of the eighteenth and nineteenth centuries.

So here you are in the library, browsing and maybe listening to the pretty music, or maybe not listening at all. It doesn't really matter. The scientific community agrees that research has shown that listening to Mozart and guys like that while you're studying can actually make you smarter, and help your chances of getting high marks in school. I am not making this up. So the music might help people concentrate, and at the same time, it could foster a psychological ambiance of elegance, charm, and serious study in the library, even if visitors are only aware of how pretty the music is.

But the genius part is what's behind the music. Now don't ask me how they make this happen, but the designers have found a clever way to sequence a second sound track onto the surface of the recording tape in such a way that, along with the music, comes a message. What message? I'm getting to that. All right, I guess I've milked this situation for all the suspense I can get.

The message is a subliminal voice telling you things as you read or browse or just, I don't know, stare out the window. Is it a male voice or a female voice? What difference does it make? Frankly, I've never actually heard a voice coming through the ceiling, except at closing time when somebody announces that people have five minutes to check out their books. I don't hear voices. I'm not Joan of Arc. Anyway, it's a voice and it says things that people don't hear with their ears but it goes straight into their minds—that's why they call it subliminal. You're not aware that you're hearing it, but you *are* hearing it.

Other questions? Bryan? Sneaky? Well, possibly a bit, but sneaky in a good way. This subliminal system is designed to calm people down and at the same time help us preserve and protect our book collection. I think this is clearly a case in which the end definitely justifies the means.

No, I don't think subliminal technology works on all people the same way. It wouldn't work on my Uncle Sherman, for example, I can guarantee you. He's deaf as a post and even two hearing aids don't help him all that much. And then, it's possible that we don't all hear the same thing. You know how they say that not everybody can be hypnotized? Sort of like that. For all I know, different people do hear different things, but when the pretty music comes out of those speakers in the ceiling throughout the building, most people will not be conscious of hearing a voice. Just the music.

Somewhere in there, though, is this hidden voice, a very persuasive voice, speaking to you, and it tells you what to do. Or rather, what not to do. Oh, don't look so alarmed. I don't *really* mean it commands you to do any-thing, but it does make some very strong suggestions, that much is true. No, it's not like being hypnotized or brainwashed. Nothing like that. Look, let me tell you what the voice says over and over—not to our consciousness but to our unconsciousness, and that should calm your fears:

> Thou Shalt Not Steal!
> Stealing Is Wrong!
> Book Thieves Will Be Prosecuted!
> Thou Shalt Not Steal!
> Stealing Is Wrong!

That's the whole message, and the tape repeats it over and over, but there's no monotony because you're not really hearing it audibly. Not on a conscious level, anyway. And it really persuades people not to steal books! Now, I think you'll agree that there are two kinds of people: honest and dishonest. Let's assume that almost all the people who come to the library are honest, so for them, all the hidden message does is validate and confirm what they already know: it's wrong to steal, for a lot of reasons. But what about the other ones? Well, people who are susceptible to the temptation to steal would be, I don't know, talked out of it, by the little voice in their minds, but they'd just think it was their conscience asserting itself, or something, if they thought about it at all.

Oh, by the way, the sales rep assured me that the recorded voice is incapable of making anyone do anything they wouldn't do normally. For example, it couldn't induce you to steal a book or vandalize a computer if you weren't already predisposed to such activities. But the few who come in here with destructive or larcenous hearts and minds? They're out there, and you know it. I'm talking about amoral people who think nothing of lifting a book or finding a way to get it out of the library without checking it out. People who don't play by the rules, because they don't care, or they think that the rules don't apply to them, or who maybe just think that they won't get caught.

Well, when the tape is running, almost all of them suddenly "realize" that stealing is wrong, like the Ten Commandments teaches us. Now, I say that's a goal worth working toward, and here's our chance to try it out. As a bonus, the same music will keep library staff honest as well, which is a pleasant side effect, given the recent incident of a staff member who had been helping herself to supplies from the storeroom, until she got caught and fired for it.

So I now move that we take that company in St. Louis up on their offer of a 90-day trial. I can see some problems, but I say it's worth a shot. I've done some extensive reading on library security. If there's a better plan out there to deter thieves that doesn't cost us any money, I don't know about it. After all, we can't have surveillance cameras and guards all over the place, and the honor system is kind of shaky. So what's more clever than subliminal gentle persuasion to talk people out of stealing library property?

Brainwashing? Nothing of the sort! This technology doesn't erase anything from your mind or replace it with anything new. It just helps you be the best person you can be, that's all it does. And comparing library staff and patrons under such a system to guinea pigs or lab rats is just plain ridiculous.

There *is* just one little problem though. Remember how I said it was a free trial? It is free of cost, yes, but free of obligation on the part of the library? Not exactly. See, there's a catch (there's always a catch, isn't there?). We have to agree to a certain proviso, and to say no to it would be a deal breaker. Marty says that if we accept his company's generous offer, we can't tell anyone what we're up to. Nobody. What you've heard here today cannot leave this room. I'd prefer that nobody here even tell his or her spouse. I know that's a lot to ask, but those are the conditions. Accepting the technology would require a licensing agreement that requires our strict secrecy.

I know. Secrecy and a public library. A strange combination, but there it is. The secrecy? Well, for at least three months, the public is not to know anything about what's happening or why, and Ann will keep it from her staff, as well. We'll make an announcement that the library is trying out musical background, and the announcement will be backed up by references to the literature attesting to the fact that listening to classical music promotes concentration, thought, and a general sense of well-being in the listener, which is all true, despite the preference of a lot of kids today for rap and other forms of musical expression that frankly make me shudder. Just out of curiosity, by the way, I asked the sales rep if the same voice could be sequenced with other types of music, but he said that I shouldn't even think about it.

Anyway, after the public announcement, the company would come in and install the tapes on a Sunday evening, when the library is closed, and nobody else but those of us in this room would know about what we're up to. Then, beginning Monday morning, everyone in the building—patrons and staff alike—would have lovely music to listen to as they went about their library errands and duties. It wouldn't be loud or intrusive, and I doubt that we'd get a lot of complaints.

But as to what's really going on? All of you have to swear an oath of secrecy or it's a no go. Marty says that alerting people to the fact that there's a voice behind or under the music reminding everybody to be good citizens would defeat the whole purpose of the experiment, and I'm persuaded that he's right. The people who are providing this subliminal technology to us need to study its operation when people are unaware that they're being studied. So if we go for this deal, it has to be our little secret, at least for now. I mean it!

Well, that's my pitch. I think we have a lot to gain from trying this offer out, and nothing much to lose as long as we all agree to the secrecy part, which I know doesn't sit well with all of us. But it's a tradeoff. Much of life is a tradeoff—you give to get. So, I call the question. All in favor?

Questions for Discussion

1. Is the subliminal messaging described in the case ethical?

2. Do you think it appropriate to subject library patrons to experimental new technologies, without their knowledge or consent, in furtherance of security objectives?

3. Do you think it appropriate to ask board members to swear to secrecy?

Case 39

Out-U-Go®

Clay Daniel, Ph.D., director of advanced research for Cybertronics, Inc., to the board, at the monthly meeting

Ladies and gentlemen of the library board, Director Bowman, and staff, I want to thank you all for the opportunity to come here this evening to demonstrate a working model and prototype of my new invention, Out-U-Go® and to demonstrate the numerous advantages that will accrue to your library if you agree to let your facility join the leading edge of library security throughout the nation.

I've brought with me a carousel of slides to illustrate the capabilities of my device, but before we get to what it is and how it works, let me underscore an important point: If your library agrees to become the demonstration library—the pioneer and innovator—it will cost you exactly nothing. I see some skeptical faces here. Perhaps you're wondering, "What's the catch?" There *is* no catch, ladies and gentlemen.

I promise you that if you allow your library to be my demonstration project, the full cost to your library and the city will be only a negligible bit of extra electrical current on the monthly bill.

Why am I doing this for you? What's in it for me? Both good questions. Well, to me, it's a win–win proposition: everybody gains; nobody loses. This library—my hometown library—will benefit greatly by becoming the first library in the world to have my state-of-the-art robotized criminal detection system, and naturally, I will benefit from the publicity when the media picks up on the story and word gets around.

So are we clear about the motivations on both sides? Good. If you're still skeptical, wait until you see what Out-U-Go® can do for you, and then—and only then—will you be asked to commit to it, by signatures on this contract. You won't be sorry if you do, I promise you that.

239

If you decide to pass on the opportunity? No harm, no foul, no hard feelings. I'll just take my invention over to the Centerville or Springfield library systems and shop it to them, but then, you'll have to explain to your city council and citizens why you let a golden opportunity—to be the first library in the world to protect people from bodily harm while actually slashing the personnel budget—pass you by.

Sound too good to be true? Well, it ain't braggin' if you can really do it. So if I can have someone darken the room, I'll begin my slide presentation to show that what I say is no brag, just fact. Please feel free to ask any questions during my presentation, and I'll try to deal with them in as much non-technical detail as you might wish. All right? Onward!

<Click> Ladies and gentlemen, introducing Out-U-Go®, a device that offers myriad benefits to the security-minded library facility that really wants to get tough on crime! Out-U-Go® is my own patented creation that I've had under development for several years. It's a new wrinkle in library security that will maximize personal safety in the library building while saving the cost of salary and benefits for security guards. I know, that's a boastful claim, but see what it can do, and you're bound to agree.

<Click> Here's how it works: What you're seeing in this slide is a photograph of me and my team of skilled technicians installing Out-U-Go® in a building's ceiling. Installation for a library this size would require a full day, during which the facility must be closed to the public. We install intersecting tracks bracketed just below the ceiling of each room; recessed in those tracks is a series of robotic arms, equipped with interchangeable extensions, adaptations, and attachments, sort of like a high-end canister vacuum cleaner. Also installed are a computerized logic center or brain and multiple, highly sensitive cameras and sensors at strategic points in the ceilings, which monitor all activity going on below.

<Click> The key feature of the system is these retractable arms, shown here in close-up, which are installed in every room open to the public—except the restrooms, of course. The arms, when not in use, are retracted and inconspicuous, and are the same white color as the ceiling. If you didn't happen to be looking up, in fact, you'd probably never even know that they were there. After installation, everything else in the library looks just as it did before, and nothing on the floors or walls is moved, removed, or rearranged during installation.

Now, what, exactly, does the system do? Let's take a hypothetical case, and watch Out-U-Go® as it counters threats and prevents or deters various forms of crime, vandalism, or aggressive behavior. Oh, did I mention? You

can customize your system from the master console to select the types of at-
tachments, options, or actions you want.

<Click> Here's step one in a progression of defensive moves. Step one
is mostly all you're going to need once people become aware of the system's
other capabilities. Now, let's say that there's this antisocial person in the library who's acting up, being disruptive. We'll call him George, although it
could just as well be Georgette. Maybe George is . . . I don't know . . . tearing
pages out of library books, or maybe he's shooting spitballs at girls, or playing with matches, or picking a fight.

It doesn't really matter, but this first type of infraction consists of misdemeanors, not really crimes, but still, nothing you want to encourage, either. In step one, George gets a polite warning. A robotic arm, ending in a
white glove with fingers and a thumb comes down silently out of the ceiling
and waggles an upraised finger (no, not *that* finger!) in George's surprised
face. Or you can customize the programming to provide a voice that says,
"Un-*uhh!*" in a tone of warning or reproof. The voice can be male, female, or
even the voice of Darth Vader, if you prefer.

I figure this first warning is going to stop the rule breaker right there,
in the vast majority of cases. I mean, if *you* were bent on mischief, and
thinking nobody was really paying any attention, but then this padded arm
dropped like a snake out of the ceiling and wagged a big finger in your face
while a deep voice said, "Un-*uhh!*" to you, what would you do? Chances are,
you'd figure that somebody is watching you closely, and you'd either become
a model citizen in a hurry or run screaming in terror out of the building.

The arm, by the way, has 360-degree mobility, and can pursue George
all the way to the exit if he tries to get away. But there's no contact in step
one. Not at this level. This first step is mostly psychological, but amazingly
effective, based on testing in my lab with paid subjects. I can give you details, if you want, but let's move on.

<Click> Now, let's hypothesize that George keeps acting up and has not
been intimidated by the gentle reproof of step one. Maybe he thinks, "Ahhh,
that wasn't so bad, so I'm just going to keep on keepin' on with what I was
doing!" What then?

Step two is activated, as determined by the higher logic center of the
system's brain. The arm descends again silently and swiftly from the ceiling,
only this time, with the thumb extended, and George becomes the recipient
of a firm tap on top of the head. What? Painful? Not really, but it'll rock your
world when you get one if you weren't expecting it. Still, it's just a warning,
but impossible to ignore. You know how somebody pokes you or taps you,

just as a way of saying, "Hey! Listen up?" Like that. Once George has been tapped, he'll probably straighten up and fly right as long as he's in the building, because he'll probably be wondering what other capabilities lay in store for him if he continues his antisocial behavior.

But let's suppose George is a hard case. Maybe enraged, or showing off for his buddies or a girl, and not about to be pushed around—especially in public—by some stupid machine. Steps one and two didn't faze him, so stronger measures are called for. George has refused to heed the two warnings he's already received. So then what happens?

<Click> Step three is what happens. This time, the arm descends with thumb and a forefinger extended ready to pinch, and that's exactly what happens. Gently but very firmly, the fingers grab George by the ear and clamp down on it. Remember, now, we're only talking about a problem patron here, one who won't listen to reason. He's had ample warning that he's been doing something against the rules, but still he's doing it.

In this step, the robotic arm drops down out of the ceiling, grabs George by the ear, and quick-marches him out the front door. I see I've alarmed some of you. Cruelty? Trust me. Nobody gets anything more than a sore ear, at this level. The fingers are well padded and the bum's rush doesn't cause him any damage as long as George submits, but any attempt to pull away or resist is going to be very painful, indeed.

Question? Yeah, we've thought about that. What if George is wearing a cap or wig or a hairdo that covers the ears? In that case, the system's brain makes the adjustment instantly, and the pinch is delivered to his nose, which, I assure you, is even less comfortable than the ear pinch because when the nose is pinched shut, breathing can become problematic. But in either case, the arm merely grabs him and hustles George (but not so quickly that he might fall and hurt himself) to—and through—the front door, and deposits him safely outside, on the front walk. The whole process takes no more than 10 seconds.

At this point, I like to think even the dullest cretin would understand that he got off easy, this time. But let's assume that stubborn George is dumb enough to try to re-enter the library and act up again. Needless to say, stronger punishment awaits him.

Question? Yes, ma'am, that's affirmative. In most cases, that's the end of the incident. George is safely outside rubbing his ear, and nobody is hurt. It's a very effective solution to your delinquency problem, I assure you, ladies and gentlemen, and the first three stages of Out-U-Go® combined, ought to handle perhaps 99 percent of all troublemakers, without injury or untoward incident. As a slogan and a selling point, I've modified something from the world of politics to fit step three: "When you've got them by the ears, their hearts and minds will follow." Isn't that cool? I think so. Came up with it, myself: a catchy slogan I plan to emphasize in marketing my device.

But there are more drastic steps that might be warranted in extreme cases, although let me stress that they're just options, and you may not want to resort to such measures. Still, I'd recommend that you get the whole package, because you never know what people might have in mind. Lots of nuts running around free, if you ask me. Read the papers, watch the evening news, and you'll see over and again incidents where somebody walks into a school, post office, fast-food joint, or even a library with a handgun or assault rifle and just starts blowing people away. Well, nothing like that could ever happen in a library where Out-U-Go® is on the job.

The pressures of society, the availability of handguns, rampant drug abuse, and the fact that some people just have bad chemicals or faulty wiring in their heads combine to make it a dangerous world. That's why you're going to feel better if you get the full package. But, hey, I'm no criminologist or sociologist. I'm just an inventor trying to make a sale. The decision is yours. Now, let's see, where was I? Oh, yeah. Step four.

<Click> Let's say George is really stubborn or still angry and he hasn't learned his lesson yet, so he comes back inside the library and begins hassling people again, picking up where he left off. Maybe push leads to shove and George loses it and pulls a weapon—gun, knife, box cutter, it doesn't matter—and attempts to use it on somebody.

Instantly, the arm in the ceiling rushes at George, forms itself into an open hand, and slaps him a good, hard one across the face or upside his head. Naturally, if he falls down from the force of such a blow, the arm would catch him before he hits the floor. And if *that* doesn't settle him down, there's step five.

<Click> In step five, the hand forms itself into a padded boxing glove and delivers a vicious roundhouse right to George's jaw. For George, that's all she wrote, I guarantee. Question? The weapon? On the floor, right next to him, possibly sitting amid quite a few of his teeth. But that's not all. The arm grabs up the weapon and whisks it high up, out of harm's way. My system has reflexes that would put a cat to shame, and it reacts to perceived threats in a fraction of a second. Let's see your overweight old security guards do that!

Maybe the best part of step five is that the system's sensors differentiate between, say, some kid using a scissors to do découpage, and a punk with a razor, threatening to cut some innocent person's throat, for whatever reason. What could be better than that?

<Click> Then, moving along the response continuum, comes step six, involving, as you can see, a long hypodermic syringe that can stab through clothing and deliver a heavy but non-lethal dose of tranquilizer directly into George's bloodstream. Nighty-night, George! He's out in seconds, and by the time he wakes up in police custody, he'll have nothing worse to show for his experience than a hangover-type headache.

<Click> Finally, there's step seven. This time, the robot hand is holding a loaded revolver. You only go to step seven when all the previous steps don't work, and you need what the cops call "stopping power" to remove the threat of assault or murder permanently. In the unlikely event that George has gotten past step six and still has some fight left in him, *Wham!* The gun takes careful aim and fires a single round into his leg, kneecapping poor George so he'll never walk again without limping. He'll live, yeah, but he'll always remember. I can, if desired, customize this option so that a stern voice first calls out, "Warning. Stop what you're doing or I'll fire!" or even, "Go ahead. Make my day!"

<Click> Finally, just for completeness—and I don't really recommend this—the system comes equipped to go to step eight (but you'll want to check with the police and city attorney before setting the controls for that one), which shoots to kill, a clean head shot. Bye-bye George! You're history. By the way, in both settings seven and eight, the system is careful not to cause collateral damage by hitting anybody else in the line of fire, even in hostage situations.

Now some of you are probably upset by some of what I've said, but distasteful as it may sound, step eight effectively eliminates the dangerous problem patron on the spot, and, afterwards, swoops up his lifeless body for disposal, returning, if necessary, to clean up any spilled blood or whatever. As you can see, I've thought of every contingency. Efficiency, effectiveness, what's not to like?

Well, that's the last slide. May we have the lights, please? Thank you. Now, I know I've taken up a lot of your time, and I guess you have more questions, but let me conclude by emphasizing that your cost for acquiring this system is exactly zero. I only ask that once I install it, you permit visitors from other library systems to come and see it in action, that's all.

So if you like what you've seen, just sign the contract, tell me which options you want installed, and by next week, my assistants and I will get busy installing the very first Out-U-Go® system ever operational in a library anywhere.

You have nothing to lose. If you aren't satisfied, we'll come back in 90 days and take it out, at no cost to the library. To recap, here are just a few of the advantages for the library:

- Your library will be a trendsetter, leading the way into a new era of library security.

- Being the demonstration library guarantees you free national and international publicity. You can't *buy* that kind of exposure, and you would be getting it at no cost.

- Because it's a demo site, you'll get everything for free, while other libraries will soon be paying hefty installation costs and monthly fees.

- Because my staff and I live in this community, we're just a toll-free telephone call away in the event of any problems, glitches, or tech support questions.

Now, I know I've given y'all a lot to think and talk about, so I'm going to leave you now. Let me wish every one of you a pleasant good evening. I hope you'll have a decision for me tomorrow, but this offer is good for 72 hours. Then I'll go looking for another library to pick up on it.

I've brought business cards and a brochure for each of you that highlights everything I've said. They're over there on that table, by the door. I look forward to doing business with this fine library. Pecan Grove is my home, after all, and I have a lot of civic pride. Once again, thanks for your attention and consideration. Good night, all! Oh, don't bother, thank you—I can find my own way out."

Questions for Discussion

1. Assuming that Out-U-Go® will work as the inventor describes, would you be willing to install it for a free trial period, thus trimming the personnel budget by getting rid of security guards?

2. What advantages can you envision if Out-U-Go® renders library buildings safer for the public to enter and use?

3. What consequences might ensue for the library if someone were to test the system's "higher" capabilities?

Case 40

Somebody Else's Problem

Sam Dick-Onuoha, computer/technical support specialist and appointed security officer, to the entire staff at an in-service workshop

Good morning, everyone. A bit early, perhaps, for many of us, I know, but we need to meet and talk as a group without the distraction of normal building operations. I think you all know me, but in case you're new, I am "Sammy D," the Nigerian chap who works in the back of the building, hunched over my computer console, either typing something into the system, or getting something out. But today, I stand before you, at the request of Director Bowman, as the ad hoc chief security officer for the library system, as well as an instructor, and a reporter on what has been accomplished in the all-important area of library security. There are some tasks and problems that still remain before us.

First, I would like to share some good news. Based on extensive assessment, this library system has—especially when you consider the scarcity of available funding to achieve the purpose—now reached a rather admirable state of building security. What that means is that we have made considerable strides in the three main areas of library security, namely, protecting our materials and equipment, protecting ourselves and the patrons who enter our buildings, and protecting our electronic computer files by keeping them off limits to prying eyes. In all three areas, we're doing much better than we were when I came aboard two and a half years ago. But it's not really about me. It was a team effort, and all of us contributed to the improvements.

I think, however, that it would be shortsighted of us to congratulate ourselves on a job well done and then relax and be less vigilant in those areas. I have not said—nor meant to imply—that we are at a high level of security.

That would be boastful, risky, and wrong. Security is not a destination, but a voyage, and we are not "there" yet, meaning that we cannot legitimately say that we have reached a high level of preparedness for any security problems that may come our way. But we can be proud of the following recent accomplishments.

- We have at least thought and talked about the varied and numerous problems of library security, and, separately and together, given consideration to various security problems.

- We have spent time and funds wisely to upgrade our overall security posture. This means that we may not be ready for whatever comes our way, but we have at least considered many of the risks and potential hazards along those lines and have erected defenses designed to interdict or at least render more difficult the task of any perpetrators of dark deeds that represent risks to our security.

- We have purchased equipment designed to foil or discourage people who attempt to threaten our library security, and have created—and frequently review—a wish list of things we hope to acquire when money becomes available.

- We conduct meetings like this one, as well as drills, workshops, simulations, and role playing intended to acquaint all library staff members with some of the situations that could arise. We have discussed both proper and improper responses to sudden emergencies or difficulties. I say "some" of the situations that may arise because we realize that no one can anticipate all risks, and in a building like this one, where the public is encouraged to enter, it is never possible to anticipate everything.

- Finally, we have trained and instructed our excellent security officers and staff to understand which problems they can handle, which require a bit of forbearance or tolerance, and which will require the summoning of armed police. Thankfully, we have had very few incidents of the latter kind during my time here at the library. But these are dangerous times, and no one can predict what threats or behavior could impact our staff, patrons, and those who trust that their confidential records will remain just that—confidential.

Speaking of the police, as the appointed chief security officer, I have made a special point of cultivating a good relationship with the local authorities, and I like to think that if they get a call from me regarding a security matter, it's indeed a serious matter, one that even our excellent security force is not equipped to handle without backup or support. That's part of my responsibility—to be the "go to" guy—and I take it seriously.

There is still one serious matter that needs emphasis, I think, and that is complacency. I tell you now that there is no such thing as perfect security, and that foolish complacency can lead to our downfall. Now most of you know that I was born in Africa, and that I emigrated to this country a dozen years ago. In my three dozen years of living prior to coming here, I saw civil wars, incessant tribal and ethnic struggle, and even genocide. This is all by way of saying that you native-born Americans tend to be naive concerning the actions of evil people in a seething world of anger and hatred.

If there is any positive aspect of the tragic events of September 11, it might be that it served to open your eyes. Perhaps you are learning now. The attacks on the World Trade Center and the Pentagon raised our consciousness of the need for eternal vigilance, and an end to being . . . what's the expression? Ah, yes! I remember—being "happy-go-lucky," and believing that everything will always turn out well. We all need to work at security preparations and actions every day, in many ways. If the bad guys out there are looking for a public place in which to commit antisocial acts or make political statements, or even just to steal a wallet or purse and then run, we must be ready for them.

But what can be said about our electronic defenses? Our prime objective is to see to it that our firewall holds and would-be hackers are turned away in despair and frustration, without gaining unlawful and destructive access to our computer files. It is true, we have upgraded our security posture together, using teamwork, ingenuity, and hard work to attain a reasonable level of electronic security. It is now truly difficult for hackers and other information thieves to puncture our defenses. I know this, because I have tried, myself, to hack into our system.

Our aim is to make it so difficult, risky, and time-consuming to get into our system that would-be hackers will give it up and decide to try breaking into *another* library's files. In this effort, however, you may see a glaring ethical problem. If our electronic defenses are so daunting and those of other libraries are not, what concern should we have for libraries that have not thought through (or spent the time and money on) the various hazards of operating a public facility like this one?

Can we just say, as the Colonial Britons used to say in my father's day back in Nigeria, "I've got mine, Jack, and devil take the hindmost"? Such a statement would imply that our concern lies only in protecting *our* library and *our* patrons and *our* staff, and as for others, well, let them emulate our example or not. We wish them well, but it's no great concern of ours.

What I am trying to ask you is whether the biblical question, "Am I my brother's keeper?" is just a passage from Genesis, or meaningful in the sense that we are all in this together, and we must not turn our backs on other libraries, however smug we may feel that we have prepared while they have not.

In the next few weeks, I plan to visit as many other libraries in this area as I can to share with them what we've learned in upgrading security here at our library. I am also preparing a practical (rather than scholarly) article on our own experience, which I hope to place in one of the excellent professional journals in our field that reaches a wide audience. You see, while I cannot go about this land, exporting our technology and problem-solving in person, I *can* acquaint others in our field with the serious problems they face and the solutions available to them.

But while we may want to export and share our knowledge, our primary emphasis should always be on *this* library and its own security posture. I think I have spoken enough, for now. In the next week, I hope to get together with the staff of each department and review the specifics of my plans for making our security even stronger than it is.

For, although we have come a long way from the confused and vulnerable institution that we were only a few years ago, there is still much left to achieve. Bear in mind that, while we have advanced from virtually *no* security in any practical sense to what may be termed pretty good security (given our circumstances, at least), there is much more to be done, with or without additional funds, to make our preparedness better. And preparedness begins not with devices and technologies but with each of us.

I ask you to join with me now in working toward that worthwhile goal, and I assure you that what we achieve will serve everyone in this community well in the years to come. Time grows short, I know. If there are any questions, I'll be happy to take them now, or we can hold another security meeting at a later date.

Alternatively, you all know where my desk is in Technical Services. Come and see me to discuss your ideas and concerns. Now, we all have jobs and posts to get to, so until we meet again as a group, I thank you all for giving me the opportunity to speak to you about this very important task of security that confronts us all. This meeting is adjourned.

Questions for Discussion

1. How can libraries—in the absence of additional funding—best protect their electronic files and information in such a way that attempts at penetrating them can be prevented or defeated?

2. Is it ethical for a library to upgrade information security in the hopes that prospective information bandits will leave it alone and go bother less well defended libraries?

3. In the event that hackers are successful in penetrating the security of other, neighboring libraries, what responsibility should your library assume in helping them to recover and strengthen their systems?

Index